Simply Delicious!

Recipes with a Dash of Distinction.

Favorite Recipes Press

Credits

President:	Thomas F. McDow III
Editorial Manager:	Mary Jane Blount
Cookbook Editors:	Georgia Brazil, Mary Cummings, Jane Hinshaw, Linda Jones, Mary Wilson
Typography:	J. David Edmondson Shirley Edmondson & Assoc.
Cover Photograph:	Favorite Recipes Press

Copyright ©1989 by
Great American Opportunities, Inc.
P. O. Box 305142
Nashville, TN 37230

Library of Congress Catalog Number: 89-1059
ISBN: 0-87197-247-6

First Printing 1989
Second Printing 1989

Contents

Keep It Simple

- As you prepare a casserole, double the recipe. Place half in a foil-lined baking dish, and cover tightly with foil. Place in the freezer. When frozen solid, lift out of the baking dish. When you need a fantastic meal in a hurry, remove from freezer, and place in the same dish for baking.

- Plan a meal with several dishes that can be baked at the same time to save both time and energy.

- Freeze chili in ice cube trays, then transfer to plastic bags for storage. Thaw and heat as needed.

- Use leftover gravy or cream soup instead of sauces in casseroles.

- Use your double boiler for maximum effectiveness by cooking vegetables in the bottom while you prepare white sauce or cheese sauce in the top.

- Use aluminum foil whenever possible to save clean-up time as well as to seal in flavor and moistness.

- Butter French bread slices, and season with garlic. Freeze slices on cookie sheet, then store in a plastic bag. Remove from freezer, and heat in the oven as needed.

- When preparing a main dish casserole that is mixed in one bowl, mix it in the baking dish instead — saves clean-up time.

- Place stale bread or crackers in blender container. Process until reduced to crumbs. Store in a covered container to use as needed.

- For a quick cake "frosting," place chocolate candy bars on top of hot cake. Let stand for several seconds, then spread evenly with a knife. Another easy topping is a sprinkling of confectioners' sugar.

- Eliminate extra trips to the pantry during meal preparation by assembling all ingredients before starting.

- Plan your meal preparation according to length of time each dish requires. Start with the dish that takes the longest, working the others in during cooking time. This will save time, and all the foods will be served at their best.

- When making waffles, prepare an extra recipe, and freeze the extras. Place frozen waffles in a hot oven for several minutes for fresh-tasting waffles at any time.

- When a recipe for sauces or custards calls for scalded milk, use cold milk instead. It blends just as well with less danger of curdling. A smoother product is the result, and you save the time you'd spend scalding milk and cleaning up the pan.

- Combine 1 cup confectioners' sugar and 2 tablespoons frozen lemonade, and mix until smooth. Use as dessert topping on cakes, puddings or custards. Topping may be stored in refrigerator or freezer.

- To cook frozen vegetables in the oven, remove frozen block from its package and place it on a square of foil. Place two pats butter on top; season with salt, pepper, and herbs as desired. Fold foil over, making tight seal, leaving room inside for steam expansion. Bake at 425 degrees for 30 to 40 minutes — no messy pans and so easy.

Appetizers

CAVIAR-CHEESE BALL

1 8-oz. package cream cheese, softened
1 4-oz. jar black caviar
2 hard-boiled eggs, separated
1 med. onion, finely chopped
Juice of 1/2 lemon

Shape cream cheese into ball. Place on serving platter; cover completely with caviar. Sieve egg yolks; chop egg whites. Surround cream cheese with onion, circle of egg yolk and circle of egg white. Squeeze lemon juice over caviar just before serving.

Mrs. W. J. Maddocks

SALMON BALL

1 15 1/2-oz. can red salmon, drained, flaked
1 tbsp. lemon juice
1 tbsp. dried onion flakes
1 8-oz. package cream cheese, softened
1/2 tsp. Worcestershire sauce
1 tsp. horseradish
1/4 tsp. salt
1/2 tsp. liquid smoke
1/3 c. finely chopped pecans

Combine all ingredients, except pecans, in bowl; mix well. Shape into ball. Chill for 2 hours or until firm. Roll in pecans. Place on serving plate; serve with crackers.

Mrs. C. S. Fabrigar

TASTY SHRIMP DIP

2 med. cans shrimp
1 8-oz. package cream cheese, softened
2 tbsp. catsup
1 c. salad dressing
1 tsp. (about) lemon juice
Dash each of onion salt, garlic powder, chili powder

Combine all ingredients in mixer bowl; mix until well blended. Chill until serving time.

Dale S. Kutz

FAVORITE ARTICHOKE DIP

1 8 1/2-oz. can artichoke hearts, drained, mashed
1/2 c. mayonnaise
1/2 c. Parmesan cheese
1/8 tsp. Worcestershire sauce
3 drops of Tabasco sauce
Paprika

Combine all ingredients except paprika in bowl; mix well. Spoon into small buttered casserole. Sprinkle with paprika. Bake at 350 degrees for 20 minutes or until bubbly. Serve hot with crackers.

Rhoda E. Serrin

DELICIOUS ARTICHOKE DIP

1 can artichoke hearts, drained, chopped
1 c. mayonnaise
1 c. Parmesan cheese
Dash of garlic salt

Combine all ingredients together in small casserole; mix well. Bake at 350 degrees for 15 minutes. Serve with taco chips.

Jo Zech

FIESTA TACO DIP

3 avocados
3 tsp. lemon juice
1/2 pkg. dry taco mix
3 tsp. each mayonnaise, sour cream
1 can jalapeno bean dip
1 c. each grated Jack cheese, Cheddar cheese
4 green onions, chopped
3 lg. tomatoes, chopped
1 sm. can chopped ripe olives

Mash avocados with lemon juice in bowl. Combine taco mix, mayonnaise and sour cream in small bowl. Layer bean dip, avocados, taco mixture, Jack cheese, Cheddar cheese, green onions, tomatoes and olives in glass serving dish. Serve with corn chips.

Laurene Peterson

DOROTHY'S SPECIAL CRAB DIP

1 *8-oz. package cream cheese, softened*
2 *tbsp. catsup*
2 *tsp. instant onion*
1 1/2 *tsp. Worcestershire sauce*
Dash of Tabasco sauce
1 *6-oz. package frozen Alaskan king crab*

Combine all ingredients except crab in bowl;
blend well. Thaw crab; reserve liquid. Chop
crab. Add reserved liquid and crab meat to
cream cheese mixture; mix well. Spoon into
casserole. Bake at 350 degrees for 15 to 20 minutes or until bubbly. Serve with crackers.

Dorothy J. Maxwell

CURRY DIP FOR CRUDITES

1/2 *c. sour cream*
1/2 *c. salad dressing*
2 *tsp. tarragon vinegar*
Dash of pepper
1/2 *tsp. each seasoned salt, curry powder*
1/8 *tsp. thyme*
2 *tsp. chili sauce*
2 *tbsp. minced onion*

Combine all ingredients in bowl; mix well. Chill
for 24 hours. Serve with fresh vegetables. Yield:
20 servings.

Dolys P. Gelke

CHAFING DISH BROCCOLI DIP

1 *pkg. frozen chopped broccoli*
1/2 *tsp. salt*
1 *sm. onion, chopped*
2 *tbsp. butter*
1 *8-oz. roll garlic cheese*
1 *can cream of mushroom soup*
1 *tsp. monosodium glutamate*
1/4 *tsp. pepper*
1 *tsp. Worcestershire sauce*
1/4 *tsp. hot sauce*
3/4 *c. sliced almonds*
1 *4-oz. can mushrooms, drained*
Tortilla chips

Cook broccoli in 1/4 cup salted water in saucepan until tender-crisp; drain. Saute onion in
butter in skillet until tender. Add next 6 ingredients; mix well. Cook over low heat until
cheese is melted. Add broccoli. Cook for 1 minute longer. Stir in almonds and mushrooms.
Serve in chafing dish with corn chips. Yield:
15-20 servings.

Mrs. David A. Brigman

SPINACH DIP

1 *pkg. frozen chopped spinach*
1 *c. sour cream*
1 *c. mayonnaise*
1 *pkg. dry leek soup mix*
1 *bunch green onions, thinly sliced*
2 *to 4 cloves of garlic, pressed*
1 *can water chestnuts, sliced*
1 *round loaf French bread*

Cook spinach, using package directions; drain
well. Combine with sour cream, mayonnaise,
soup mix, green onions, garlic and water chestnuts in bowl; mix well. Chill in refrigerator
overnight or longer to blend flavors. Serve in
round loaf of French bread from which center
has been scooped to form bowl. Cut bread from
top and center into bite-sized pieces for dip-
ping. Yield: 20 servings.

Susan F. Chelini

CREAMY ARTICHOKE FONDUE

1 *c. mayonnaise*
1 *8-oz. package cream cheese*
1 *c. shredded Jack cheese*
1/2 *c. Parmesan cheese*
1/4 *tsp. garlic salt*
2 *6-oz. jars marinated artichoke*
    hearts, chopped
1 *tbsp. chopped parsley*

Combine mayonnaise, cheeses and garlic salt in
saucepan. Cook over low heat until cheeses
melt, stirring constantly. Stir in artichoke
hearts and parsley. Spread on toast points or
Melba rounds. Yield: 15 servings.

Lois Carson

CHEESE FONDUE

2 c. sparkling grape juice
1 lb. imported Swiss cheese, shredded
3 tbsp. flour
Salt and freshly ground pepper to taste
Grated fresh nutmeg to taste
5 tbsp. orange juice
Italian bread cubes

Heat grape juice in chafing dish. Add cheese; sprinkle with flour, salt, pepper and nutmeg. Stir until cheese melts. Add orange juice. Serve with Italian bread. Yield: 5-6 servings.

Linda Bailey

LOBSTER FONDUE

1 can frozen cream of shrimp
   soup, thawed
1 7 1/2-oz. can lobster, drained, flaked
1/4 c. milk
1/2 c. shredded American cheese
2 tsp. lemon juice
Dash each of paprika, white pepper

Combine soup and lobster in fondue pot; mix well. Heat, covered, over moderate flame, stirring frequently. Fold in remaining ingredients. Heat over low flame to serving temperature. Serve as appetizer with Melba toast. Add additional milk if needed. Yield: 2 3/4 cups.

Deborah Jones

BONBRIGHT CHEESE SPREAD

2 3-oz. packages cream cheese, softened
1/3 c. butter, softened
1/4 c. finely chopped onion
1/2 tsp. Worcestershire sauce
3/4 tsp. salt
1 tbsp. caraway seed
1 bottle of capers

Blend cream cheese and butter together in bowl. Add remaining ingredients, except capers; mix well. Drain capers, reserving 1 tablespoon liquid. Fold capers and reserved liquid into cream cheese mixture. Serve with crackers.

Mary Hansen

MOCK BOURSIN CHEESE

1 8-oz. package cream cheese, softened
1/4 lb. butter
1 clove of garlic, minced
1/2 tsp. oregano
1/4 tsp. each marjoram, dillweed, thyme
1/4 tsp. pepper

Combine all ingredients in blender container. Process until fluffy and smooth. Serve with crackers. Store in refrigerator. May be frozen.

Mrs. E. Denley Rafferty

BAKED CRAB SPREAD

1 3/4 c. crab meat
1 8-oz. package cream cheese, softened
1/4 c. slivered almonds
2 tbsp. milk
2 tbsp. minced onion
1 tsp. horseradish
1/2 tsp. each salt, pepper

Combine all ingredients in medium bowl; mix well. Spoon into 1-quart casserole. Bake at 375 degrees for 20 minutes. Serve hot with assorted crackers.

Mary K. Halvorsen

EASY CRAB SPREAD

2 8-oz. packages cream cheese, softened
2 tbsp. powdered horseradish
2 dashes of Worcestershire sauce
Dash each of onion salt, garlic powder
Dash of lemon juice
1/2 to 2/3 jar chili sauce
1 6 1/2-oz. can crab meat,
   drained, flaked
Parsley flakes

Combine first 6 ingredients in bowl; mix well. Spread on serving plate. Layer chili sauce and crab meat over cream cheese mixture. Sprinkle with parsley flakes. Chill, covered, overnight. Serve with crackers arranged around edge of cheese.

Paula D. Younkin

PARTY ARTICHOKE SPREAD

>   2   14-oz. cans artichoke hearts in
>   water, drained
>   1 c. Parmesan cheese
>   1 c. mayonnaise

Chop artichokes. Combine all ingredients; mix well. Spread in quiche dish or other ovenproof serving dish. Bake, uncovered, at 350 degrees for 20 minutes or until heated through. Serve artichoke spread on white Melba rounds.

Mrs. C. Thomas Bell

RON'S MOM'S CHEESE SPREAD

>   3 eggs, well beaten
>   1 tsp. salt
>   1/2 c. (scant) oil
>   1/2 c. sugar
>   1/2 c. vinegar
>   1 tsp. each dry mustard, celery salt
>   6 oz. smoked cheese, grated
>   1/2 lb. Velveeta cheese, grated
>   1 sm. bottle of stuffed olives, chopped
>   4 hard-boiled eggs, chopped

Combine first 5 ingredients in saucepan; mix well. Cook over medium heat until thick. Do not boil. Add more oil if too thick; remove from heat. Mix in dry mustard and celery salt; cool. Combine cheeses, olives and eggs in bowl. Stir in cooled sauce. Chill for several hours. Serve on small rye rounds. Yield: 30 servings.

Rosanne Brown

VERNA'S SHRIMP SPREAD

>   1   7-oz. can shrimp, mashed
>   1   8-oz. package cream cheese, softened
>   1 tbsp. horseradish
>   1 tbsp. lemon juice
>   1 tbsp. grated onion
>   4 dashes of Tabasco sauce

Combine all ingredients in bowl; mix well. Spoon into small baking dish. Bake at 375 degrees for 20 minutes. Garnish with paprika. Serve warm with crackers. Yield: 8 servings.

Dana Lee Walker

JEZEBEL SPREAD

>   18 oz. pineapple preserves
>   18 oz. apple jelly
>   12 oz. horseradish
>   1   6-oz. jar mustard
>   1 tsp. pepper

Combine all ingredients in saucepan; mix well. Cook over medium heat for 5 minutes, stirring constantly. Pour into hot jars; cool to room temperature. Chill in refrigerator for 2 days before serving. Serve over block of cream cheese surrounded with crackers. May store in refrigerator for 3 months.

Joyce Nelson

CHICKEN TIDBITS CHINESE

>   3 tbsp. each dry Sherry, soy sauce
>   3 tbsp. cornstarch
>   2 whole chicken breasts, boned, cut
>   into bite-sized pieces
>   Salt to taste
>   1/4 tsp. each garlic powder, thyme
>   3 tbsp. margarine
>   1 tbsp. chopped fresh parsley

Combine Sherry, soy sauce and cornstarch in bowl; mix well. Add chicken. Marinate for 30 minutes. Remove chicken; sprinkle with salt, garlic powder and thyme. Cook in margarine in skillet for 5 minutes. Sprinkle with parsley. Serve in chafing dish.

Elizabeth B. Williams

EAST INDIA MIX

>   2 tbsp. mustard seed
>   2 tbsp. butter, melted
>   1 tsp. (heaping) curry powder
>   Dash of pepper
>   2 cans potato sticks
>   1 c. peanuts

Saute mustard seed in butter in saucepan until mustard seed pop. Add remaining ingredients; mix well. Cook until heated through.

Pat Hollingsworth

ANGOSTURA LIVER PATE

2 lb. beef liver
2 env. unflavored gelatin
3 vegetable bouillon cubes
3 tbsp. lemon juice
1 sm. onion, grated
1 tbsp. salt
1 tbsp. angostura bitters

Place liver in enough water to cover in saucepan. Simmer about 10 minutes until tender; drain. Put through food chopper; set aside. Sprinkle gelatin into 1 cup cold water in saucepan. Let stand for 5 minutes. Add bouillon cubes. Cook over low heat until gelatin and bouillon are dissolved, stirring constantly. Stir in lemon juice, onion, salt and 2 cups cold water. Chill until partially set. Fold in liver and angostura bitters. Beat until well blended. Pour into lightly oiled 9 x 5-inch loaf pan. Chill until firm. Unmold. Cut into cubes. Serve on crackers or bread squares.

Photograph for this recipe on page 5.

CHEESE STRAWS
FOR COOKIE PRESS

1 lb. Cheddar cheese, grated
1/2 c. butter, softened
2 c. flour
1 tsp. salt
1/4 tsp. pepper

Combine cheese and butter in bowl; mix well. Add sifted dry ingredients; mix until crumbly. Mix in 4 tablespoons water. Force through cookie press onto baking sheet. Bake at 425 degrees for 10 minutes.

Jill Wiegand

CHEESE DATES

2 sticks pie crust mix
1 jar Old English sharp Cheddar cheese
  spread, softened
1 tbsp. oil
1 c. pecan halves

1 16-oz. package pitted dates
Cayenne pepper or paprika to taste

Combine first 3 ingredients in bowl; mix well. Shape into small marble-sized balls. Break pecan halves in half lengthwise. Stuff into center of date. Place in center of each flattened ball of dough. Roll and pinch off ends. Arrange on ungreased baking sheet without touching. Sprinkle with cayenne pepper or paprika. Bake at 325 degrees for 20 minutes. May be stored in freezer. Yield: 6 1/2 dozen.

Peg Henderson

CRAB NIBBLES

1 1/2 tsp. mayonnaise
1 stick margarine, melted
1 jar Old English Cheddar cheese
  spread, softened
1 6-oz. can crab meat, well drained
1/2 tsp. each garlic salt, seasoned salt
6 English muffins, split

Combine first 6 ingredients in bowl; mix well. Spread on muffin halves; cut each into 8 pie-shaped pieces. Place on baking sheet. Broil for 5 to 10 minutes or until bubbly. Yield: 6 dozen.

Laurene Peterson

CRAB-SPINACH CANAPES

1 bunch green onions, chopped
6 tbsp. butter, melted
2 pkg. frozen chopped spinach, cooked,
  well drained
4 oz. Parmesan cheese
1 8-oz. can crab meat
1/4 tsp. garlic powder
Several drops of Tabasco sauce
Salt and pepper to taste

Saute green onions in butter in skillet. Add spinach; mix well. Add remaining ingredients; mix well. Serve hot with corn chips. May be prepared day ahead and reheated before serving.

Carol Padalino

CHILES RELLENOS

>   6 4-oz. cans green chilies, seeded
>   1 1/2 lb. Jack cheese, cut into
>   thick strips
>   1 1/2 lb. Cheddar cheese, grated
>   6 eggs, beaten
>   1 1/4 c. evaporated milk
>   1/4 c. flour

Stuff chilies with Jack cheese. Place side by side in greased rectangular baking dish. Sprinkle Cheddar cheese over chilies. Combine eggs, milk and flour in bowl; beat well. Pour over cheese. Bake at 350 degrees for 25 to 30 minutes or until set. Yield: 12 servings.

Kitty Allen

JALAPENO SQUARES

>   8 to 10 jalapenos, seeded, chopped
>   10 eggs, beaten
>   1 to 1 1/2 c. grated Cheddar cheese

Arrange jalapenos in greased 9 x 13-inch baking pan. Pour eggs over top. Sprinkle with cheese. Bake at 325 degrees for 20 minutes; cool. Cut into squares. Yield: 36 servings.

Peg Henderson

CRISP WON TONS

>   1/2 lb. ground pork
>   4 med. shrimp, cooked, peeled, chopped
>   4 water chestnuts, chopped
>   1 green onion, finely chopped
>   1/4 tsp. sugar
>   1/2 tsp. each salt, MSG
>   1 pkg. won ton wrappers
>   Oil for deep frying

Combine first 4 ingredients with seasonings in bowl; mix well. Place 1/2 teaspoonful on won ton wrapper. Dampen edges with a small amount of water. Fold into triangle to enclose filling. Fold corners to center, pressing to seal. Deep-fry in oil until golden brown on both sides. Drain on paper towels. Serve hot.

Patricia Rabago

ARTICHOKE QUICHE HORS D'OEUVRES

>   2 6-oz. jars marinated artichoke hearts
>   1 sm. onion, chopped
>   1 clove of garlic, chopped
>   4 eggs, beaten
>   1/4 c. bread crumbs
>   1/4 tsp. salt
>   1/8 tsp. pepper
>   1/8 tsp. oregano
>   1/8 tsp. Tabasco sauce
>   1/2 c. grated Cheddar cheese

Drain artichoke hearts, reserving marinade. Saute onion and garlic in reserved marinade in skillet until tender; remove from heat. Add artichokes and remaining ingredients; mix well. Spoon into greased 7 x 11-inch baking dish. Bake at 325 degrees for 30 minutes or until set. Cool. Cut into 1-inch squares. Yield: 6 dozen.

Dorothy J. Maxwell

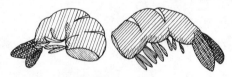

BITE-SIZED CREAM PUFFS WITH SHRIMP

>   1/2 pkg. pie crust mix
>   2 eggs
>   5 oz. cooked shrimp
>   1 tbsp. finely chopped chives
>   1/4 tsp. salt
>   2 tsp. lemon juice
>   1/2 c. mayonnaise
>   Several drops of Tabasco sauce

Combine pie crust mix and 2/3 cup boiling water in saucepan. Cook until mixture leaves side of pan, stirring constantly. Stir for 30 seconds longer. Remove from heat. Beat in eggs 1 at a time. Drop by tablespoonfuls 1 inch apart onto greased baking sheet. Bake at 400 degrees until brown. Combine remaining 6 ingredients in bowl, mixing well. Fill cooled puffs with shrimp mixture. Heat filled puffs in hot oven for 3 minutes before serving. Yield: 35-40 servings.

Mrs. Cary A. Kennedy

INDIVIDUAL SHRIMP QUICHES

  1 8-oz. package butter flake
     refrigerator rolls
24 sm. cooked shrimp
1 1/3 oz. Swiss cheese, grated
1 egg, beaten
1/2 c. half and half
1 tbsp. Brandy
1/2 tsp. salt
Pinch of white pepper (opt.)

Place 1/2 of each roll in greased miniature muffin cup, shaping to fit. Place 1 shrimp in each cup. Sprinkle with grated cheese. Combine remaining ingredients in bowl; mix well. Spoon evenly into individual quiches. Bake at 375 degrees for 10 to 12 minutes or until lightly browned. May substitute one 4-ounce can shrimp. Yield: 24 small appetizers.

Janet L. LaGrassa

TUNA BUNWICHES

2 tbsp. minced onion
1/2 c. chopped celery
2 tbsp. butter
2 tbsp. flour
1/4 tsp. salt
3/4 c. evaporated milk
1 tbsp. lemon juice
1 7-oz. can tuna, drained, flaked
1 hard-boiled egg, chopped
1 10-count can refrigerator biscuits
2 oz. cheese, cut into 20 strips

Saute onion and celery in butter in saucepan until tender. Blend in flour and salt. Stir in evaporated milk gradually. Cook until thickened, stirring constantly. Stir in lemon juice, tuna and egg. Roll each biscuit into 4-inch circle on lightly floured surface. Place 1 heaping tablespoonful tuna mixture on each biscuit. Pull edges to center to enclose filling; seal. Place on baking sheet. Bake at 375 degrees for 12 to 15 minutes or until lightly browned. Place 2 strips cheese in crisscross pattern on each roll. Bake for 2 minutes longer or until cheese melts. Yield: 10 servings.

Helen Jackson

SAUSAGE SNACKS

1 8-oz. can refrigerator crescent rolls
2 tbsp. margarine, softened
1/4 c. Parmesan cheese
1 to 2 tsp. oregano
8 brown and serve sausage links

Separate crescent dough into 4 rectangles; press perforations to seal. Brush with margarine. Sprinkle with cheese and oregano. Cut dough into squares. Place sausage on each square; roll to enclose sausage. Cut rolls into 3 or 4 pieces; secure with toothpicks. Place cut side down on baking sheet. Bake in preheated 370-degree oven for 12 to 15 minutes or until golden brown. Yield: 2 dozen.

Ellin Martin

SIZZLERS

1 lb. hot sausage
10 oz. shredded cheese
3 1/2 c. biscuit mix

Combine all ingredients in bowl; mix well. Shape into bite-sized balls. Place on baking sheets. Bake at 350 degrees for 20 minutes or until brown. May be frozen before baking. Yield: 2 dozen.

Frances B. Lindquist

STUFFED SNOW PEAS

100 snow peas
1 8-oz. package cream cheese, softened
1/4 c. Parmesan cheese
3 tbsp. catsup
2 tsp. dried dillweed
1 tsp. dry mustard
1 tsp. Worcestershire sauce
1/2 tsp. each salt, white pepper

Arrange snow peas in shallow pan. Cover with boiling water. Let stand for 1 minute; drain. Cover with ice cold water; drain. Cut 1/4 inch from each stem end. Combine remaining ingredients in bowl; mix well. Pipe cream cheese mixture into pea pods using pastry bag. Arrange on serving tray. Chill until serving time.

Norma McDonald

Salads &
Salad Dressings

APRICOT SALAD

2 lg. packages orange gelatin
1 c. apricot juice
1 c. pineapple juice
1 lg. can apricots
1 med. can crushed pineapple
Miniature marshmallows
2 tbsp. flour
2 tbsp. butter
1 egg, beaten
1 c. whipping cream, whipped
Grated cheese

Dissolve gelatin in 2 cups boiling water. Add 1/2 cup apricot juice, 1/2 cup pineapple juice, apricots and pineapple. Pour into 9 x 13-inch dish. Sprinkle with marshmallows. Chill until partially set. Combine remaining juices with flour, butter and egg in saucepan. Simmer until thickened, stirring constantly; cool. Add whipped cream; spread over gelatin. Top with cheese. Chill until firm. Yield: 15 serving .

Rosanne Brown

SHERRIED FRUIT SALAD

1 pineapple
1 cantaloupe
1 papaya
3 apples, sliced
1 bunch seedless grapes
1 pt. strawberries
1 c. slivered almonds
1 3-oz. package cream cheese, softened
1 tbsp. lime juice
1 tbsp. sugar
3/4 c. Sherry
Dash of salt

Chill fruit overnight. Cut pineapple, cantaloupe and papaya into bite-sized pieces. Combine all fruit with almonds in serving bowl, reserving enough papaya and almonds to garnish. Toss gently. Chill in refrigerator. Combine cream cheese with remaining ingredients in bowl; blend well. Combine with fruit; toss gently. Garnish with remaining papaya and almonds. Serve with light crackers and white wine.

Deb Fuller

LIME PARTY SALAD

1/4 lb. marshmallows
1 c. milk
1 pkg. lime gelatin
2 3-oz. packages cream cheese, softened
1 20-oz. can crushed pineapple
1 c. whipped cream
2/3 c. mayonnaise

Combine marshmallows and milk in double boiler. Heat until melted, stirring constantly. Pour over gelatin in bowl; stir until dissolved. Add cream cheese; stir until melted. Mix in pineapple; cool. Fold in whipped cream and mayonnaise. Chill until firm.

Laurene Peterson

ORANGE AND AVOCADO SALAD

4 lg. oranges, peeled, sectioned
2 med. avocados, sliced
Watercress sprigs
1/4 c. salad dressing
1/4 c. catsup
2 tbsp. sugar
3 tbsp. oil
2 tbsp. cider vinegar

Arrange oranges and avocados in lettuce-lined serving plates. Top with watercress. Combine remaining ingredients in small bowl; mix well. Pour over salad. Yield: 8 servings.

Mrs. George W. Rhyne

STUFFED HONEYDEW MELONS

3 honeydew melons
1 c. watermelon balls
1 c. cantaloupe balls
1 c. honeydew balls
1 c. Port

Cut 1 inch off top of each honeydew melon. Scoop out seeds; fill with mixed melon balls. Pour 1/3 cup wine into each melon; replace tops. Chill for 2 hours. Cut each melon in half; serve with melon balls and marinade. May use lime juice for Port. Yield: 6 servings.

Mrs. John A. Simonds

SUMMER LUNCHEON SALAD

1 c. halved pitted fresh Bing cherries
1 1/2 c. fresh orange wedges
1 1/2 c. fresh pineapple wedges
1 c. banana slices
1 c. green grapes
4 c. cottage cheese
1/2 c. orange juice
1 1/2 c. mayonnaise
1 jigger Cointreau
1/2 c. whipping cream, whipped

Arrange fruit and cottage cheese on serving plates. Fold juice, mayonnaise and Cointreau into whipped cream. Spoon over salad. Yield: 6 servings.

Mrs. Kermit Jamison

TINGEY HOUSE CHIFFON MOLD

1 1/2 c. sugar
2 env. unflavored gelatin
1/4 tsp. salt
4 eggs, separated
1 c. pureed frozen mango
1 c. pureed frozen pineapple
2 c. whipping cream, whipped

Combine 1 cup sugar with gelatin, salt, egg yolks and 1 cup cold water in saucepan. Simmer for about 5 minutes until slightly thickened, stirring constantly. Add frozen juices, mixing well. Chill until partially set. Beat egg whites until soft peaks form. Add remaining 1/2 cup sugar; beat until stiff. Fold in gelatin mixture; fold in whipped cream. Pour into 10-cup mold. Chill until set. Unmold on serving plate; garnish with fresh fruit. Two cans frozen orange juice concentrate may be substituted for frozen mango and pineapple. Yield: 10 servings.

Mrs. Thomas B. Hayward

STRAWBERRY SOUFFLE SALAD

2 10-oz. packages frozen sliced
*   strawberries*
2 3-oz. packages strawberry gelatin

1/2 c. dry Sauterne
1 c. mayonnaise
1/4 tsp. salt
1 c. canned pineapple tidbits, drained
1 c. chopped pecans

Fasten collar of double thickness waxed paper around souffle dish extending collar 1 1/2 inches above rim. Thaw strawberries, reserving 1/2 cup juice. Pour 2 cups boiling water over gelatin in mixer bowl. Stir until gelatin is dissolved. Add reserved strawberry juice, Sauterne, mayonnaise and salt. Beat until well blended. Pour into freezer tray. Freeze for 20 to 25 minutes or until firm 1 inch from edge. Spoon into mixer bowl; beat until fluffy and thick. Fold in strawberries, pineapple and pecans. Spoon into souffle dish. Chill in refrigerator for 1 hour or until firm. Remove collar at serving time. Garnish with whole strawberries and chicory. Yield: 8-12 servings.

Photograph for this recipe on page 13.

GREEN GODDESS SALAD

Romaine lettuce, torn
Iceberg lettuce, torn
Spinach leaves
Avocado wedges
Grapefruit sections
Whole white seedless grapes
1 c. salad dressing
1/2 c. sour cream
1 clove of garlic, crushed
4 anchovies, chopped
4 tbsp. parsley, chopped
3 tbsp. chopped chives
1 tbsp. lemon juice
1 tbsp. tarragon vinegar
1/2 tsp. salt
Dash of pepper

Place lettuce, spinach, avocado, grapefruit sections and grapes in salad bowl; toss to mix. Combine remaining ingredients in small bowl; mix well. Pour over salad; toss gently. Yield: 8 servings.

Mrs. Carleton V. Hansen

NOODLE CAESAR SALAD

1 clove of garlic, minced
3/4 c. oil
1/4 c. vinegar
1 tsp. salt
1 tsp. anchovy paste
3/4 tsp. sugar
1/4 tsp. each pepper, dry mustard
1 clove of garlic, cut in half
8 oz. medium egg noodles, cooked,
    well drained
1 egg yolk
1 head romaine lettuce, torn
2 c. garlic-flavored croutons
1/4 c. Parmesan cheese

Combine minced garlic, next 5 ingredients, pepper and dry mustard in bowl; mix well. Chill in refrigerator. Rub large salad bowl with garlic halves. Add noodles and egg yolk; mix well. Add lettuce, chilled dressing and 1 cup croutons; toss to mix. Sprinkle remaining 1 cup croutons and cheese over salad.

Photograph for this recipe on this page.

CATALINA SALAD

1 clove of garlic, chopped
6 tbsp. oil
2 c. bread cubes
1 lg. head lettuce, torn
1 head romaine, torn
3 tbsp. quartered pickled onions
1/4 c. sliced pitted black olives
1/4 tsp. salt
1/8 tsp. pepper
1/3 c. grated Parmesan cheese
1 egg
3 tbsp. lemon juice

Soak garlic in oil in bowl overnight. Strain and remove garlic. Brown bread cubes in 2 tablespoons garlic oil in skillet; set aside. Place lettuce and romaine in salad bowl. Add onions, olives, remaining 1/4 cup garlic oil, salt, pepper and cheese. Drop egg on top. Pour lemon juice over egg; toss well. Add croutons; toss to mix. Garnish with tomato wedges. Yield: 6 servings.

Mrs. John Giraudo

CAESAR SALAD

1 clove of garlic, mashed
1/2 c. oil
1/2 head lettuce
1/2 bunch curly endive
1 c. croutons
3 or 4 tomatoes, chopped
1 egg, beaten
1/2 c. grated Parmesan cheese
1/4 c. lemon juice
1 tsp. Worcestershire sauce
1/2 tsp. salt
Pepper to taste

Combine garlic and oil in small bowl. Let stand for several minutes; strain. Place lettuce and endive in bowl. Add croutons and tomatoes. Pour garlic oil over greens. Combine remaining ingredients in bowl; mix well. Pour over salad; toss to mix. Yield: 4-6 servings.

Mrs. Joseph Bourassa

GREEN PEA SALAD

1 can green peas, drained
Pimento to taste
1 tsp. garlic salt
2 stalks celery, chopped
2 hard-boiled eggs, chopped
1/2 c. cubed American cheese
Mayonnaise

Combine first 6 ingredients in bowl. Add mayonnaise to taste; mix well.

Mrs. Chester Kuras

ASPARAGUS MOLD

2 pkg. frozen asparagus, cooked
1 tbsp. gelatin
1/2 c. mayonnaise
1/2 c. heavy cream, whipped
1 tsp. salt
2 tbsp. lemon juice
1 c. blanched almonds

Drain asparagus, reserving 1 cup liquid. Soften gelatin in 1/4 cup cold water in bowl. Add hot asparagus liquid; stir until gelatin is dissolved. Chill until partially set. Fold in remaining ingredients and asparagus. Pour into mold. Chill until set. Yield: 12 servings.

Mrs. Robert E. Edmonds

BEET AND HORSERADISH SALAD

1 pkg. lemon gelatin
1 c. hot beet juice
1/2 tsp. salt
2 tbsp. horseradish
2 tbsp. sugar
1 c. chopped celery
2 tbsp. minced onion
1 c. diced beets
3 tbsp. vinegar

Dissolve gelatin in hot beet juice in bowl. Add 1/2 cup cold water and remaining ingredients; mix well. Pour into 1-quart mold. Chill until firm. Unmold on serving plate. Yield: 8 servings.

Mrs. George M. Karl

BEST-EVER POTATO SALAD

4 c. diced cooked potatoes
1 1/2 c. chopped celery
1/2 c. chopped scallions
1/4 c. sliced radishes
2 tbsp. chopped parsley
1 c. mayonnaise
1 tbsp. vinegar
2 tsp. prepared mustard
1/2 tsp. celery seed

1 1/2 tsp. salt
1/8 tsp. pepper

Combine all ingredients in bowl; mix well. Chill until serving time. Serve on shredded lettuce. Garnish with tomato, hard-boiled egg, sliced stuffed olives, grated carrots or sweet pickles. Yield: 6 servings.

Betty Bell

LUNCHEON TOMATOES

6 med. ripe tomatoes
12 oz. small curd cottage cheese
1 med. onion, chopped
4 stalks celery, chopped
3 tbsp. mayonnaise
1/4 tsp. Worcestershire sauce
1/8 tsp. Tabasco sauce

Cut tops from tomatoes. Scoop out pulp, reserving shells. Chop pulp and combine with remaining ingredients in bowl; mix well. Spoon into tomato shells. Place on lettuce leaf-lined plate. Garnish with additional mayonnaise and paprika. Yield: 6 servings.

Mrs. Frank G. Ratliff

SESAME-SPINACH SALAD

1 2-lb. package fresh spinach
1 head Boston lettuce
1 sm. head iceberg lettuce, torn
1 bunch watercress
1 cucumber, thinly sliced
1 10-oz. jar mandarin oranges, drained
1 avocado, sliced
1/3 c. oil
2 1/2 tbsp. cider vinegar
1 1/4 tbsp. sugar
2 tsp. soy sauce
1 1/2 tsp. sesame seed

Place spinach, lettuce, watercress, cucumber, oranges and avocado in salad bowl. Chill in refrigerator. Combine remaining ingredients in jar with lid. Shake to mix well. Pour over salad. Yield: 6-8 servings.

Mrs. Lawrence V. Greene

FOUR-SEASONS SPINACH SALAD

6 c. fresh spinach
1 sm. Bermuda onion, sliced
1/4 c. diced celery
4 hard-boiled eggs, sliced
1/8 tsp. pepper
1/2 c. sour cream
1/2 tsp. garlic salt
1 1/2 oz. bleu cheese, crumbled
1 1/2 tbsp. lemon juice

Place spinach, onion, celery, eggs and pepper in salad bowl; toss well. Chill in refrigerator. Combine remaining ingredients in bowl. Chill salad and dressing until serving time. Toss salad with dressing to mix well. Yield: 4 servings.

Mrs. Dean S. Laird

POLYNESIAN SALAD

1 head romaine, torn
3 tomatoes, cut into wedges
1 ripe avocado, sliced
Salt and pepper to taste
2 tbsp. sesame seed, toasted
6 tbsp. oil
2 tbsp. wine vinegar
2 tbsp. chutney juice
2 tsp. finely minced chutney

Place romaine and tomatoes in salad bowl. Chill, covered, for 1 hour. Top with avocado slices; sprinkle with salt and pepper. Combine remaining ingredients in small bowl; mix well. Pour over salad; toss gently. Yield: 6 servings.

Mrs. Richard C. Smith

SPRING SALAD

3 sm. heads Boston lettuce, quartered
1 c. mayonnaise
2 hard-boiled eggs, chopped
1 tbsp. mixed chopped chives and parsley

Soak lettuce in ice water in bowl for 1 hour. Drain; dry thoroughly. Arrange 2 wedges on individual salad plates. Pour a small amount of mayonnaise over lettuce. Combine egg and herbs in small bowl. Sprinkle over mayonnaise.

Mrs. John E. Clark

CLASSY TOSSED SALAD

1/3 c. slivered almonds
5 tbsp. sugar
3 tbsp. vinegar
1 can mandarin oranges, drained
1 c. chopped celery
1 head lettuce, torn

Caramelize almonds in 2 tablespoons sugar in heavy skillet over low heat; cool on waxed paper. Dissolve 3 tablespoons sugar in vinegar in small bowl. Combine remaining ingredients in salad bowl. Add vinegar mixture and almonds; toss to mix. Yield: 8 servings.

Rhoda E. Serrin

TOSSED LETTUCE SALAD

1 med. head lettuce, torn into
    bite-sized pieces
2 lg. tomatoes, cut into chunks
5 med. green onions, chopped
4 slices crisp-cooked bacon, crumbled
3 slices American cheese, cubed
2 tbsp. vinegar
2 tbsp. mayonnaise
1/2 tsp. each salt, pepper

Combine lettuce, tomatoes, onions, bacon and cheese in bowl. Mix vinegar, mayonnaise, salt and pepper in small bowl. Pour dressing over salad; toss to mix. Yield: 6 servings.

Mrs. Henry E. Chriceol

CURRIED CHICKEN AND GRAPE SALAD

3 c. chopped cooked chicken
1 1/2 c. thinly sliced celery
1 c. seedless green grapes
2 tbsp. lemon juice
1 1/4 tsp. salt
1/4 tsp. freshly ground pepper
1 1/2 tsp. curry powder
6 tbsp. mayonnaise

Combine all ingredients in bowl; toss lightly. Chill thoroughly. Serve on lettuce. Garnish with toasted slivered almonds. Yield: 6 servings.

Linette Peterson

COLD BEEF SALAD

2 c. slivered roast beef
1 c. chopped celery
1 c. chopped peeled tart apple
1/4 c. mayonnaise
1 tbsp. prepared mustard
1/2 tsp. salt

Combine beef, celery and apple in salad bowl. Combine mayonnaise, mustard and salt in small bowl; mix well. Add to beef mixture; toss lightly until well coated. Serve on lettuce leaves.

Dorian Rutherford

SALMON-MACARONI SALAD

1 can salmon, drained
1 med. cucumber, chopped
1 tsp. grated onion
1 tbsp. chopped parsley
2 c. cooked macaroni
1 c. mayonnaise
Salt and pepper to taste

Combine all ingredients in salad bowl; toss gently. Chill, covered, until serving time.

Ann Milner

LOBSTER-CHICKEN SALAD

1 chicken breast, cooked, slivered
1/2 lb. lobster, chopped
3 hard-boiled eggs, separated
1 c. finely chopped celery
French dressing
1 c. mayonnaise
2 tbsp. chili sauce
1 tbsp. chopped chives
Salt to taste
1/2 c. whipped cream

Combine chicken, lobster, chopped egg white and celery in bowl. Add a small amount of French dressing; mix well. Let stand for 1 hour. Combine mayonnaise and chili sauce with chives and salt in small bowl; mix well. Stir in mashed egg yolk. Fold in whipped cream. Chill until serving time. Combine chicken mixture with mayonnaise mixture in bowl; toss lightly. Serve on crisp lettuce.

Shirley Crofts

CRAB LOUIS

1 lg. head lettuce
3 c. chilled crab meat
2 lg. tomatoes, cut in wedges
2 hard-boiled eggs, cut in wedges
Salt to taste
1 c. mayonnaise
1/4 c. sour cream
1/4 c. chili sauce
1/4 c. chopped green onion
1 tsp. lemon juice

Line 4 large plates with lettuce leaves. Shred remaining lettuce; arrange on leaves. Arrange crab meat on lettuce; circle with tomato wedges and egg wedges. Sprinkle with salt. Combine mayonnaise, sour cream, chili sauce, green onion and lemon juice in bowl; season with salt. Chill thoroughly. Pour 1/4 cup mayonnaise mixture over each salad. Garnish with paprika. Serve with remaining dressing. Yield: 4 servings.

Hellene Handcock

SHRIMP MOUSSE WITH TOMATO ASPIC

1 pkg. unflavored gelatin
1 c. mayonnaise
2 hard-boiled eggs, chopped
1 c. diced celery
3 1/2 c. shrimp
1/2 pt. whipping cream, whipped
1 pkg. lemon gelatin
2 c. hot tomato juice
2 tbsp. wine vinegar
2 tbsp. grated onion
1/2 tsp. each salt, pepper, basil,
    celery seed

Soften gelatin in 1/4 cup cold water in bowl. Stir in 1/4 cup boiling water until gelatin dissolves. Add mayonnaise, eggs, celery and shrimp; mix gently. Fold in whipped cream. Spoon into 9 x 13-inch dish. Chill until set. Dissolve lemon gelatin in hot tomato juice in bowl. Add remaining ingredients; mix well. Pour over congealed gelatin mixture. Chill until set. Yield: 12 servings.

Liz Waldin

SHRIMP-STUFFED AVOCADOS

1/4 c. tarragon vinegar
2 tbsp. horseradish mustard
1 tbsp. catsup
1 1/2 tsp. paprika
1/2 tsp..salt
1/4 tsp. cayenne pepper
1/2 c. oil
1/4 c. minced celery
1/4 c. minced green onions and tops
2 lb. shrimp, cleaned, cooked
8 med. avocado halves, peeled

Combine first 6 ingredients in bowl. Add oil gradually, beating constantly. Stir in celery and onion. Pour over shrimp in shallow dish. Chill for 4 hours or longer. Drain shrimp, reserving marinade. Arrange shrimp in avocado halves. Garnish with chilled asparagus spears and carrot sticks. Serve with reserved marinade or French dressing.

Nancy B. White

Salad Dressings

MAKE-AHEAD ROQUEFORT DRESSING

2 c. mayonnaise
2 cloves of garlic, minced
1 c. sour cream
1/2 c. wine vinegar
2 tbsp. lemon juice
1/2 lb. Roquefort cheese
Cracked pepper

Combine mayonnaise, garlic and sour cream in bowl. Thin mixture with wine vinegar and lemon juice. Crumble Roquefort cheese into mixture. Season to taste with coarsely ground pepper. Chill for 24 hours.

Mrs. John McEachern

HONEY-LIME DRESSING

1   6-oz. can frozen limeade concentrate
3/4 c. oil
1/2 c. honey
1/4 tsp. salt
2 tsp. celery seed

Combine limeade concentrate, oil, honey and salt in blender container; process until well blended. Stir in celery seed. Serve over fruit salad. Yield: 2 cups.

Roxanne Farnsworth

SPROUT DRESSING

1 c. alfalfa sprouts
1 tbsp. honey
1 tbsp. lemon juice
1 tsp. poppy seed
1 tsp. sesame seed
1/2 tsp. salt

Place all ingredients in blender container; process until smooth. Chill until serving time. Serve over sauteed watercress.

Kathleen Carrington

TABASCO VINAIGRETTE DRESSING

3/4 c. olive oil
1/2 c. tarragon vinegar
3/4 tsp. salt
1/4 tsp. Tabasco sauce
2 tsp. minced chives
2 tsp. minced fresh chervil
2 tsp. capers
1 hard-boiled egg, chopped (opt.)

Combine all ingredients in bowl; beat well. Yield: About 1 1/3 cups.

Luanne Brock

YOGURT DRESSING

1 c. yogurt
1 tbsp. lemon juice
1 tbsp. minced onion
2 tsp. sugar
1/4 tsp. salt
Dash of cayenne pepper
Dash of cumin

Combine all ingredients in bowl; blend well. Yield: 4 servings.

Charlene Rafferty

Meats
for Everyone

PEACH-GLAZED CORNED BEEF

  1 *3-lb. corned beef brisket*
  4 sm. apples, halved, cored
  1/3 c. peach preserves
  1/4 tsp. ground ginger

Rinse brisket in cold water. Place fat side up on rack in shallow roasting pan containing 2 cups water. Bake, covered, at 325 degrees for 2 hours; drain. Arrange apples skin side up around brisket with 1/2 cup water. Bake, uncovered, for 30 minutes longer. Blend preserves and ginger in bowl. Turn apples skin side down. Spoon preserves over brisket and apples. Bake until glaze is heated through.

Elaine Frost

BEEF STROGANOFF

  3 cloves of garlic, minced
  2 lg. onions, chopped
  1/2 c. butter
  2 lb. lean sirloin, cut into thin strips
  2 tbsp. flour
  1 bay leaf
  2 tsp. soy sauce
  1 1/2 c. tomato juice
  1 lb. fresh mushrooms
  2 tsp. Worcestershire sauce
  Salt and pepper to taste
  Paprika to taste
  2 pt. sour cream

Saute garlic and onions in butter in skillet until tender. Add sirloin. Cook until brown. Stir in flour and next 8 ingredients. Cook until sirloin is tender. Stir in sour cream. Cook until heated through; cool. Chill overnight. Cook until heated through at serving time. May substitute half bottle of catsup for tomato juice.

Mrs. W. E. Cummins

DELICIOUS BEEF WITH WINE

  1 1/2 lb. beef, cubed
  Flour
  Salt and pepper to taste
  Shortening

  1 c. chopped celery
  1/2 c. chopped onion
  1/2 pkg. oxtail soup mix
  1 8-oz. can mushrooms
  1/2 c. red wine

Dredge beef in flour seasoned with salt and pepper. Brown in shortening in skillet; drain. Add celery, onion, soup mix, mushrooms and 2 cups water; mix well. Simmer for several hours or until beef is tender. Add wine just before serving. Serve over rice.

Mrs. Richard P. Pawson

FIVE-HOUR STEW

  4 lb. boneless chuck, cubed
  6 med. potatoes, cubed
  6 carrots, coarsely chopped
  2 c. coarsely chopped celery
  2 lg. onions, coarsely chopped
  1 lg. green pepper, coarsely chopped
  2 cloves of garlic, minced
  1 lg. can tomatoes, cut up
  1 tbsp. sugar
  1 bay leaf
  1 20-oz. can tomato sauce
  2 slices white bread, shredded
  1 tbsp. seasoned salt
  3 tbsp. tapioca
  1/2 c. Sherry
  1 sm. can mushrooms
  1 10-oz. package frozen peas

Combine all ingredients except peas in Dutch oven; mix well. Bake, covered, at 300 degrees for 5 hours. Do not stir or peek. Stir in peas 5 minutes before serving. Simmer for 5 minutes. Yield: 8-12 servings.

Dolys P. Gelke

CARBONNADE FLAMANDE

  3 lb. beef chuck, cubed
  Flour
  Salt and pepper to taste
  5 lg. onions, sliced
  3 to 4 tbsp. olive oil

3 sprigs of parsley
Several celery tops
1 bay leaf
2 sprigs of thyme
3 or 4 peppercorns, crushed
3 cloves of garlic, minced
1 to 2 c. strong beef broth
1 to 2 c. dark beer
1 tbsp. brown sugar
1 tbsp. wine vinegar

Dredge beef in flour seasoned with salt and pepper; shake off excess. Brown beef with onions in olive oil in stock pot; drain. Combine parsley, celery tops, bay leaf, thyme and peppercorns in cheesecloth; tie with string. Add to beef mixture with garlic and enough broth and beer to cover beef. Simmer, covered, for 2 to 2 1/2 hours or until beef is tender. Add additional broth and beer if necessary. Remove bouquet garni. Stir in brown sugar and wine vinegar. Simmer for 10 minutes longer.

Mrs. J. W. Williams

GOURMET BEEF ELEGANTE

1   6-oz. can tomato paste
1   3-lb. rump roast
2 c. cold chicken stock
1 c. dry white wine
1/4 c. dry Sherry
1 lg. onion, sliced
1 stalk celery, chopped
1 bay leaf
1/2 tsp. oregano
2 tbsp. finely chopped caraway seed
3 tbsp. flour
Salt and pepper to taste
MSG to taste
1/2 c. sour cream

Spread tomato paste over roast. Place in shallow bowl with next 7 ingredients. Marinate overnight in refrigerator, turning once. Drain, reserving marinade. Place roast in Dutch oven. Bake at 450 degrees for 30 to 40 minutes or until brown. Remove from oven. Add reserved marinade. Simmer for several minutes. Add caraway seed; mix well. Blend flour into 1 cup

cold water. Add gradually to simmering marinade, stirring constantly. Stir in seasonings. Simmer for 2 1/2 hours or until roast is tender. Remove onion, celery and bay leaf. Stir in sour cream gradually. Yield: 4-6 servings.

Mrs. John M. Kiernan, Jr.

MARINADE FOR MEAT

1 c. Italian dressing
1/4 c. soy sauce
1/4 c. red cooking wine
1 to 1 1/2 tsp. meat tenderizer
1/2 tsp. each onion salt, garlic salt
1 tsp. charcoal grill seasoning
2 to 3 lb. chuck roast

Combine all ingredients except roast in large shallow dish; mix well. Add roast. Marinate overnight in refrigerator, turning frequently. Cook roast over hot coals to desired degree of doneness.

Mary Pat Thuma

PERFECT TENDERLOIN

1 1/2 c. oil
3/4 c. soy sauce
1/4 c. Worcestershire sauce
2 tbsp. dry mustard
2 to 3 tsp. salt
1/4 tsp. pepper
1/2 c. white vinegar
1/3 c. lemon juice
1 tbsp. chopped parsley
1 tbsp. garlic powder
1   2 1/2 to 3-lb. beef tenderloin
1/4 lb. butter

Combine first 10 ingredients in bowl; mix well. Pour over tenderloin in shallow dish. Chill for 24 hours. Remove tenderloin from marinade. Pat dry with paper towels. Place in shallow baking pan. Dot with butter. Bake at 450 degrees for 15 minutes. Reduce temperature to 350 degrees. Bake for 15 to 30 minutes longer or to desired degree of doneness.

Emily Pennington

TENDERLOIN WITH MUSHROOM STUFFING

1/2 sm. onion, chopped
1 4-oz. can mushrooms
1/4 c. butter
1 1/2 c. soft bread crumbs
1/2 c. chopped celery
Salt and pepper to taste
1 3-lb. beef tenderloin, split,
  flattened
4 slices bacon

Saute onion and mushrooms in butter in skillet until lightly browned. Add bread crumbs, celery, seasonings and enough water to moisten; mix well. Spread over bottom half of tenderloin; fold to enclose filling, securing edges. Place in roasting pan. Top with bacon. Bake at 350 degrees for 1 hour. Yield: 6 servings.

Mrs. Kenneth H. McChesney

GRILLED CHUCK STEAK

1 1 1/2 to 2-in. thick chuck steak
Meat tenderizer
1 tsp. each thyme, marjoram
2 tbsp. minced onion
1/2 c. oil
1/2 c. vinegar
1/2 c. red wine
1 bay leaf, crushed
Salt and pepper to taste

Sprinkle both sides of steak generously with meat tenderizer; pierce with fork. Place in shallow dish. Refrigerate for 1 hour. Combine remaining ingredients in bowl; mix well. Pour over steak. Marinate for 3 to 4 hours, turning occasionally. Drain; reserve marinade. Grill over hot coals, basting frequently with reserved marinade, to desired degree of doneness.

Gail Pringle

GRILLED DILL STEAK

3/4 c. olive oil
3/4 c. dill pickle liquid
1/3 c. sliced dill pickles

1 clove of garlic, minced
1 3-lb. London Broil, 1 1/2 to
  2 in. thick
Salt and pepper to taste

Combine oil, pickle liquid, pickles and garlic in large shallow dish; mix well. Add London Broil; turn to coat. Marinate, covered, overnight in refrigerator, turning once. Drain, reserving marinade. Grill 6 inches from heat source for 14 to 17 minutes per side, basting frequently with reserved marinade. Season with salt and pepper. Cut diagonally across grain into thin slices. Yield: 8 servings.

Malinda Fort

CHICKEN-FRIED STEAK WITH CREAM GRAVY

2 lb. round steak
1 egg
Flour
Salt
Pepper
1/2 c. shortening
2 c. milk

Pound steak; cut into 4 pieces. Beat egg with 1 tablespoon water in shallow bowl. Dip steak in egg. Dredge in 1/3 cup flour seasoned with 1/2 teaspoon each salt and pepper. Brown steak on both sides in hot shortening in skillet. Simmer for 20 minutes. Remove steak to serving platter. Blend 3 tablespoons flour with 3 tablespoons pan drippings in skillet. Add 1/2 teaspoon each salt and pepper. Cook until flour is lightly browned, stirring constantly. Stir in milk gradually. Cook until thick, stirring constantly. Boil for 4 to 5 minutes. Serve over steak. Yield: 4 servings.

Kathleen Carrington

LONDON BROIL WITH ONIONS

1 lb. flank steak
2 med. onions, thinly sliced
3/4 tsp. salt
1 tbsp. butter

2 tbsp. oil
1 tsp. lemon juice
2 cloves of garlic, crushed
1/4 tsp. pepper

Place steak on rack in broiler pan. Score both sides of steak in diamond pattern 1/8 inch deep. Saute onions with 1/4 teaspoon salt in butter in skillet until tender. Set aside; keep warm. Combine remaining ingredients with 1/2 teaspoon salt in bowl; mix well. Brush steak with half the mixture. Broil 2 to 3 inches from heat source for 5 minutes. Turn steak and brush with remaining sauce. Broil for 5 minutes longer. Slice across the grain into thin slices. Serve with onions.

Linda Beazley

STEAK ROLL-UPS

1 1-lb. round steak, pounded thin
Salt and pepper to taste
Dash of garlic salt
1 pkg. stuffing mix
1 can cream of mushroom soup

Cut steak into 6 pieces. Sprinkle with seasonings. Prepare stuffing using package directions. Spoon 1 tablespoonful onto each piece of steak. Roll to enclose filling; secure with toothpick. Brown in a small amount of shortening in skillet. Add soup and 1 soup can water. Simmer for 1 hour, basting occasionally.

Cheryl King

STUFFED FLANK STEAK

2 c. chopped onion
4 cloves of garlic, pressed
Butter
2 c. sliced green olives
2 c. sliced mushrooms
2 c. chopped salami
4 flank steaks, pounded
2 c. dry red wine

Saute onion and garlic in a small amount of butter in skillet. Add next 3 ingredients. Cook until tender. Spread over steaks. Roll to enclose filling. Secure with string. Brown in butter in skillet, turning frequently. Remove to roasting pan. Stir wine into pan drippings. Pour over steaks. Bake at 400 degrees for 20 minutes or to desired degree of doneness. Yield: 4 servings.

Mrs. P. X. Kelley

SHISH KABOBS

4 steaks, cut into 1-in. cubes
Cherry tomatoes
Green peppers, cut into chunks
Onions, cut into chunks
1 lg. bottle of Catalina salad dressing
Fresh mushrooms

Place first 4 ingredients in large shallow dish. Cover with Catalina dressing. Marinate for 4 hours in refrigerator. Add mushrooms to marinade. Marinate for 1 hour. Thread all ingredients on skewers. Grill over hot coals. Yield: 5-6 servings.

Eloise Parker

SIMPLY DELICIOUS BEEF WELLINGTON

1 4-lb. beef fillet
Salt and freshly ground pepper to taste
Brandy
Bacon slices
1 c. braunschweiger
1 pkg. frozen patty shells, thawed
1 egg, beaten

Rub beef with salt, pepper and Brandy; place in baking dish. Arrange bacon slices over top. Bake at 325 degrees for 40 minutes or to desired degree of doneness. Remove from oven; let cool. Spread braunschweiger over beef. Roll out patty shells very thin; arrange over beef in single thickness, covering completely and sealing edges. Do not overlap; trim off excess pastry. Place on baking sheet. Brush pastry carefully with egg; cut several diagonal slashes in top of pastry. Bake at 425 degrees for 30 minutes or until pastry is golden.

Mrs. Charles A. Bell

BEEF AND WILD RICE SUPREME

1 lb. ground beef
1/4 c. melted margarine
2 cans beef bouillon
1 pkg. long grain and wild rice
1 can mushrooms, drained

Brown ground beef in skillet, stirring until crumbly; drain. Combine with remaining ingredients in 2-quart casserole; mix well. Bake, covered, at 375 degrees for 1 1/2 hours or until rice is tender.

Judy Smith

DEEP-DISH PIZZA

1 lb. ground beef
1/4 c. each chopped onion, green pepper
1 16-oz. can tomatoes
1 pkg. pizza mix
2 6-oz. packages mozzarella cheese,
  sliced
Parmesan cheese

Brown ground beef in skillet, stirring until crumbly; drain. Add onion and green pepper. Cook until tender. Stir in tomatoes and sauce from pizza mix. Simmer for 15 minutes. Prepare pizza dough using package directions. Press dough onto bottom and halfway up sides of greased 9 x 13-inch baking pan. Layer mozzarella cheese and tomato sauce alternately over dough until all ingredients are used. Sprinkle with Parmesan cheese. Bake at 425 degrees for 20 to 25 minutes or until heated through. Yield: 6-8 servings.

Jean F. Reavis

DANISH MEAT LOAF

2 lb. lean ground beef
1 c. bread crumbs
Salt
Pepper
1 tsp. sugar
4 eggs, beaten
5 slices bacon
3 tbsp. flour

2 c. milk
2 bouillon cubes
3 tbsp. apple jelly
Kitchen Bouquet to taste

Combine ground beef, bread crumbs, 1 tablespoon salt, 1 teaspoon pepper, sugar and eggs in bowl; mix well. Shape into loaf. Arrange 3 slices bacon in bottom of baking dish. Place meat loaf over bacon. Make 8 finger-sized holes in top of loaf. Fill each with 1/4 slice bacon. Bake at 375 degrees for 10 minutes. Blend flour with 1/3 cup water in saucepan. Stir in milk, 1 cup water and bouillon cubes. Cook until thick, stirring constantly. Add jelly, Kitchen Bouquet, salt and pepper to taste. Pour over meat loaf. Bake for 1 hour longer.

Marianne T. Swanson

MEAT ROLL SUPREME

2 lb. ground chuck
1 onion, chopped
2 eggs, beaten
3 slices bread, crumbled
1/2 c. tomato sauce
Parsley to taste
1/2 tsp. oregano
1/4 tsp. each salt, pepper
8 thin slices baked ham
6 oz. mozzarella cheese, shredded
3 slices Swiss cheese

Combine first 9 ingredients in bowl; mix well. Spread into rectangle on foil. Layer ham and mozzarella cheese over rectangle. Roll as for jelly roll. Place seam side down on foil in shallow baking pan. Bake at 350 degrees for 1 1/4 hours. Cut Swiss cheese into triangles. Arrange over roll. Bake for 5 minutes longer or until cheese melts.

Emily Anderson

COMPANY MANICOTTI

2 lb. ground beef
1 onion, chopped
1 tsp. salt
2 tbsp. chopped parsley

1/2 tsp. each oregano, garlic salt
2 eggs, beaten
2 c. dry cottage cheese
1/2 c. Parmesan cheese
3/4 lb. mozzarella cheese, shredded
1 pkg. manicotti shells, cooked, drained
1 med. jar prepared spaghetti sauce

Brown ground beef with onion in skillet, stirring until crumbly; drain. Stir in seasonings; mix well. Add next 3 ingredients and 1/3 of the mozzarella cheese; mix well. Stuff manicotti shells with mixture. Arrange in baking dish. Top with remaining ground beef mixture, spaghetti sauce and remaining cheese. Bake at 350 degrees for 30 minutes.

Susanne Simmons

PITA BREAD WITH MEDITERRANEAN MIX

1 lb. ground beef
1 cucumber, peeled, seeded
1 med. onion, chopped
1/2 jar green olives, chopped
1/2 jar ripe olives, chopped
1 stalk celery, chopped
2 med. tomatoes, chopped
1/2 lb. Cheddar cheese, shredded
1/2 lb. Swiss cheese, shredded
1 clove of garlic, crushed
1 slice bread, cubed
2 slices hard salami, chopped
Pepper to taste
2 to 3 tbsp. olive oil
Pita bread

Brown ground beef in skillet, stirring until crumbly; drain. Add remaining ingredients except pita bread; mix well. Chill for 2 to 3 hours. Cut pita bread into halves to form pockets. Fill with ground beef mixture.

Glenda Gibbs

FAVORITE TAGLIARINI

1 lb. ground round steak
1 lg. onion, chopped

1 clove of garlic, chopped
1 green pepper, chopped
2 tbsp. olive oil
1 can tomato soup
Salt and pepper to taste
2 sm. cans chopped mushrooms
1 c. Parmesan cheese
1 No. 2 can cream-style corn
1/2 c. chopped ripe olives
1/4 c. parsley flakes
1 tsp. each Accent, basil, oregano
1 5-oz. package thin egg noodles

Sear ground beef; remove from skillet. Saute onion, garlic and green pepper in oil until browned. Combine all ingredients except noodles; stir in 2 soup cans water. Mix well. Stir in uncooked noodles; spoon into greased 4-quart casserole. Bake, uncovered, in 350-degree oven for 1 hour or until heated through. Yield: 8 servings.

Mrs. Willis M. Simmons

MEATBALLS IN SOUR CREAM SAUCE

2 lb. ground beef
2 med. onions, ground
1 egg
1 tsp. salt
1/4 tsp. pepper
1/2 tsp. Italian seasoning
Cracker crumbs
Butter
1 can mushroom soup
1 pt. fresh mushrooms, sliced
2/3 c. sour cream
1/2 c. dry white wine

Combine first 6 ingredients in bowl; mix well. Shape into small balls; coat with crumbs. Brown in butter in Dutch oven. Combine remaining ingredients in bowl; mix well. Pour over meatballs. Bake, covered, at 350 degrees for 30 minutes or until heated through. Garnish with additional sour cream and chopped dill. Yield: 8 servings.

Mrs. Charles Lamback

BARBECUED MEATBALLS

2 lb. ground beef
1 pkg. dry onion soup mix
2 eggs
1 c. seasoned dry bread crumbs
1 c. barbecue sauce
1/4 c. honey
4 drops of Tabasco sauce

Combine ground beef, onion soup mix, eggs and bread crumbs in bowl; mix well. Shape into small balls. Place in shallow baking pan. Bake in 350-degree oven for 20 to 30 minutes or until brown. Drain; place in chafing dish. Mix barbecue sauce, honey and Tabasco sauce in bowl. Pour over meatballs. Yield: 3 dozen.

Linda Fisher

BAKED HONEY HAM PIQUANTE

1 10-lb. ham
6 whole cloves
1/2 c. cider vinegar
2 c. pickled peach juice
1 c. honey
1 c. packed brown sugar
1 c. white grapes, seeded, cut in half
1 c. chopped oranges
1 c. pineapple chunks

Place ham fat side up in baking pan; stud with cloves. Pour vinegar and peach juice over ham. Brush with honey; press brown sugar over ham. Bake at 300 degrees for 1 hour. Bake, covered, for 2 hours, basting frequently. Arrange grapes, oranges and pineapple in pan. Bake for 1 hour longer or until ham is tender. Serve sliced ham with fruit sauce.

Mrs. Paul E. Ross

HOLIDAY HAM

1 boneless ham
Whole cloves
1 lg. can crushed pineapple
1 1/2 c. white wine

Stud ham with cloves. Combine pineapple and wine in blender container. Process until well blended. Place ham on large sheet of heavy foil in baking dish. Pour pineapple mixture over ham. Seal tightly. Marinate for 24 hours or longer in refrigerator. Bake at 320 degrees until heated through. Let stand, wrapped, for 1 hour or longer before slicing

Melba Walker

HAM WITH CHEESE STRATA

12 slices bread
3/4 lb. sharp American cheese, sliced
1 10-oz. package frozen broccoli,
    cooked, drained
2 c. finely diced cooked ham
6 eggs, slightly beaten
3 1/2 c. milk
2 tbsp. instant minced onion
1/2 tsp. salt
1/4 tsp. dry mustard
Shredded cheese (opt.)

Cut bread with doughnut cutter; reserve holes and rings. Layer bread scraps, cheese, broccoli and ham in 9 x 13-inch baking dish. Cover with reserved rings and holes. Combine eggs, milk, onion, salt and mustard in bowl; mix well. Pour over bread. Chill, covered, for 6 hours or longer. Bake, uncovered, at 325 degrees for 50 minutes. Sprinkle with shredded cheese. Bake for 5 minutes longer. Let stand for 10 minutes before serving. Yield: 12 servings.

Mrs. L. E. Gaskins

HAM AND VEGETABLE MEDLEY

1 1-lb. cooked ham, shredded
1 sm. green pepper, sliced
1 sm. red pepper, sliced
1 yellow squash, sliced
1 med. zucchini, sliced
1 onion, sliced
3 tbsp. oil
1 env. chicken bouillon
2 tsp. basil
1/2 tsp. salt
1/4 tsp. pepper
2 lg. tomatoes, cut into wedges

Stir-fry first 6 ingredients in oil in skillet over high heat for 5 minutes. Add bouillon, seasonings and 1/2 cup water. Cook over medium heat for 5 minutes or until vegetables are tender-crisp, stirring occasionally. Add tomatoes. Cook until heated through. Yield: 4 servings.

Sandra Damiani

PARTY TORTILLAS

>8 slices boiled ham
>8 slices Monterey Jack cheese
>8 slices green chili
>8 flour tortillas
>Cream mustard to taste
>2 c. light cheese sauce

Place 1 slice ham, cheese and chili on each tortilla; roll up. Arrange seam side down in greased 7 x 11-inch baking dish. Blend mustard with cheese sauce; pour over tortilla rolls. Bake at 350 degrees for 30 minutes. Yield: 4 servings.

Ann Myers

LAMB-APPLE CURRY

>3 lg. apples, thinly sliced
>1 lg. onion, sliced, separated
>1 clove of garlic
>Butter
>2 to 3 tbsp. flour
>1 tbsp. curry powder
>1 tbsp. lemon juice
>2 c. beef bouillon
>1 tsp. gravy flavoring (opt.)
>Grated rind of 1/2 lemon
>1/2 c. raisins
>3 whole cloves
>2 c. chopped cooked lamb

Saute apples, onion and garlic in a small amount of butter in skillet until golden brown; remove garlic. Blend in flour and curry powder. Mix lemon juice, bouillon and gravy flavoring in bowl. Stir into apple mixture gradually. Stir in lemon rind, raisins and cloves. Simmer, covered, for 30 minutes. Add lamb. Cook until heated through. Serve with rice and chutney.

Evelyn Day

LAMB CROWN ROAST WITH RICE STUFFING

>1 crown roast of lamb
>Seasoned salt and pepper
>1 6-oz. package curried rice mix
>1 lb. ground lamb
>1/2 c. chopped green pepper
>1/2 tsp. salt
>1/3 c. dark seedless raisins
>12 sm. whole onions, cooked
>1/2 c. chicken broth
>2 tbsp. lemon juice

Sprinkle roast with seasoned salt and pepper. Place on rack in shallow roasting pan. Roast at 325 degrees for 30 minutes per pound or to 175 degrees on meat thermometer. Prepare rice mix according to package directions using 2 1/2 cups water. Brown ground lamb and green pepper in skillet; drain. Combine rice, lamb, salt, 1/2 teaspoon seasoned salt, 1/8 teaspoon pepper, raisins, onions, broth and lemon juice in bowl; mix well. Fill center of roast with rice mixture 1 hour before lamb is done. Cover with foil. Place remaining stuffing in 1-quart casserole. Bake, uncovered, for 1 hour, stirring occasionally. Yield: 7-8 servings.

Photograph for this recipe on page 21.

MINTED GRAPEFRUIT LEG OF LAMB

>1 onion, sliced
>1 carrot, sliced
>1 stalk celery, sliced
>1 7-lb. leg of lamb
>1 tsp. salt
>1/4 tsp. pepper
>3 c. grapefruit juice
>1 tsp. dried mint

Arrange vegetables over bottom of roasting pan. Rub lamb with salt and pepper. Place on top of vegetables. Pour grapefruit juice mixed with mint over lamb. Bake at 325 degrees for 2 hours, basting frequently with pan drippings. Serve with strained pan drippings.

Ladonna Allen

VEAL STEAK CORDON BLEU

4 veal cutlets, pounded thin
2 slices cooked ham
2 slices Swiss cheese
1 egg, beaten
Fine dry bread crumbs
2 to 4 tbsp. margarine

Top 2 veal cutlets with ham and cheese slices. Dip remaining cutlets in egg; place firmly on top of each cheese slice. Dip each stack in egg; coat with bread crumbs. Cook cutlets in margarine over medium heat for about 5 minutes on each side or until golden brown and tender. Garnish with lemon slices and parsley. Yield: 2 servings.

Photograph for this recipe above.

VEAL SCALLOPINI SAUTERNE

2 lb. veal thinly sliced
Seasoned flour
3 tbsp. olive oil
1 c. beef broth
1 can mushrooms, drained
1 tsp. tarragon vinegar
1 tbsp. chopped parsley
1 bay leaf

1/2 c. Sauterne
Grated Parmesan cheese (opt.)

Coat veal lightly with flour. Cook in oil in skillet over medium-low heat until lightly browned. Stir in broth gradually. Add mushrooms. Bring to a boil. Simmer, covered, for 20 minutes, turning veal occasionally. Add vinegar, parsley, bay leaf and Sauterne. Bring to a boil; remove from heat. Serve immediately with Parmesan cheese. Yield: 4-6 servings.

Dorothy Crook

VEAL CUTLET SUPREME

12 thin slices veal
Salt and pepper to taste
6 thin slices Swiss cheese
6 thin slices ham
Flour
3 eggs, beaten
3/4 c. bread crumbs
3/4 c. butter
24 asparagus tips, cooked

Flatten veal slices with meat mallet; sprinkle with salt and pepper. Place 1 slice cheese and 1 slice ham on each of 6 veal slices; cover with remaining veal slices. Pound edges together. Coat with flour; dip into eggs. Coat with crumbs. Fry in butter in skillet for 8 minutes. Serve with asparagus tips.

Mrs. A. Voegele

VEAL GOURMET

1/2 c. Sherry
1/2 tsp. salt
1/8 tsp. marjoram
Monosodium glutamate
4 3/4-in. thick veal chops
2 tbsp. shortening
1 5-oz. can sliced water chestnuts
1 3-oz. can sliced mushrooms
2 tbsp. cornstarch

Combine first 4 ingredients in dish; mix well. Add chops. Marinate for 1 hour or longer. Drain chops, reserving marinade. Brown chops in shortening in skillet. Add reserved marinade. Simmer, covered, for 30 to 45 minutes or until chops are tender. Drain water chestnuts and mushrooms, reserving liquid. Mix reserved liquids with cornstarch. Stir into veal mixture. Add water chestnuts and mushrooms. Simmer until thickened. Garnish with paprika.

Mrs. Cushing Snider

SHIRLEY'S GINGER BASTE FOR PORK

2/3 c. packed brown sugar
2 tbsp. cornstarch
2 tsp. freshly grated ginger
2 cloves of garlic, crushed
1/4 c. wine vinegar
2/3 c. soy sauce

Combine all ingredients in bowl; stir until sugar is dissolved. Let stand for 1 hour to blend flavors. Stir well before brushing on pork while cooking.

Candy Barnes

PORK TENDERLOIN JAVANESE

6 Brazil nuts, grated
1 c. minced onion
2 cloves of garlic, minced
1/4 c. lemon juice
1/4 c. soy sauce
2 tbsp. brown sugar
2 tbsp. ground coriander
1/4 tsp. red pepper
1/4 c. olive oil
2 lb. pork tenderloin, trimmed, cut
   into 1-in. cubes

Combine all ingredients except pork in bowl; mix well. Add pork. Marinate for 10 minutes. Place pork on skewers; reserve marinade. Grill over hot coals for about 10 minutes on each side, basting once with reserved marinade. Serve with rice. Yield: 4-5 servings.

Sally Bice

ROTISSERIE-STYLE BONELESS PORK LOIN

1 3 to 6-lb. boneless pork loin roast
Barbecue sauce

Insert rotisserie rod through exact center of roast; use prongs to hold roast in place. Insert meat thermometer so bulb is centered in roast but not in fat or on rod. Cook at low temperature on rotisserie for 2 to 3 hours or to 170 degrees on meat thermometer. Brush with barbecue sauce during last 30 minutes of cooling.

Esther Blake

HOT SWEET AND SOUR SZECHWAN-STYLE PORK

Cornstarch
Soy sauce
2 egg whites
1 lb. boneless pork, cut into
   1/2-in. pieces
1/2 c. corn syrup
1/2 c. vinegar
1/4 c. sugar
1/4 c. halved pitted canned cherries
1/4 c. pineapple chunks
1/4 c. cherry juice
1/2 c. coarsely chopped green pepper
2 tbsp. red pepper seed
1 c. oil
1 tbsp. minced fresh ginger
4 green onions, cut into 1-in. pieces
3 stalks celery, cut into 1-in. pieces
1/4 c. blanched peanuts
1/4 c. white wine

Combine 2 tablespoons cornstarch, 2 tablespoons soy sauce, 2 tablespoons water and egg whites in bowl; mix well. Add pork; stir to coat. Let stand for 1/2 hour. Combine next 7 ingredients, 1/4 cup cornstarch and 2 tablespoons soy sauce in saucepan. Cook over low heat until thick, stirring constantly. Set aside; keep warm. Stir-fry pepper seed in oil in wok until well browned. Add drained pork to wok. Stir-fry until brown; drain. Add ginger. Stir-fry over high heat until well mixed. Add onions, celery and peanuts. Stir-fry until well mixed. Add wine; stir-fry until liquid is reduced by 1/2. Remove to serving platter. Serve over rice or Chinese noodles with warm sweet and sour sauce. Yield: 8 servings.

Jo Ann Clark

HAM-STUFFED PORK CHOPS

3 c. fresh bread crumbs
1 c. chopped cooked ham
1/8 tsp. pepper
1/4 tsp. nutmeg
1 egg
1 can beef broth
6 pork chops, 1 1/2 in. thick
1 tsp. salt
1/4 tsp. each sage, thyme
Oil
Cornstarch

Combine bread crumbs, ham, pepper, nutmeg, egg and 1/2 cup beef broth in bowl; mix well. Cut pocket in each pork chop; rub with salt, sage and thyme. Stuff with ham mixture; brush with oil. Place in large baking pan. Bake at 450 degrees for 30 minutes or until brown; turning chops once. Reduce temperature to 400 degrees; drain. Mix 1 cup water with remaining broth; pour over pork chops. Bake, covered, for 50 to 60 minutes longer or until pork chops are tender. Place pork chops on platter. Thicken pan liquid with cornstarch mixed with water; serve with pork chops. Garnish pork chops with watercress and lemon slices.

Mrs. Herminio Hernandez

SWEET AND SOUR PORK CHOPS SUCCESS

6 pork chops
2 tbsp. shortening
1 tsp. salt
1/4 tsp. pepper
1 c. sliced carrots
1   16-oz. can pineapple chunks
1/2 c. lemon juice
1/4 c. honey
1/4 c. chopped onion
1 tbsp. soy sauce
1 tsp. beef bouillon
3 tbsp. cornstarch
6 green pepper rings

Brown pork chops in shortening in skillet; remove to baking pan. Season with salt and pepper. Add carrots. Drain pineapple, reserving syrup. Combine next 5 ingredients and half the reserved pineapple syrup in saucepan; mix well. Blend cornstarch with remaining pineapple syrup in small bowl. Add to lemon mixture; mix well. Cook until thick, stirring constantly. Pour over pork chops. Bake, covered, at 350 degrees for 50 to 60 minutes or until pork chops are tender. Add 1 cup pineapple. Top with green pepper rings. Bake, covered, for 10 minutes longer.

Debbie Melnick

SAUSAGE-MUSHROOM SOUFFLE

1 1/2 lb. pork sausage, crumbled
8 slices white bread, trimmed, cubed
3/4 lb. Cheddar cheese, cubed
4 eggs, beaten
Milk
1 tsp. salt
3/4 tsp. dry mustard
1 can cream of mushroom soup

Brown sausage in skillet, stirring until crumbly; drain. Layer bread, cheese and sausage in baking dish. Mix eggs, 2 1/2 cups milk and seasonings in bowl. Pour over sausage. Chill overnight. Mix soup with 1/3 soup can milk in small bowl. Spoon over casserole. Bake at 350 degrees for 1 hour.

Bonnie Albright

DELICIOUS SAUSAGE AND RICE CASSEROLE

1 lb. sausage, crumbled
1 med. onion, chopped
2 cans beef consomme
1 c. rice

Brown sausage in skillet, stirring until crumbly; drain. Combine with remaining ingredients in 9 x 13-inch casserole. Bake, covered with foil, at 375 degrees for 40 minutes. Yield: 10 servings.

Miriam M. Adair

Seafood Unlimited

OYSTER STEW

2 c. oysters
4 c. milk, scalded
3 tbsp. butter
Salt and pepper
Paprika

Place oysters in saucepan with water to cover. Simmer until edges curl; drain. Heat milk to scalding in saucepan. Add oysters, butter and seasonings; mix well. Yield: 6 servings.

Mary Gibson

SEAFOOD GUMBO

1 1/2 c. tomato juice
1/4 c. cooked okra
1/4 c. chopped green pepper
1/2 c. chopped celery
2 tbsp. onion flakes
2 tsp. shrimp boil
1/4 tsp. garlic salt
Salt and pepper to taste
1/4 c. each cooked shrimp, crab

Boil tomato juice in saucepan until thick. Add remaining ingredients except shrimp and crab; mix well. Simmer for 15 minutes. Add shrimp and crab. Heat to serving temperature. Serve over rice. Yield: 1 serving.

Nancy Drake

SHRIMP BISQUE

1/4 c. each finely chopped onion, celery
2 tbsp. flour
1 tsp. butter-flavored salt
1/4 tsp. paprika
Dash of white pepper
4 c. skim milk
14 oz. cooked shrimp, coarsely chopped

Combine first 2 ingredients with 1/4 cup water in saucepan. Simmer until vegetables are tender. Add remaining ingredients except shrimp; mix well. Simmer until thick, stirring constantly. Fold in shrimp. Heat to serving temperature. Yield: 6 servings.

Karen Douglas

BAKED FISH ITALIANO

1 c. finely chopped onion
1 clove of garlic, minced
1/2 c. chopped celery
1   15-oz. can tomato sauce
1/8 tsp. ground cloves
1 bay leaf
1 1/2 c. shredded carrots
3/4 c. chicken broth
Salt and pepper to taste
2 lb. fish fillets

Saute onion, garlic and celery in skillet until tender. Add remaining ingredients except fish; mix well. Simmer, covered, for 30 minutes; stir occasionally. Roll up fish, securing with pick. Arrange in greased shallow baking dish. Cover with sauce. Bake at 350 degrees for 35 minutes or until fish flakes easily. Garnish with parsley.

Wanda Lovern

COD FILLETS SUPREME

1 pkg. frozen cod fillets
1   6 1/2-oz. can crab meat
1 can cream of mushroom soup
1/2 c. shredded Swiss cheese

Place cod fillets in buttered casserole. Sprinkle with crab meat. Spoon soup over crab meat. Sprinkle Swiss cheese over top. Garnish with almonds. Bake, covered, at 350 degrees until fish flakes easily. Yield: 4 servings.

Henrietta Henderson

HALIBUT STEAKS PARMESAN

2 lb. halibut steaks
Juice of 1 lemon
2 tbsp. butter, melted
2 tbsp. flour
1/2 tsp. nutmeg
1/2 tsp. paprika
1/2 tsp. salt
1/2 tsp. pepper
1   8-oz. can mushrooms
Milk
1/2 c. grated Parmesan cheese

Place halibut in well-greased casserole. Add lemon juice. Combine next 6 ingredients in saucepan; mix well. Drain mushrooms, reserving liquid. Add enough milk to mushroom liquid to measure 1 cup. Stir into flour mixture. Simmer until thickened, stirring constantly. Pour over halibut; sprinkle with mushrooms and cheese. Bake at 350 degrees for 1/2 hour.

Mrs. F. W. Vannoy

FLAMING FISH

1   4-lb. mackerel
Lemon juice
Salt and freshly ground pepper
2 c. red wine
1 onion, sliced
2 cloves of garlic, mashed
1 tsp. salt
4 peppercorns
1 clove
2 bay leaves
Dash of thyme
1/4 c. Brandy

Rub mackerel cavity with lemon juice, salt and pepper. Combine next 8 ingredients in glass bowl; mix well. Add mackerel. Marinate in refrigerator for 3 hours or overnight. Place mackerel in baking dish. Strain marinade; pour over mackerel. Bake at 350 degrees for 30 minutes or until mackerel flakes easily. Place on serving platter; garnish with lemon slices and parsley. Heat Brandy in small saucepan; ignite and pour over mackerel just before serving. Yield: 8 servings.

Mrs. Bobby C. Wilks

FLOUNDER STUFFED WITH MUSHROOMS

6 lg. flounder fillets
1 1/2 c. chopped mushrooms
2 tbsp. chopped onion
4 tbsp. butter, melted
1/2 c. lightly toasted chopped almonds
1/4 c. minced parsley
Salt and pepper to taste

Coil each fish fillet on side in muffin cup. Saute mushrooms and onion in 2 tablespoons butter in skillet until tender. Stir in almonds, parsley, salt and pepper. Spoon mixture into center of each fish coil. Drizzle with remaining butter. Bake at 375 degrees for 35 minutes or until fish flakes easily. Lift onto serving dish with 2 spoons. Spoon pan juices over tops. Yield: 6 servings.

Carole Humphreys

GRILLED BARBECUED CATFISH

1/4 tsp. each salt, pepper
1 tsp. Worcestershire sauce
1/8 tsp. paprika
1/2 c. oil
1/4 c. each white vinegar, catsup
2 tbsp. sugar
6 med. catfish fillets

Combine all ingredients except catfish in bowl; mix well. Pour marinade over catfish in shallow dish. Let stand for 20 minutes. Drain, reserving marinade. Cook 4 inches above hot coals on greased grill for 5 minutes on each side or until fish tests done, basting frequently with reserved marinade. Yield: 6 servings.

Shannon Brown

SALMON ROMANOFF

1/2 c. chopped green onions
1 clove of garlic, crushed
2 tbsp. butter
1 c. cottage cheese
2 c. sour cream
5 dashes of Tabasco sauce
1/2 tsp. salt
1 lb. fresh cooked salmon
1   6-oz. package noodles, cooked
1 c. shredded cheese

Saute onions and garlic in butter in skillet until tender. Combine with remaining ingredients except cheese in bowl; mix well. Place in casserole. Bake at 350 degrees for 15 minutes. Top with cheese. Bake for 15 minutes longer or until bubbly.

Irene Hunter

SEAFOOD-STUFFED SALMON

1/2 lb. crab meat, chopped
1/2 lb. cooked shrimp, chopped
2 tbsp. parsley flakes
1/2 c. chopped celery
1/4 c. chopped onion
4 c. bread crumbs
Melted butter
1/2 c. (or more) chicken bouillon
1   4 to 6-lb. salmon
1/4 c. fresh lemon juice

Combine first 6 ingredients with 1/2 cup butter and enough bouillon to make stuffing consistency in bowl; mix well. Fill salmon cavity; fasten with skewers. Bake at 300 degrees for 2 hours, basting several times with lemon juice and butter. Yield: 8-10 servings.

Mrs. Robert P. Cady

WESTERN-BROILED SALMON

1/4 c. minced onion
1/4 c. minced celery
2 tbsp. minced green pepper
1 clove of garlic, minced
1 tbsp. oil
1/2 tsp. salt
1/8 tsp. pepper
1 c. tomato sauce
1/2 c. Parmesan cheese
4 salmon steaks

Saute onion, celery, green pepper and garlic in oil in skillet until soft. Add salt, pepper and tomato sauce. Simmer for 3 minutes. Stir in Parmesan cheese. Broil salmon steaks 2 inches from heat for about 4 minutes; turn. Broil for 2 minutes. Pour sauce over salmon. Broil for 2 minutes or until sauce is bubbly and fish flakes easily. Yield: 4 servings.

Mrs. James E. Baker

PARTY SALMON CREPES

1 c. pancake mix
3 1/2 c. milk
Butter, melted
1 egg, slightly beaten
1/4 c. minced onion
1/2 c. chopped celery
1/4 c. flour
1/2 tsp. salt
2/3 c. grated Parmesan cheese
2 c. salmon
1   8-oz. can peas

Combine pancake mix, 1 1/4 cups milk, 1 tablespoon butter and egg in bowl; mix until just moistened. Pour 1/3 cup batter at a time onto hot, lightly buttered griddle. Bake until set. Turn to brown other side. Saute onion and celery in 1/4 cup butter in skillet until tender. Blend in flour and salt to make smooth paste. Add 2 1/4 cups milk gradually, stirring constantly. Cook until thick, stirring constantly. Remove from heat; add cheese. Cook until cheese is melted, stirring constantly. Set aside 1 1/3 cups sauce; keep warm. Add salmon and peas to sauce in pan. Cook until heated through, stirring constantly. Spread pancakes with salmon mixture; roll up. Place in 9 x 11-inch baking dish. Bake at 350 degrees for 15 to 20 minutes or until heated through. Serve with remaining sauce.

Dana Condellone

GRILLED RED SNAPPER

1/2 c. butter, melted
1/4 c. lemon juice
3/4 tsp. Worcestershire sauce
1/4 tsp. onion salt
2 lb. red snapper

Mix first 4 ingredients in small bowl. Grill snapper over hot coals for 5 to 8 minutes on each side, basting with lemon mixture frequently. Serve snapper with remaining lemon mixture. Yield: 6-8 servings.

Lucille Jackson

SAN FRANCISCO SOLE SUPERB

2 lb. sole fillets
1 1/4 tsp. salt
Dash of white pepper

1 8 3/4-oz. can seedless green grapes
2 tbsp. butter
1/2 c. chopped onion
1/4 c. dry white wine
3/4 c. half and half
1 egg yolk, beaten
1 tbsp. flour
Dash of nutmeg
Paprika

Sprinkle both sides of fillets with 1 teaspoon salt and pepper. Roll fillets; secure with toothpicks. Drain grapes, reserving liquid. Melt butter in 10-inch pan; add onion. Cook until tender. Place fish rolls in baking pan. Add reserved grape liquid and wine. Simmer, covered, for 8 minutes or until fish flakes. Place fish on serving platter; remove toothpicks. Keep fish warm. Combine half and half, egg yolk, flour, 1/4 teaspoon salt and nutmeg in bowl. Add gradually to hot liquid. Cook until thickened, stirring constantly. Add grapes. Pour sauce over fish. Sprinkle with paprika. Broil 5 inches from heat source for 4 minutes or until lightly browned. Yield: 6 servings.

Photograph for this recipe on page 33.

TROUT MARYLAND

1 c. stuffing mix
1/2 c. walnuts
4 10-oz. packages frozen rainbow trout
Butter, melted
Lemon juice

Prepare stuffing using package directions; mix with walnuts. Fill cavity of each trout with about 3 tablespoons stuffing. Secure with string or poultry pins. Arrange in shallow casserole. Mix butter with small amount of lemon juice; brush over trout. Bake at 350 degrees for 15 to 20 minutes or until fish flakes, basting often. Brown quickly under broiler. Serve with lemon wedges. Yield: 8 servings.

Mrs. Alice Downer

TUNA-MACARONI BAKE

4 tbsp. butter
4 tbsp. flour

2 c. milk
1/2 tsp. salt
1 tsp. dry mustard
2 c. shredded cheese
2 c. macaroni, cooked, drained
1 can tuna, drained

Melt butter in saucepan. Blend in flour, stirring until smooth. Stir in milk, blending well. Simmer until thickened, stirring constantly. Add salt, mustard and cheese; blend well. Stir in remaining ingredients; mix well. Pour into greased casserole. Bake at 325 degrees for 30 minutes or until bubbly. Yield: 4-6 servings.

Margie Hyde

SMOKY TUNA POTAGE

2 cans green pea soup
2 7-oz. cans tuna
1 8-oz. can sliced carrots
1 tsp. liquid smoke
1/2 tsp. marjoram
1/4 tsp. salt

Blend soup with 2 cups water in 2-quart saucepan. Add remaining ingredients; mix well. Simmer, covered, for 15 minutes. Garnish with paprika. Yield: 6 servings.

Photograph for this recipe on page 33.

SEVICHE

3 lb. halibut, cubed
Lime juice
1 can tomatoes
1 jar sliced olives
1 lg. onion, chopped
1/2 c. catsup
1/2 c. olive oil
2 tsp. salt
1 tsp. oregano
1 tsp. Tabasco sauce

Marinate halibut in juice overnight in refrigerator. Drain and rinse. Place on serving dish. Combine remaining ingredients in bowl; mix well. Spoon over halibut; serve cold.

Candy Barnes

CLAM STEW

1   16-oz. can stewed tomatoes
1   6 1/2-oz. can minced clams
1 tsp. grated Romano cheese

Combine tomatoes and clams in saucepan; mix well. Bring to a boil. Sprinkle with cheese to serve. Yield: 2 servings.

Adele Poe

WHITE CLAM SAUCE

1 med. onion, chopped
2 cloves of garlic, minced
1/2 c. butter
1/2 c. oil
1/4 c. chopped parsley
1/2 lb. mushrooms, sliced
Juice of 1 lemon
1/2 c. white wine
2   10-oz. cans baby clams with broth
1 lb. thin spaghetti, cooked
Parmesan cheese

Saute onion and garlic in butter and oil in skillet. Add parsley and mushrooms. Cook until vegetables are tender. Add lemon juice, wine and clams; mix well. Pour sauce over hot spaghetti. Sprinkle with Parmesan cheese.

Virginia Frye

CRAB MEAT DIVAN

1   10-oz. package frozen broccoli,
      cooked, drained
1   6 1/2-oz. can king crab meat, drained
1/3 c. mayonnaise
1 1/2 tsp. lemon juice
1/2 tsp. prepared mustard
1 tsp. grated onion
1/4 c. grated process cheese

Arrange broccoli on baking dish. Cover with crab meat broken into pieces. Combine next 4 ingredients in bowl; mix well. Spoon over crab; top with cheese. Bake at 350 degrees for 20 minutes. Yield: 4 servings.

Mrs. Paul G. Jones

CRAB QUICHE

1/2 c. mayonnaise
2 tbsp. flour
2 eggs, beaten
1/2 c. milk
1/2 lb. crab meat, flaked
8 oz. Swiss cheese, shredded
1/3 c. chopped scallions
1 unbaked pie shell

Combine first 4 ingredients in bowl; mix well. Stir in crab meat, cheese and scallions. Pour into pie shell. Bake at 350 degrees for 40 to 45 minutes or until set.

Mary Pat Thuma

SEAFOOD MEDLEY

2 tbsp. chopped shallots
1 c. chopped mushrooms
Butter
1 tsp. dry mustard
1/2 tsp. chopped tarragon leaves
1 c. chopped cooked shrimp
1 c. cooked scallops
1 c. chopped cooked lobster
1 c. cream
1 tbsp. cornstarch
Salt and pepper to taste

Saute shallots and mushrooms in a small amount of butter in skillet for 5 minutes. Stir in next 6 ingredients. Bring to a boil. Blend cornstarch with a small amount of water. Stir into mixture. Cook until thick, stirring constantly; season to taste. Yield: 4 servings.

Tamara Heath

LOBSTER CATALANA

6 cloves of garlic
2 lg. onions, finely chopped
1/2 lb. green peppers, finely chopped
4 oz. olive oil
4 oz. dry Sherry
2 lb. ripe tomatoes, chopped
1 lb. eggplant, diced
1 tsp. paprika
3 lb. cooked lobster, cut in pieces

1 sm. can green peas
1   12-oz. can pimento

Saute garlic, onions and green peppers in oil in saucepan. Add Sherry, tomatoes, eggplant and paprika. Simmer for 30 to 40 minutes or until eggplant is tender. Add lobster. Heat to serving temperature. Serve over rice; top with peas and pimento.

Mrs. James M. Diehl

LOBSTER NEWBURG

2 sm. lobsters
4 tbsp. butter
1 tsp. salt
1/4 tsp. pepper
Dash of cayenne pepper
Dash of mace
3 egg yolks, beaten
1 c. cream
Sherry to taste

Cut lobster meat into bite-sized pieces. Saute in butter in saucepan for 5 minutes. Add seasoning. Saute for 5 minutes longer. Stir in remaining ingredients. Heat to serving temperature. Serve on toast points. May substitute shrimp or crab for lobster. Yield: 4 servings.

Mrs. P. X. Kelley

OYSTERS IN CASSEROLE

4 doz. oysters
4 tbsp. dry Sherry
1 lg. clove of garlic, crushed
6 tbsp. butter
1 1/3 c. fresh white bread crumbs
1 1/2 tbsp. freshly chopped parsley
2 tsp. finely grated lemon rind
Salt and freshly ground pepper to taste

Arrange oysters in individual casseroles; drizzle with Sherry. Saute garlic in butter in skillet until golden. Add remaining ingredients. Saute until bread crumbs are golden. Spoon over oysters. Bake at 400 degrees for 5 minutes or until heated through. Serve at once garnished with decorated lemon half.

Trish Lewis

OYSTERS ROCKEFELLER

5 tbsp. butter, melted
1/2 c. strained spinach
2 tbsp. minced onion
2 tsp. minced celery
3 tbsp. fine dry crumbs
1/4 tsp. herb blend for fish
1/4 tsp. anchovy paste
1/4 tsp. salt
Pepper to taste
2 doz. oysters on the half shell
Rock salt

Combine all ingredients except oysters and rock salt in bowl; mix well. Arrange oysters in 4 pie plates filled with rock salt. Broil for 5 minutes. Spoon spinach mixture onto oysters. Broil until bubbly. Serve immediately. Yield: 4 servings.

Gwen Schofield

SCALLOPS AND MUSHROOMS

12 oz. frozen scallops
1/4 lb. fresh mushrooms, sliced
1 sm. onion, sliced
1/2 green pepper, sliced
Salt and pepper to taste

Microwave scallops in covered casserole on High for 3 minutes. Add vegetables. Microwave on High for 8 to 10 minutes. Season with salt and pepper. Yield: 2 servings.

Gillian Edwards

SAVORY SCALLOPS

1/4 c. butter
1 1/2 tsp. Worcestershire sauce
1/4 c. minced onion
1 pt. scallops
1/4 c. white wine

Melt butter in small frying pan with Worcestershire sauce. Add onion; cook until golden. Pick over and rinse scallops; divide into 4 large scallop shells or individual bakers. Divide onion mixture evenly over scallops. Pour 1 tablespoon wine over each. Bake in 500-degree oven for 10 minutes. Serve immediately. Yield: 4 servinngs.

Mrs. C. Thomas Bell

SHRIMP SCAMPI

2 lb. large shrimp, shelled, deveined
2 cloves of garlic, minced
1/4 c. butter, melted
2   16-oz. cans apricot halves, drained
1/3 c. chopped parsley
2 tbsp. lemon juice
3/4 tsp. salt
1/4 tsp. pepper

Saute shrimp and garlic in butter in large skillet for 3 to 5 minutes or until shrimp turns pink. Stir in apricots and remaining ingredients. Cook for 2 to 3 minutes or until heated through, stirring gently. Serve immediately.

Photograph for this recipe above.

SHRIMP CASSEROLE HARPIN

2 lb. shrimp
1 tbsp. lemon juice
3 tbsp. oil
1/4 c. chopped green pepper
1/2 c. chopped onion
2 tbsp. butter
1 c. heavy cream
1 tsp. salt
1/4 tsp. pepper
1/8 tsp. mace
Dash of cayenne pepper
1 can tomato soup
1/2 c. Sherry
1 1/2 c. cooked rice
1/4 slivered almonds

Combine shrimp, lemon juice and oil in buttered casserole; mix well. Saute green pepper and onion in butter in skillet until tender. Add with remaining ingredients except almonds to shrimp mixture; mix gently. Top with almonds. Bake at 350 degrees for 1 hour.

Janice Andrews

SHRIMP CREOLE

2 med. onions, chopped
1 green pepper, chopped
1 1/2 c. celery, cut into lg. pieces
1/4 c. oil
1   29-oz. can tomatoes
1 can Spanish-style tomato sauce
1 clove of garlic, mashed
1 bay leaf
4 tsp. chili powder
3 dashes of hot sauce
2 tsp. salt
2 1/2 lb. cooked shrimp, chilled

Saute onions, green pepper and celery in oil in skillet until tender; add 1/2 cup water and remaining ingredients except shrimp. Simmer for 30 minutes. Add shrimp. Chill for 30 minutes. Reheat over low heat. Yield: 5-6 servings.

Mrs. John D. Servis

SHRIMP DE JONGHE

1 c. butter, melted
2 cloves of garlic, minced
1/3 c. parsley, chopped
1/2 tsp. paprika
Dash of cayenne pepper
1/2 c. Sherry
4 to 5 lb. cooked shrimp, shelled
2 c. soft bread crumbs

Combine butter, garlic, parsley, paprika, cayenne pepper and Sherry in saucepan; mix well. Simmer, covered, for 25 minutes to blend flavors. Toss shrimp with crumbs; pour butter mixture over top. Stir lightly. Combine all ingredients in casserole. Bake at 325 degrees for 25 to 30 minutes. Garnish with additional chopped parsley. Yield: 8 servings.

Mrs. Dorothy DuBose

Poultry
Pleasers

BARBECUE SAUCE FOR CHICKEN

1/2 c. oil
1 lg. onion, chopped
2 cloves of garlic, minced
3 tbsp. mustard
3 tbsp. Worcestershire sauce
1 tbsp. salt
1 6-oz. can orange juice, thawed
Lemon juice (opt.)
2 tbsp. vinegar

Combine first 6 ingredients and 1 cup water in saucepan. Cook for 1 hour over low heat. Add juices and vinegar. Simmer for 1/2 hour longer.

Margaret L. Knee

CHINESE CHICKEN LIVERS

1 1/2 lb. chicken livers
Soy sauce
1/3 c. peanut oil
1 c. pineapple chunks
3/4 c. blanched almonds, slivered
3 tbsp. cornstarch
1/3 c. wine vinegar
1 2/3 c. pineapple juice
1/2 tsp. salt
1/3 c. (about) sugar

Marinate chicken livers in a small amount of soy sauce in bowl. Brown lightly in peanut oil in skillet; remove livers. Add pineapple chunks and almonds to skillet; cook for several minutes, stirring constantly. Remove pineapple and almonds; mix with livers in serving dish. Blend cornstarch with vinegar in small bowl. Add pineapple juice, salt and sugar; mix well. Pour into pan drippings. Cook until thick, stirring constantly. Pour over liver mixture. Serve hot with rice. Yield: 3-4 servings.

Mrs. Lee V. Twyford

ROAST CHICKEN DELUXE

1 4-lb. chicken
2 tbsp. Brandy
7 whole cloves
1 med. onion, peeled
1 lemon, peeled
1 orange, peeled
2 tbsp. butter, softened

Wash chicken; pat dry inside and out. Pour Brandy in cavity; turn chicken to coat. Insert cloves in onion. Place with lemon and orange in cavity; close with skewers. Rub chicken with butter; wrap in foil. Roast at 350 degrees for about 1 1/2 hours or until tender. Roast, uncovered, for several minutes longer or until browned. Yield: 4 servings.

Mrs. Harold L. Dix

ALPINE CHICKEN

6 chicken breasts, skinned, boned
1 6-oz. package sliced Swiss cheese
1 can cream of chicken soup
1/2 soup can Sherry (opt.)
1 8-oz. package herb-seasoned
  stuffing mix
3/4 c. melted margarine

Arrange chicken in shallow greased baking dish. Layer Swiss cheese slices over chicken. Combine soup and Sherry in bowl. Pour over chicken. Toss stuffing mix with margarine in bowl; spread over mixture. Bake, covered, at 350 degrees for 1 hour. Bake, uncovered, for 1/2 hour longer.

Candy Barnes

BREAST OF CHICKEN ROYALE

4 whole chicken breasts, skinned, boned
1 14-oz. can hearts of palm, drained
Melted butter
Salt and pepper to taste
1 can cream of mushroom soup
1 8-oz. package cream cheese, softened

Flatten chicken breasts. Wrap around hearts of palm stalks. Place in baking dish. Brush with butter. Season with salt and pepper. Bake at 400 degrees for 30 to 35 minutes, basting occasionally. Combine soup and cream cheese in saucepan. Cook over low heat until cheese melts and sauce is smooth, stirring frequently. Serve with chicken. Yield: 4 servings.

Arlene Fulmer

CARIBBEAN CHICKEN

2 whole chicken breasts, split
1 tsp. salt
1/2 tsp. dried leaf tarragon
1/4 c. butter
2 tbsp. lime juice
1/2 tsp. Tabasco sauce

Season chicken with 1/2 teaspoon salt and 1/4 teaspoon tarragon. Cook in butter in skillet over medium heat for 10 minutes or until brown. Turn chicken; sprinkle with remaining salt and tarragon. Cook for 10 minutes or until brown. Combine lime juice, 2 tablespoons water and Tabasco sauce in small bowl. Pour over chicken. Simmer, covered, for 10 minutes longer or until tender. Serve with hot cooked rice. Yield: 4 servings.

Photograph for this recipe on page 41.

CHICKEN BREASTS WITH ALMOND RICE

4 lb. chicken breasts, skinned, boned
Butter
1/2 lb. mushrooms, sliced
1/4 c. chopped onion
1/3 c. chopped parsley (opt.)
2 tbsp. flour
Dash of pepper
1 3/4 c. chicken bouillon
1/2 c. light cream
Sherry to taste
1/4 c. slivered blanched almonds
1 1/3 c. minute rice, cooked

Brown chicken in 1/2 cup butter in skillet over medium heat. Add mushrooms and onion. Saute until lightly browned. Remove chicken. Blend in parsley, flour and pepper. Add bouillon and cream gradually, stirring constantly. Cook until thick, stirring constantly. Add chicken. Simmer, covered, until chicken is tender. Stir in Sherry. Saute almonds in 2 tablespoons butter in skillet; add to rice. Place chicken breasts on rice on serving plate; top with sauce. Yield: 4-6 servings.

Mrs. M. A. Shadday

CHICKEN-ARTICHOKE CASSEROLE

6 boned chicken breasts
1 tsp. salt
1/2 tsp. each pepper, paprika
1/2 c. melted butter
12 to 15 artichoke hearts, drained
1/4 lb. mushrooms, sliced
2 tbsp. flour
2/3 c. chicken broth
3 tbsp. Sherry

Season chicken with salt, pepper and paprika. Brown in 6 tablespoons butter in skillet. Place with artichokes in 9 x 13-inch casserole. Add remaining 2 tablespoons butter and mushrooms to pan drippings. Cook for 15 minutes. Place mushrooms in casserole. Stir flour into pan drippings until smooth. Add broth and Sherry. Cook for 5 minutes or until thick, stirring constantly. Pour over chicken. Bake, covered, at 375 degrees for 40 minutes. Yield: 6 servings.

Mrs. Royle P. Carrington, III

CHICKEN BREASTS AND MUSHROOMS

3 chicken breasts, halved, boned
2 tbsp. lemon juice
Salt and white pepper to taste
1/2 lb. fresh mushrooms, sliced
1/2 c. finely chopped onion
3 tbsp. margarine
1/3 c. flour
2 tbsp. oil
1/2 c. dry white wine
1 bay leaf
1/2 tsp. tarragon, crumbled

Season chicken with lemon juice, salt and pepper; set aside. Saute mushrooms and onion in margarine in skillet for 5 minutes; remove vegetables. Coat chicken with flour. Brown in oil added to pan drippings for 10 to 15 minutes. Stir in sauteed vegetables and remaining ingredients. Simmer until chicken is tender. Yield: 6 servings.

Danielle Smith

CHICKEN PATERMO

6 chicken breasts, halved, skinned, boned
3 slices mozzarella cheese
1/2 c. fine dry bread crumbs
1/4 c. grated Parmesan cheese
1/4 c. melted butter
1 env. spaghetti sauce mix
1 16-oz. can tomato paste
1 can mushroom stems and pieces

Pound chicken breasts between sheets of plastic wrap. Cut each slice of cheese into 4 strips. Place 2 or 3 strips in middle of each piece of chicken. Fold chicken around cheese tucking in ends; secure with wooden picks. Combine bread crumbs and Parmesan cheese. Roll chicken in butter; coat with crumb mixture. Place in baking pan with remaining butter. Bake, uncovered, at 400 degrees for 20 minutes. Combine spaghetti sauce mix, tomato paste, mushrooms and 1 1/2 cups water in saucepan. Simmer for 10 minutes, stirring occasionally. Pour over chicken. Bake 5 minutes longer.

Candy Barnes

CHICKEN BREASTS MAGNIFIQUE

4 whole chicken breasts, halved
1/8 tsp. ginger
1/4 tsp. nutmeg
1/4 tsp. garlic powder
White pepper to taste
1/2 c. white wine
3 tbsp. lemon juice
2 8-count pkg. crescent dinner rolls
1 carton soft cream cheese with chives
1 egg, beaten
3 1-oz. packages Durkee white sauce mix
1 lg. can mushroom stems and pieces,
   drained

Place chicken breasts in baking dish. Combine next 6 ingredients in bowl; mix well. Pour over chicken breasts; cover. Bake at 350 degrees for 40 minutes or until tender. Let cool in pan juices. Remove chicken breasts to drain; set pan juices aside for future use as stock. Remove skin and bones from breasts. Pat 2 dinner roll sections together to make a 5 x 8-inch rectan-

gle. Spread each chicken breast with cheese; place each in rectangle. Fold dough over to cover; seal edges. Place in 2 foil-lined jelly roll pans; cover with plastic wrap until ready to use. Bake, uncovered, in 375-degree oven for about 40 minutes. Brush with egg; bake until golden brown and heated through. Prepare medium white sauce according to package directions. Stir in mushrooms; heat through. Serve sauce over chicken breasts. Yield: 8 servings.

Mrs. Charles A. Bell

CRUNCHY CHICKEN CRESCENTS

2 tbsp. margarine, softened
2 3-oz. packages cream cheese with
   chives, softened
1 1/2 c. chopped cooked chicken
1 8-count pkg. crescent dinner rolls,
   separated
3/4 c. melted margarine
1 c. seasoned stuffing mix

Cream softened margarine and cream cheese in bowl. Add chicken; mix well. Spoon 1/4 cup chicken mixture onto each roll. Wrap dough to enclose filling, sealing well. Dip each roll into melted margarine. Coat with stuffing mix. Place on baking sheet. Bake at 375 degrees for 20 minutes.

Rachel Hooper

CHICKEN WITH WALNUTS

1 tbsp. cornstarch
1/2 tsp. each salt and pepper
3 drops of Tabasco sauce
1 tsp. sugar
2 tbsp. soy sauce
3 tbsp. oil
4 whole chicken breasts, boned, cut
   into 1-in. pieces
2/3 c. coarsely chopped walnuts
2 tbsp. sesame oil
1/2 to 3/4 c. chopped ham
1/2 c. chicken stock

Combine first 5 ingredients, 1 tablespoon soy sauce and 2 tablespoons oil in bowl; mix well. Add chicken; stir to coat. Saute walnuts in remaining 1 tablespoon oil in small skillet until lightly browned. Stir-fry chicken in hot sesame oil in skillet over medium-high heat for 2 to 3 minutes. Add sauteed walnuts and ham. Stir-fry for 4 to 5 minutes longer. Add chicken stock and remaining 1 tablespoon soy sauce; stir for 1 minute. Serve with rice. Yield: 8 servings.

Joan Waal

COMPANY CHICKEN

4 boneless chicken breasts, split
1 3-oz. can sliced mushrooms
1 can cream of mushroom soup
1/2 soup can dry Sherry
1 c. sour cream
Paprika

Arrange chicken in single layer in shallow 9 x 13-inch baking dish. Combine mushrooms, soup, Sherry and sour cream in bowl; mix well. Pour over chicken; dust with paprika. Bake at 350 degrees for 1 hour. Bake, covered, for 1/2 hour longer. May use cream of celery soup for mushroom soup and seedless white grapes for mushrooms. Yield: 4 servings.

Libby Singleton

CURRY-GLAZED CHICKEN

8 to 10 chicken breasts, skinned
8 tbsp. flour
1 1/2 tsp. salt
1 tsp. ginger
6 tbsp. melted butter
1 med. onion, chopped
6 slices bacon, chopped
1 tbsp. curry powder
1 tbsp. sugar
1 can condensed beef broth
2 tbsp. applesauce
2 tbsp. flaked coconut
2 tbsp. catsup
2 tbsp. lemon juice

Coat chicken with mixture of 6 tablespoons flour, salt and ginger; roll in butter. Place in baking pan. Combine 2 tablespoons flour with remaining ingredients in saucepan; mix well. Simmer for 15 minutes, stirring often. Bake chicken at 400 degrees for 20 minutes; baste with half the curry sauce. Bake for 20 minutes longer; pour remaining curry sauce on chicken. Bake for 20 minutes longer. Serve with rice and desired condiments. Yield: 8 servings.

Mrs. Roland W. Marshal

GREAT CHICKEN CASSEROLE

8 chicken breasts, boned
2 jars chipped beef
2 cans cream of mushroom soup
2 cartons sour cream
4 or 5 slices bacon

Wrap chicken breasts in chipped beef. Place in 9 x 13-inch casserole. Mix soup and sour cream in bowl. Spoon over chicken. Bake, covered, at 225 degrees for 3 hours. Top with bacon. Bake, uncovered, for 1 hour longer or until bacon is crisp. Yield: 8 servings.

Miriam M. Adair

ORIENTAL CHICKEN

1/2 lb. dried beef
8 chicken breasts, boned
4 slices bacon, halved
1 can mushroom soup
1 8-oz. carton sour cream
1/4 c. white wine
1/4 c. milk

Line shallow 9 x 13-inch casserole with dried beef. Place chicken breasts on top. Place 1/2 strip bacon on each breast. Mix soup with sour cream, wine and milk in bowl. Pour over chicken; sprinkle with paprika. Bake, covered, at 300 degrees for 1 1/2 hours. Yield: 8 servings.

Judie Silvasy

STIR-FRY CHICKEN

3 chicken breasts, cooked, cut into
    2-in. strips
1 tbsp. soy sauce
1/4 c. chopped onion
2 sm. cloves of garlic, minced
1/2 green pepper, cut in strips
1 c. diagonally sliced celery
1 c. frozen snow peas
1 c. drained bean sprouts
1/2 c. sliced drained mushrooms
1/4 c. bamboo shoots
2 pkg. instant chicken broth

Combine first 4 ingredients with 1 cup water in large nonstick skillet. Cook until tender, stirring occasionally. Add green pepper, celery and snow peas; mix well. Cook for 3 to 5 minutes or until tender-crisp. Stir in remaining ingredients. Heat to serving temperature. Serve over rice. Yield: 3 servings.

Catherine French

CHICKEN-ASPARAGUS CASSEROLE

1/2 c. mayonnaise
1 can cream of chicken soup
1 can cream of mushroom soup
2 c. diced cooked chicken
1 can cut asparagus
1 c. diced Velveeta cheese
1/2   7-oz. package narrow noodles
1/2 c. cashews
1 c. diced celery
1 sm. can mushrooms
1 sm. jar pimento, diced
1/4 c. chopped green pepper
1/4 c. chopped green onion
1/2 c. chopped ripe olives

Combine mayonnaise and soups in bowl; mix well. Layer remaining ingredients in 9 x 13-inch baking dish. Top with soup mixture; mix gently. Bake at 325 degrees for 45 minutes. Garnish with chow mein noodles or crushed potato chips. Bake for 15 minutes longer. Yield: 10-12 servings.

Diane Vasilou

CHICKEN BOMBAY BAKE

1/3 c. flour
1 tsp. paprika
Salt to taste
8 chicken pieces
4 tbsp. butter
1 med. onion, sliced
4 chicken bouillon cubes
1 1/2 c. instant rice
1/2 c. white raisins
1/2 c. flaked coconut
1 sm. can mandarin oranges
1 tsp. curry powder
1/2 c. sliced almonds

Combine flour, paprika and salt in small bowl; mix well. Coat chicken in flour mixture. Brown chicken in butter in large skillet; remove and drain. Saute onion in pan drippings. Dissolve bouillon cubes in 1 1/2 cups boiling water; stir into onion mixture. Add remaining ingredients except almonds; mix well. Pour into casserole. Arrange chicken over top. Bake at 350 degrees for 1 hour. Sprinkle with almonds. Bake for 15 minutes longer.

Ellen Miles

BAKED CHICKEN WITH PECANS

1 c. flour
1 c. chopped pecans
1/4 c. sesame seed
3/4 tsp. salt
1 tbsp. paprika
1/2 tsp. pepper
1 c. buttermilk
1 egg, slightly beaten
1/2 c. butter
1 frying chicken, cut up

Combine first 6 ingredients in bowl; mix well. Combine buttermilk and egg in bowl; mix well. Melt butter in casserole. Dip chicken into milk mixture. Coat with pecan mixture. Place in melted butter, turning to coat both sides. Bake at 350 degrees for 1 1/2 hours or until brown and tender, basting several times.

Melanie Lawson

CHERRY-ALMOND CHICKEN

3 tbsp. cornstarch
2 c. chicken broth
1 1/2 tbsp. lemon juice
1/2 tsp. salt
1/4 tsp. celery salt
2 c. chopped cooked chicken breast
1 20-oz. can pitted white cherries,
    drained
1 8-oz. can white grapes, drained
1 c. canned chopped peaches
1/3 c. slivered blanched almonds

Combine cornstarch with a small amount of broth in saucepan; mix until smooth. Stir in remaining broth. Cook over medium heat until thick, stirring constantly. Add lemon juice, salt and celery salt; mix well. Add chicken, fruits and almonds. Place in chafing dish over low heat. Serve with rice dusted with cinnamon. Yield: 6 servings.

Mrs. Jean Hodge

CHICKEN PUFFS

1 can boned chicken, finely chopped
1/3 c. chopped toasted almonds
1 c. chicken broth
1/2 c. oil
2 tsp. seasoned salt
1/2 tsp. cayenne pepper
1 tsp. celery seed
1 tbsp. parsley flakes
2 tbsp. Worcestershire sauce
1 c. sifted flour
4 eggs

Combine chicken, almonds, broth, oil and seasonings in saucepan; mix well. Bring to a boil; add flour. Cook over low heat, beating vigorously until dough forms smooth ball. Remove from heat. Beat in eggs 1 at a time. Drop by 1/2 teaspoonfuls onto greased baking sheet. Bake at 450 degrees for 10 to 15 minutes or until browned. May be frozen and reheated at 250 degrees for 10 minutes when thawed. Yield: 8 dozen.

Lisa Miller

CHICKEN A L'ORANGE

1 3-lb. chicken, quartered
Salt, pepper, paprika to taste
1/4 c. flour
2 tbsp. butter
1 lg. onion, sliced
1/4 c. chopped green pepper
1/2 c. sliced mushrooms
1 c. orange juice
2 tbsp. Sherry
1 tbsp. brown sugar
1 tsp. salt
1 tsp. grated orange rind
1 tbsp. cornstarch

Wash and dry chicken. Sprinkle with salt, pepper and paprika; coat with flour. Line shallow 2-quart casserole with foil. Melt butter in casserole. Arrange chicken in casserole; sprinkle with onion, green pepper and mushrooms. Mix orange juice, Sherry, brown sugar, salt and orange rind in saucepan. Blend 2 tablespoons water with cornstarch in small bowl; stir into juice mixture. Simmer until thickened, stirring constantly. Pour over chicken. Bake at 375 degrees for 1 hour. Garnish with fresh orange slices and parsley.

Sandra Young

CHICKEN CACCIATORE

1 2 to 3-lb. chicken, cut up
1 clove of garlic, sliced
1/2 c. olive oil
1 sm. can tomatoes, drained
1 1/4 tsp. salt
1 tsp. rosemary
1 tsp. chopped parsley
1 tsp. pepper
1 sm. can mushrooms, drained
1 c. white cooking wine
1 sm. jar green olives, drained, chopped

Brown chicken with garlic in hot oil in Dutch oven; drain. Add remaining ingredients; mix well. Simmer for 15 minutes. Bake at 375 degrees for 1/2 hour or until chicken is tender. Serve over rice. Yield: 4 servings.

Diane Nichols

CHICKEN-FILLED CREPES

4 eggs
1 c. flour
1 c. milk
1 tsp. salt
2 tbsp. melted butter
1   29-oz. can boned chicken with broth
1 stalk celery, finely chopped
1/2 med. onion, finely chopped
Pepper to taste
1/2 c. cream
2 cans mushrooms, sliced
Parmesan cheese

Combine half the first 5 ingredients in blender container. Process until smooth. Repeat with remaining eggs, flour, milk, salt and butter. Pour a small amount of batter in buttered crepe pan, tilting to coat bottom. Cook until firm. Repeat with remaining batter. Drain chicken, reserving broth. Heat broth in saucepan. Add celery, onion, salt and pepper to taste. Simmer for 20 minutes or until vegetables are tender. Add cream and mushrooms; mix well. Fill crepes with chicken and sauce; roll to enclose filling. Place in baking dish. Cover with remaining sauce; sprinkle with cheese. Bake at 350 degrees for 25 minutes. Yield: 12 servings.

Mrs. Sam Young

CHICKEN CREPES WITH ALMONDS

3 eggs, beaten
2 1/2 c. milk
1/2 c. pancake mix
Butter
1 c. sliced fresh mushrooms
1/4 c. flour
1/4 tsp. pepper
2 chicken bouillon cubes, crushed
2 c. chopped cooked chicken
Toasted sliced almonds

Combine eggs, 1/2 cup milk and pancake mix in bowl; beat until smooth. Heat a small amount of butter in 8-inch skillet until bubbly. Pour a small amount of batter into hot skillet; tilt to cover bottom. Brown lightly on both sides.

Stack crepes between waxed paper. Saute mushrooms in 2 tablespoons butter in skillet. Blend 4 tablespoons melted butter with flour and pepper in medium saucepan. Cook over low heat for 1 minute, stirring frequently. Stir in 2 cups milk and bouillon cubes. Cook until thick, stirring constantly. Add mushrooms and chicken. Heat through. Spoon 1/3 cup chicken mixture on each crepe; roll to enclose filling. Arrange in 10 x 15-inch baking dish. Sprinkle with almonds. Bake at 325 degrees for 10 minutes.

Photograph for this recipe above.

CHICKEN TETRAZZINI

8 oz. spaghetti
1 tbsp. oil
2 tbsp. chopped onion
3 tbsp. butter
1 tbsp. flour
1 c. chicken broth
1 tsp. salt
1 c. milk
1 can mushroom soup
1 c. shredded sharp cheese
3 tbsp. chopped pimento
2 tbsp. parsley
2 1/2 to 3 c. diced cooked chicken
1/2 c. slivered almonds
1/4 c. Sherry
1 c. buttered cracker crumbs

Cook spaghetti in boiling salted water for 8 to 10 minutes. Stir in oil; drain. Saute onion in butter in saucepan until tender. Blend in flour. Stir in broth gradually. Cook until thick, stirring constantly. Add next 4 ingredients; mix well. Cook until cheese melts. Combine with spaghetti and remaining ingredients except crumbs; mix gently. Place in large shallow baking dish. Cover with buttered crumbs. Bake at 350 degrees for 45 minutes or until crumbs are golden brown.

Barbara Jones

ALMOND CHICKEN BAKED IN CREAM

> 1 tsp. each celery salt, paprika, salt
> 1/2 tsp. each curry powder, crushed
>   oregano, pepper
> 7 tbsp. melted butter
> 3 1/2 lb. chicken pieces
> Flour
> 3/4 c. sliced almonds
> 1 1/2 c. half and half
> 1/2 c. sour cream
> 3 tbsp. fine dry bread crumbs

Blend seasonings with 6 tablespoons butter in bowl. Coat chicken with flour; dip in seasoned butter. Arrange in single layer in large baking dish. Sprinkle with almonds. Pour half and half around chicken pieces. Bake, covered, at 350 degrees for 45 minutes. Spoon 1/2 cup pan drippings into sour cream in bowl; mix well. Pour evenly over chicken. Sprinkle with crumbs mixed with remaining tablespoon butter. Bake, uncovered, for 15 minutes.

Georgia Madison

OLD-FASHIONED CHICKEN AND DRESSING

> 1 4-lb. chicken
> Salt
> 2 c. white cornmeal
> 1 1/4 c. buttermilk
> 5 eggs
> 1 1/2 tbsp. bacon drippings
> 3 slices white bread, torn
> 1 med. onion, chopped

> 1/2 tsp. sage
> 1 tbsp. mayonnaise
> 1/4 c. grated cheese
> 1/4 c. chopped celery
> 1/4 tsp. pepper
> 1 hard-boiled egg, chopped

Cook chicken in salted water to cover in saucepan until tender. Drain, reserving broth. Cut chicken into serving pieces. Combine cornmeal, buttermilk, 2 beaten eggs and bacon drippings in bowl; mix well. Pour into baking dish. Bake at 425 degrees for 25 minutes. Break into small pieces. Combine with white bread in baking pan. Add 2 to 3 cups broth, 1/2 teaspoon salt, 3 beaten eggs and remaining ingredients except hard-boiled egg. Bake at 350 degrees for 1/2 hour. Arrange chicken over top. Bake for 5 minutes longer. Thicken remaining broth for gravy. Stir in hard-boiled egg. Season to taste. Serve over chicken.

Mrs. Bernice Johnson

STIR-FRY CHICKEN AND BROCCOLI

> 1/3 c. soy sauce
> 2 tbsp. brown sugar
> 3 tbsp. Sherry
> 1 clove of garlic, crushed
> 1 tsp. ginger
> 1 tsp. cornstarch
> 1 1/2 lb. chicken, cut into bite-sized
>   pieces
> 3 tbsp. oil
> 1 bunch broccoli, cut into flowerets
> 1 lg. onion, cut into wedges

Combine first 6 ingredients with 1/4 cup water in bowl; mix well. Marinate chicken in sauce for 10 minutes or longer. Drain chicken, reserving marinade. Stir-fry chicken, several pieces at a time, in hot oil in skillet until brown. Remove chicken. Add broccoli and onion to hot pan drippings. Add 1/4 cup water; mix well. Cook, covered, for 3 minutes or until broccoli is tender-crisp. Add chicken and reserved marinade. Cook until heated through, stirring constantly. Serve over rice.

Jane Barnes

CHILI CHICKEN

1/2 c. milk
1 can cream of chicken soup
1   8-oz. jar Cheez Whiz
1 sm. can chopped chilies, drained
2 tbsp. dried onion
2 c. chopped cooked chicken
1 bag corn chips

Combine first 5 ingredients in saucepan. Cook until Cheez Whiz melts. Add chicken; mix well. Layer corn chips and chicken mixture in casserole, beginning and ending with chips. Bake at 350 degrees for 20 minutes. Yield: 6 servings.

Ann P. Thode

COQ AU VN

2   2 1/2-lb. fryers, cut up
3 tbsp. flour
2 tsp. salt
1/2 tsp. black pepper
6 tbsp. butter, melted
16 sm. whole white onions
1/4 c. chopped onion
4 shallots, minced
2 cloves of garlic, minced
16 mushroom caps
2 c. red Burgundy
1/4 tsp. thyme
1 bay leaf

Coat chicken with mixture of flour, salt and pepper. Brown in butter in large skillet. Add onions, shallots, garlic and mushrooms. Cook over low heat until onions are lightly browned. Add Burgundy, thyme and bay leaf. Simmer, covered, for 1/2 hour or until chicken is tender.

Mrs. James R. Kennedy

TARRAGON CHICKEN

1 c. dry white wine
1/4 c. lemon juice
2 tbsp. red wine vinegar
2 tbsp. oil
1 1/2 tsp. tarragon, crushed

1 tsp. Beau Monde seasoning
Salt and pepper
2 lg. garlic cloves, crushed
1   3-lb. chicken, cut up
3 c. frozen sm. whole onions, thawed
3 med. zucchini, cut into strips
2 med. tomatoes, cut into wedges

Combine first 8 ingredients with 1 clove of garlic in bowl; mix well. Marinate chicken in mixture in refrigerator overnight; turn occasionally. Broil chicken on grill 4 to 5 inches from coals for 45 minutes or until tender, basting frequently with marinade. Turn chicken occasionally. Saute onions, zucchini and 1 garlic clove in skillet until tender-crisp. Season with salt and pepper. Add tomatoes. Cook until heated through. Arrange chicken on large serving dish surrounded by vegetables.

Joyce Gentry

CORNISH HENS A L'ORANGE

3/4 c. chopped onion
1 3/4 c. melted butter
4 1/2 c. cooked wild rice
2/3 c. chopped toasted almonds
1/2 tsp. thyme
Salt
8 Cornish hens
1/4 tsp. pepper
1/2 c. orange juice
1/2 c. bouillon
1/2 c. marmalade, melted

Saute onion in 4 tablespoons butter in skillet. Add rice, almonds, thyme and salt to taste; mix well. Stuff hens with wild rice mixture. Place breast side up in shallow baking dish. Mix 1/2 cup butter, 1 1/2 teaspoons salt and pepper; pour over hens. Roast at 425 degrees for 20 minutes, basting with orange juice and remaining butter every 5 minutes. Reduce temperature to 350 degrees. Roast for 1/2 hour, basting twice. Turn hens breast side down. Roast for 15 minutes, basting several times; add bouillon if liquid evaporates. Turn hens; pour marmalade over top. Roast for 1/2 hour longer.

Mrs. Richard L. Hennessy

CORNISH HENS WITH BLUEBERRIES

> 8 Cornish hens, thawed
> Salt and pepper to taste
> 1/4 c. oil
> 1/4 c. lemon juice
> 4 c. fresh blueberries, rinsed, drained
> 4 tsp. sugar
> 1/2 c. butter, softened
> 8 bay leaves

Sprinkle hens inside and out with salt and pepper. Mix oil and lemon juice in bowl. Brush inside and outside of hens. Fill each hen with 1/2 cup blueberries and 1/2 teaspoon sugar. Skewer opening; place on shallow baking pan. Spread butter over breasts of hens; place one bay leaf on each breast. Roast in 350-degree oven for 1 hour or until hens test done. Garnish with additional blueberries. Yield: 8 servings.

Alexandra Barnes

GLAZED CORNISH HENS

> 2 tbsp. honey
> 2 tbsp. unsalted margarine, melted
> Orange juice
> 4 Rock Cornish hens
> 1/4 c. chopped celery
> 1/4 c. chopped onion
> 2 tbsp. chopped parsley
> 1 tsp. grated orange peel
> 1/8 tsp. rosemary leaves, crushed
> 1/8 tsp. thyme leaves, crushed
> 1 c. dry-roasted unsalted peanuts
> 1 c. rice

Combine first 2 ingredients with 2 tablespoons orange juice in small bowl. Place Cornish hens on rack in broiler pan. Bake at 375 degrees for 1 hour or until tender, basting frequently with honey mixture. Saute celery and onion in saucepan until tender. Add remaining ingredients with 1/2 cup orange juice and 1 1/2 cups water; mix well. Simmer, covered, until liquid is absorbed. Place Cornish hens on serving platter surrounded by seasoned rice. Yield: 4 servings.

Nancy Miller

ROAST PLUM DUCK

> 1 onion, minced
> Butter
> 1 17-oz. can purple plums, pureed
> 1 6-oz. can frozen lemonade, thawed
> 1/3 c. chili sauce
> 1/4 c. soy sauce
> 1 tsp. Worcestershire sauce
> 1 tsp. ginger
> 2 tsp. mustard
> Onion salt and garlic salt to taste
> Tabasco sauce to taste
> 2 ducks
> Oranges, sliced

Saute onion in small amount of butter in saucepan until tender. Add plums with next 6 ingredients. Season with onion salt, garlic salt and Tabasco sauce to taste; blend well. Simmer for 15 minutes. Wash ducks; wipe dry inside and out. Place ducks on rack in baking pan; cover with orange slices. Bake, covered, at 350 degrees for 1 1/2 hours. Spoon half the sauce over ducks. Bake for 1 1/2 hours longer or until tender. Serve with remaining sauce.

Carolyn Holt

CURRIED TURKEY SOUP

> 1 c. diced celery
> 1 c. diced peeled apple
> 1/2 c. chopped onion
> 1/4 c. butter
> 1/4 c. flour
> 2 tsp. curry powder
> 1 1/2 tsp. salt
> 1/8 tsp. pepper
> 4 c. milk
> 2 c. diced cooked turkey

Saute celery, apple and onion in butter in saucepan until tender. Blend in flour, curry powder, salt and pepper. Stir in milk gradually. Simmer until thickened, stirring constantly. Add turkey. Heat to serving temperature.

Cheryl Lewis

TURKEY CHOP SUEY

1/2 c. sliced onions
1 1-lb. can bean sprouts
1 1/2 to 2 c. diced cooked turkey
1 c. sliced celery
1 6-oz. can sliced water chestnuts,
    drained
1/2 c. turkey broth
2 tbsp. cornstarch
1/4 tsp. salt
1/4 tsp. monosodium glutamate
2 tbsp. soy sauce
4 c. hot cooked rice
1/2 c. blanched slivered almonds, toasted

Saute onions in saucepan until tender. Drain
bean sprouts, reserving liquid. Add next 4 ingredients and reserved liquid to sauteed onions;
mix well. Combine cornstarch with seasonings,
1/4 cup water and soy sauce in bowl; mix well.
Stir into turkey mixture. Simmer until thickened, stirring constantly. Add bean sprouts,
stirring until heated through. Serve over rice.
Garnish with almonds. Yield: 4-6 servings.

Kit Tarkington

FANTASTIC TURKEY CASSEROLE

1 lb. sliced fresh mushrooms
1 med. onion, chopped
3 tbsp. butter
2 tsp. salt
1/4 tsp. pepper
1 pkg. white and wild rice mix with
    seasoning packet
3 c. diced cooked turkey
1/2 c. chopped blanched almonds
3 c. chicken broth
1 1/2 c. heavy cream

Saute mushrooms and onion in butter in skillet
for 10 minutes. Combine with remaining ingredients in order listed in large greased casserole.
Bake at 350 degrees for 1 1/2 hours. Yield: 6-8
servings.

Mickie Franklin

SMOKED TURKEY

1 13-lb. turkey
Dry white wine
1 lb. margarine
1 c. lemon juice
1 c. Worcestershire sauce
1 tbsp. salt
Red pepper to taste
Tabasco sauce
1 tbsp. paprika
1 tsp. monosodium glutamate
1/4 c. dry Sherry

Place turkey in deep roasting pan. Fill cavity
with 1/2-inch white wine. Combine remaining
ingredients except Sherry in saucepan. Bring to
a boil. Stir in Sherry; mix well. Cook turkey in
barbecue grill with hood closed over hot coals
and hickory chips for 4 to 6 hours or until
turkey tests done. Baste frequently with Sherry
sauce during cooking.

Mrs. W. H. Ladd

TURKEY POULET OVEN-BAKE

Cooked turkey slices
4 c. cooked rice
6 slices bacon
2 tbsp. chopped onion
1 can condensed cream of chicken soup
1/4 c. milk
2 tbsp. chopped parsley
1 tbsp. cooking Sherry
1 tbsp. lemon juice
Parmesan cheese, grated

Arrange turkey slices over rice in 8-inch square
baking dish. Saute bacon in skillet until lightly
browned; remove bacon. Cook onion in 2 tablespoons bacon drippings until tender. Blend in
soup, milk, parsley, Sherry and lemon juice.
Cook until heated through. Pour over turkey.
Sprinkle with cheese; top with bacon. Bake at
325 degrees for 20 to 25 minutes or until
bubbly. Yield: 6 servings.

Mrs. John H. Buzard

Garden Vegetables & Side Dishes

ARTICHOKE HEARTS IN PARMESAN CUSTARD

2 pkg. frozen artichoke hearts
1/2 c. drained canned tomatoes
Salt and pepper to taste
Garlic salt and chopped parsley to taste
1/4 to 1/2 c. Parmesan cheese
1/4 to 1/2 c. olive oil
6 eggs

Arrange artichoke hearts in bottom of oiled 2-quart casserole. Cut up tomatoes; layer over artichokes. Sprinkle with salt, pepper, garlic salt, parsley and Parmesan cheese. Add 1/2 to 3/4 cup water and olive oil. Bake, covered, at 350 degrees for 1 hour. Beat eggs until light and fluffy; pour over artichokes. Bake, uncovered, for 15 to 20 minutes or until eggs are set.

Mrs. Santo P. Giunta

ASPARAGUS ANGELIQUE

2 lb. asparagus
4 tbsp. butter
6 tbsp. bread crumbs
1/2 tsp. salt
1/8 tsp. pepper
2 tbsp. grated Cheddar cheese
2 tbsp. Parmesan cheese
3/4 c. pancake batter
3 egg whites, stiffly beaten

Parboil asparagus until tender-crisp. Melt butter in shallow baking dish; add bread crumbs. Combine salt and pepper; blend 1/4 teaspoon mixture with bread crumbs. Arrange asparagus over bread crumbs. Combine cheeses and remaining salt mixture with pancake batter in bowl; fold in egg whites. Spread over asparagus. Bake at 400 degrees for 15 minutes. Yield: 8 servings.

Margery A. Herbert

ASPARAGUS FABIEN

1 tbsp. prepared white mustard
1/4 tsp. salt
Juice of 1/2 lemon, strained
3/4 c. olive oil

2 tsp. finely chopped fresh parsley
2 tsp. each tarragon, chervil
2 tsp. finely chopped shallots
1 can white asparagus, drained

Combine mustard, salt and lemon juice in bowl. Add olive oil gradually, beating constantly with wire whisk. Whisk in parsley, tarragon, chervil and shallots. Arrange asparagus on serving plate. Pour sauce over asparagus.

Mildred Krech

EMPRESS ASPARAGUS

3   10-oz. packages frozen asparagus
*   spears*
1 can bean sprouts, drained
2 cans French-fried onion rings
2 cans cream of mushroom soup
1 tbsp. soy sauce
1 c. slivered almonds

Cook asparagus for half the time as directed; drain. Place alternate layers of asparagus, bean sprouts and onion rings in buttered 10-inch casserole, reserving last layer of onion rings. Mix soup and soy sauce together; spread over bean sprouts. Top with reserved onion rings; sprinkle with almonds. Bake in 350-degree oven for 30 minutes or until bubbly. Yield: 8 servings.

Betty Bell

ASPARAGUS WITH HOLLANDAISE TABASCO

2 egg yolks
2 tbsp. lemon juice
1/4 tsp. dry mustard
1/4 tsp. sugar
1/4 tsp. salt
1/4 tsp. Tabasco sauce
1/2 c. butter
Cooked asparagus spears

Combine egg yolks, lemon juice, mustard, sugar, salt and Tabasco sauce in small heavy earthenware mixing bowl; mix well. Add 1/3 of the butter to egg mixture; place bowl in hot water in saucepan. Cook over low heat until butter is melted, stirring constantly. Repeat

GREEN BEAN CASSEROLE DELUXE

   2 cans julienne green beans, drained
   1 4-oz. can mushrooms, drained
   1 1-lb. can bean sprouts, drained
   1 8-oz. can sliced water chestnuts,
      drained
   1/2 tsp. salt
   1 can mushroom soup
   1 c. grated Cheddar cheese

Combine all ingredients except cheese in casserole; mix well. Top with cheese. Bake at 350 degrees for 25 minutes.

Mrs. Sam R. Sellers

BAKED BEANS

   2 28-oz. cans pork and beans
   1 lb. lean sliced bacon, cut in half
   2 onions, chopped
   2 tbsp. Worcestershire sauce
   1 c. packed brown sugar
   1 c. catsup
   1 tsp. dry mustard
   1/4 c. molasses

Combine all ingredients in baking dish. Bake, covered, at 325 degrees for 1 1/2 hours; stir twice and spoon off excess bacon drippings. Bake, uncovered, for 1/2 hour longer. Yield: 10-12 servings.

Regina Bedarf

BEETS IN SOUR CREAM

   2 1/2 c. cooked whole sm. beets
      and liquid
   2 tbsp. butter
   1/4 tsp. allspice
   1 c. sour cream
   2 tbsp. chopped parsley

Place beets and liquid in saucepan. Heat through; drain off liquid. Add butter, allspice and sour cream. Heat through, stirring well; do not boil. Sprinkle parsley over top.

Mrs. Peter Olenchuk

twice more with remaining butter, stirring constantly as butter melts and sauce thickens. Remove from heat. Serve over asparagus.

Photograph for this recipe above.

BARBECUED BEANS

   1 1-lb. can pork and beans
   1 1-lb. can kidney beans, drained
   1 1-lb. can green lima beans, drained
   1 lg. onion, chopped
   1 clove of garlic, minced
   1 tbsp. Worcestershire sauce
   Dash of Tabasco sauce
   2 tbsp. cumin seed
   2 to 3 tbsp. cold coffee
   1/4 c. packed brown sugar
   1/2 c. catsup
   Pinch of oregano
   Pinch of basil
   3 slices bacon

Combine all ingredients except bacon in large shallow baking dish; mix well. Place bacon strips on top. Bake, covered, at 350 degrees for 1 hour. Bake, uncovered, for 15 minutes longer.

Candy Barnes

SPECIAL BROCCOLI CASSEROLE

1/2 can cream of mushroom soup
1/2 c. mayonnaise
2 tbsp. chopped onion
1/2 c. shredded sharp cheese
Salt and pepper to taste
1 egg, well beaten
1   10-oz. package frozen chopped
*   broccoli, thawed*
Buttered crumbs

Combine first 7 ingredients in bowl; mix well. Fold in broccoli. Spoon into greased baking dish. Top with crumbs. Bake at 350 degrees for 1/2 hour.

Mary Pat Thuma

BROCCOLI DELIGHT

2 pkg. frozen broccoli spears,
*   cooked, drained*
1/3 c. mayonnaise
2 egg whites, stiffly beaten
Grated Cheddar cheese

Arrange broccoli spears on plate like wheel spokes with stem ends toward center. Blend mayonnaise into egg whites. Spoon sauce into center of broccoli. Arrange circle of grated cheese around sauce. Very pretty for a buffet.

Rosemary Sanders

BRUSSELS SPROUTS AND ARTICHOKES

1   10-oz. package frozen Brussels
*   sprouts, cooked, drained*
1   14-oz. package frozen artichoke
*   hearts, cooked, drained*
2/3 c. mayonnaise
1/2 tsp. celery salt
1/4 c. Parmesan cheese
1/4 c. margarine, melted
2 tsp. lemon juice
1/4 c. sliced almonds

Arrange vegetables in 1-quart casserole. Combine remaining ingredients in small bowl; mix well. Spoon over vegetables. Bake at 425 degrees until hot and bubbly.

Mrs. Laura Teague

NOODLE BROCCOLI

1 stick butter
2 pkg. tiny noodles, cooked
2 bunches green onions, finely chopped
2 pkg. chopped frozen broccoli, cooked
1 can cheese soup
1/2 tsp. rosemary
1 tsp. Worcestershire sauce
Dash of Tabasco sauce
1 c. grated cheese

Add 1/2 stick butter to hot noodles. Saute onions in 1/2 stick butter in skillet. Combine noodles and onions with broccoli, cheese soup, rosemary, Worcestershire sauce and Tabasco sauce in casserole; mix well. Top with cheese. Bake at 350 degrees for 50 minutes.

Mrs. Jerry Tune

BROCCOLI RING

4 c. cooked chopped broccoli
2 c. thick white sauce
2 c. mayonnaise
Onion juice
Cayenne pepper
Salt
Accent
12 eggs, beaten

Mix broccoli, white sauce and mayonnaise. Season with onion juice, cayenne pepper, salt and Accent. Add eggs; mix well. Pour into buttered 2-quart ring mold; set in pan of water. Bake in 350-degree oven for about 1 hour or until firm. Remove from mold; serve.

Mrs. Henry Viccellio

DILLED CARROTS

2 lb. carrots, sliced
1/2 stick butter
1/4 c. sugar
1/4 c. Sherry
1 or 2 tsp. dillseed

Combine all ingredients in saucepan. Simmer until carrots are tender-crisp. Refrigerate overnight to enhance flavor.

Bunny Waddell

CARROTS AMANDINE

1 1/2 tsp. cornstarch
1/4 c. packed brown sugar
1/4 tsp. salt
1 tbsp. butter
1/2 c. orange juice
1 lb. carrots, sliced diagonally
2 tbsp. slivered almonds

Combine cornstarch, brown sugar, salt, butter and orange juice in saucepan. Cook until thick, stirring constantly. Arrange carrots and almonds in 1 1/2-quart casserole. Pour orange sauce over carrots. Bake, covered, at 350 degrees for 1 hour. Yield: 6 servings.

Mrs. Clifford C. Segerstrom

CAULIFLOWER CHEESE SOUFFLE

4 tbsp. flour
2 tbsp. butter
1 tsp. baking powder
1 c. milk
1/2 tsp. salt
Dash of pepper
2 c. grated cheese
3 egg yolks, beaten
2 c. cooked cauliflower, chopped
3 egg whites, stiffly beaten

Add flour to melted butter in saucepan. Stir in next 4 ingredients. Simmer until thickened, stirring constantly. Stir in cheese until melted; cool. Add egg yolks and cauliflower; mix well. Fold in egg whites. Pour into greased baking dish. Bake at 350 degrees for 50 minutes.

Mrs. W. J. Macpherson

CREAMED CELERY WITH PECANS

4 c. celery, cut diagonally into
* 1/2-in. pieces*
2 tbsp. flour
2 tbsp. butter, melted
2 c. milk
1 tsp. salt
3/4 c. pecan halves
Buttered bread crumbs

Boil celery in water to cover in saucepan until tender; drain. Blend flour into melted butter in skillet; add milk slowly. Simmer until thick and smooth, stirring constantly. Add salt and celery; mix well. Spoon into greased 1 1/2-quart casserole. Top with pecans; cover with buttered crumbs. Bake at 400 degrees for 15 minutes.

Mrs. Scott McGee

SCALLOPED CORN

1 can cream-style corn
1 c. milk
1 egg, well beaten
3/4 tsp. salt
1/4 c. chopped onion
1/4 c. sliced pimento (opt.)
1 1/2 c. coarse cracker crumbs
1 tbsp. melted butter

Mix first 6 ingredients and 3/4 cup cracker crumbs in bowl. Pour into buttered 1 1/2-quart casserole. Top with remaining crumbs mixed with melted butter. Bake at 350 degrees for 30 to 45 minutes or until knife inserted into center comes out clean. Yield: 4 servings.

Mrs. Judith A. Curinga

BAKED CUCUMBERS

6 cucumbers, peeled
2 tbsp. wine vinegar
1 1/2 tsp. salt
1/8 tsp. sugar
1 tbsp. melted butter
1/2 tsp. dill
3 to 4 tbsp. minced green onions
1/8 tsp. pepper

Cut cucumbers in half lengthwise; scoop out seeds. Cut into 3/8-inch wide strips; cut strips in half. Combine with vinegar, salt and sugar in bowl. Marinate for 1/2 to several hours. Mix cucumber mixture with remaining ingredients in 12-inch round baking dish. Bake at 375 degrees for 1 hour or until tender-crisp, stirring several times. Yield: 6 servings.

Mrs. Arthur C. Agan, Jr.

MARINATED VIDALIA ONIONS

1 c. sugar
1/2 c. white vinegar
4 lg. Vidalia onions, sliced
1/4 c. mayonnaise
Celery salt to taste

Combine sugar, vinegar and 2 cups water in large bowl; stir until sugar dissolves. Separate onion slices into rings; stir into vinegar mixture. Marinate overnight. Drain onions thoroughly. Add mayonnaise and celery salt; mix well.

Marietta Randolph

CURRIED PECAN AND GREEN PEA SHORTCAKES

2 c. biscuit mix
Butter
Milk
2 tbsp. minced onion
1   10-oz. package frozen green peas
Salt
1 c. pecan halves
2 tbsp. flour
1/2 tsp. paprika
1/2 to 1 tsp. curry powder
1/2 c. half and half

Prepare biscuit mix according to package directions using 1/3 cup butter and 2/3 cup milk. Roll to 1/4 inch thickness on lightly floured surface. Cut with 3-inch biscuit cutter. Cut 1 1/2-inch round from half the biscuits and place on uncut biscuits on baking sheet. Bake using package directions. Saute onion in 4 teaspoons butter in saucepan. Add 3 tablespoons water, peas and 1/2 teaspoon salt. Simmer, covered, until peas are tender, stirring occasionally. Add pecans. Heat thoroughly. Add flour to 2 tablespoons melted butter in saucepan. Stir in paprika, curry powder, half and half, 3/4 cup milk and 1/2 teaspoon salt. Simmer until thickened, stirring constantly. Place biscuit shells in serving plate; spoon curry sauce into centers and top with pea mixture. Yield: 4 servings.

Joan Waters

CHINESE PEAS WITH WATER CHESTNUTS

2 c. cubed cooked chicken
1 tbsp. oil
2 c. Chinese green peas
1/2 c. thinly sliced water chestnuts
1 tsp. monosodium glutamate
1 can beef broth or bouillon
2 tbsp. cornstarch
Soy sauce to taste

Cook chicken in oil in skillet until heated through. Add next 4 ingredients; mix well. Cook, covered, over high heat for 3 minutes. Mix cornstarch with 1/4 cup cold water. Push vegetables to side. Stir in cornstarch mixture. Cook until slightly thick, stirring constantly. Stir in soy sauce. Serve with steamed rice. Yield: 4 servings.

Mrs. J. Richard Gouthey

CREOLE BLACK-EYED PEAS

2 1-lb. cans black-eyed peas
1 1-lb. can jalapeno black-eyed peas
1 lg. can tomatoes
1 c. chopped onion
1 c. chopped celery
1 1-lb. bag cut-up frozen okra
   (not breaded)

Combine all ingredients in slow cooker. Cook on High for 4 hours. Yield: 8 servings.

Dona Caldwell

CHEESE-PUFFED POTATOES

4 eggs, separated
4 c. seasoned mashed potatoes
1 c. shredded sharp Cheddar cheese
2 tsp. finely chopped onion
2 tsp. finely chopped green pepper
1/2 tsp. celery salt
Salt to taste
Paprika

Combine egg yolks and mashed potatoes in bowl; beat until well mixed. Stir in cheese, onion, green pepper, celery salt and salt. Fold in stiffly beaten egg whites. Spoon into well-greased 7 x 13-inch casserole; sprinkle with paprika. Bake at 375 degrees for 25 minutes. Yield: 6 servings.

Mrs. Oliver W. Fix

GRATED POTATO BAKE

1/2 c. milk
3 eggs
1/2 tsp. salt
1/8 tsp. pepper
1 c. cubed sharp process cheese
1/4 c. butter
3 1/2 med. onions
3 med. potatoes, peeled, cubed

Place all ingredients in blender container. Process on high until potatoes are grated. Pour into 6 x 10-inch baking dish. Bake at 375 degrees for 35 to 40 minutes. Garnish with green pepper rings. Yield: 6 servings.

Mrs. George E. Rippey

POTATO AND CELERY MOLD

12 stalks celery, peeled
1 leek
6 lg. potatoes, cubed
4 tbsp. butter, softened
2 egg yolks
1/2 c. grated Swiss cheese

Cook vegetables in salted water in saucepan until tender; drain. Put through food mill. Combine with 2 tablespoons butter, egg yolks and 1/4 cup cheese in blender container. Process until smooth. Butter 1-quart pudding mold with remaining butter. Pour vegetable mixture into prepared mold. Bake at 350 degrees for 15 minutes. Unmold on heatproof serving plate. Sprinkle with remaining cheese. Broil until lightly browned.

Mrs. Pierre J. Dolan

HEAVENLY HASHED BROWNS

1 lg. package frozen hashed brown
    potatoes, thawed
1 can cream of celery soup
1 can cream of potato soup
3 tbsp. chopped onions or onion flakes
3 tbsp. dried celery flakes
8 oz. sour cream
Paprika to taste

Combine first 6 ingredients in greased 9 x 13-inch casserole. Sprinkle with paprika. Bake, covered, at 325 degrees for 1 to 1 1/2 hours. May be frozen. Yield: 8-10 servings.

Mrs. Willis M. Simmons

POTATO DRESSING

3 lb. potatoes, boiled, mashed
4 to 6 slices bread, cubed
1 med. onion, chopped
2 c. chopped celery
Salt and pepper to taste

Combine all ingredients in large bowl; mix well. Place in casserole. Bake, covered, at 350 degrees for 1 hour. May also be used to stuff turkey or round steak.

Janna French

SINFUL POTATOES

2 lb. frozen hashed brown potatoes,
    thawed
1/2 c. melted margarine
1 tsp. salt
1/4 tsp. pepper
1 can cream of mushroom soup
2 c. grated cheese
1/2 c. chopped onion
2 c. sour cream
Bread crumbs

Combine all ingredients except bread crumbs in large bowl; mix well. Spread in 9 x 13-inch baking pan. Top with bread crumbs. Bake at 350 degrees for 1 hour.

Marge Janssen

SPINACH DIANA

2 pkg. frozen chopped spinach
2 tbsp. flour
4 tbsp. butter
2 tbsp. chopped onion
1/2 c. evaporated milk
3/4 tsp. celery salt
1/2 tsp. black pepper
3/4 tsp. garlic powder
1/2 tsp. salt
1 tsp. Worcestershire sauce
Red pepper to taste
1 6-oz. roll jalapeno cheese, chopped
Buttered crumbs

Cook spinach using package directions. Drain, reserving 1/2 cup liquid. Add flour to melted butter in top of double boiler; mix well. Add onion. Cook until tender, stirring constantly. Add spinach liquid and evaporated milk. Cook until thickened, stirring constantly. Stir in seasonings with cheese. Add spinach; mix well. Spoon into casserole; top with buttered crumbs. Bake at 350 degrees for 1/2 hour or until bubbly.

Mary Pat Thuma

SUPER SQUASH CASSEROLE

2 lb. yellow squash, cooked, mashed
1 carton sour cream
1 can cream of mushroom soup
1 onion, grated
1 stick margarine, melted
1 carrot, grated
1/4 pkg. herb-seasoned stuffing mix

Combine all ingredients in casserole; mix well. Top with additional stuffing mix. Bake at 350 degrees until bubbly. Yield: 8 servings.

Lisa Miller

SWEET POTATO BALLS

1/4 c. butter, softened
3/4 c. packed brown sugar

2 tbsp. milk
1/4 tsp. salt
1/2 tsp. grated orange rind
Chopped nuts (opt.)
3 c. mashed cooked sweet potatoes
8 marshmallows
1 c. crushed cornflakes

Add butter, sugar, milk, salt, orange rind and nuts to sweet potatoes; mix well. Shape sweet potato mixture around each marshmallow. Roll each ball in cornflakes. Place on buttered baking dish. Cover with foil. Freeze until needed. Bake at 325 degrees for 20 minutes. Yield: 8 servings.

Zena Brandeis

SWEET POTATO SOUFFLE

2 c. cooked mashed sweet potatoes
4 tbsp. butter, melted
2 tbsp. brown sugar
2 tbsp. orange juice
1/3 c. light cream
1/2 tsp. cinnamon
3 eggs, separated
Marshmallows

Combine first 6 ingredients with beaten egg yolks in bowl; mix well. Fold in stiffly beaten egg whites. Spread in greased casserole; top with marshmallows. Bake at 325 degrees for 1 hour. Yield: 6 servings.

Mrs. William Henson

EASY SCALLOPED TOMATOES

1 16-oz. can tomatoes
1 tsp. instant minced onion
1 tbsp. sugar
1/2 tsp. salt
Dash of Tabasco sauce
1 tbsp. Worcestershire sauce
4 slices toasted bread, cubed
1/4 c. melted butter
1/4 c. shredded Cheddar cheese

Combine tomatoes, onion, sugar, salt, Tabasco sauce and Worcestershire sauce in bowl; mix well. Alternate layers of toast cubes and tomato mixture in buttered 1 1/2-quart casserole, ending with toast cubes. Pour butter over toast. Sprinkle with cheese. Bake at 375 degrees for 35 minutes. Yield: 4 servings.

Mrs. James G. Towle

BOURBON TOMATOES

2 cans stewing tomatoes
3 slices white bread, broken into pieces
2 tbsp. margarine
2 c. sugar
1 tsp. nutmeg
1/8 tsp. cinnamon
1/2 c. Bourbon

Combine all ingredients in casserole; mix well. Bake at 350 degrees for 30 minutes, stirring once after margarine has melted. Yield: 6-8 servings.

Mrs. Neil Craighead

BUFFET VEGETABLE BAKE

2 10-oz. packages frozen mixed
    peas and carrots
1 9-oz. package frozen green beans
1 5-oz. can sliced water chestnuts,
    drained
1 3-oz. can broiled sliced mushrooms,
    drained
1 can cream of mushroom soup
3 to 4 tbsp. Sherry
1 tsp. Worcestershire sauce
Dash of hot pepper sauce
2 c. shredded sharp process cheese
1/4 c. buttery cracker crumbs

Cook frozen vegetables using package directions until tender-crisp; drain. Add water chestnuts and mushrooms. Combine remaining ingredients except crumbs in bowl; mix well. Add to vegetables; toss to mix. Turn into 2-quart casserole. Bake at 350 degrees until bubbly, stirring occasionally. Sprinkle with crumbs. Yield: 10-12 servings.

Mrs. Bobby B. Spoonemore

CHINESE ZUCCHINI

1 sm. onion, sliced
1 clove of garlic, minced
2 tbsp. bacon drippings
4 zucchini, sliced
1/4 c. soy sauce

Saute onion and garlic in bacon drippings in skillet until golden. Add remaining ingredients and 2 tablespoons water. Simmer, covered, for 5 to 8 minutes or until tender-crisp. Yield: 4-6 servings.

Mrs. William J. Gammon

Side Dishes

BAKED PINEAPPLE

1 20-oz. can crushed pineapple, drained
2 eggs, beaten
1 c. (scant) sugar
1/2 c. milk
1/4 c. melted butter
1/2 c. crushed saltine crackers

Drain pineapple, reserving half the juice. Combine eggs and sugar; mix well. Stir in remaining ingredients and reserved juice. Pour into shallow buttered 9-inch baking dish. Bake at 350 degrees for 1 hour.

Marjorie T. Pastino

PARTY GRITS

1 c. grits
1 tsp. salt
1 roll garlic cheese
1/2 c. milk
2 eggs, beaten
2 tbsp. butter, melted
1 c. cornflakes, crushed

Cook grits in salted water in saucepan for 5 minutes; remove from heat. Stir 3/4 of the cheese into grits until cheese melts. Mix milk and eggs; beat into grits. Combine butter, cornflakes and remaining cheese; mix well. Stir into grits mixture. Turn into casserole. Bake at 350 degrees for 45 minutes.

Toby G. Mahin

BARLEY WITH MUSHROOMS

3/4 to 1 c. sliced mushrooms
3/4 to 1 c. chopped onion
1/4 c. butter
2 c. pearlox barley
4 c. chicken broth

Saute mushrooms and onion in butter in skillet over medium heat until tender. Stir in barley and chicken broth. Simmer, covered, for 30 minutes or until liquid is absorbed.

Mary K. Halvorsen

PASTA PESTO

3/4 c. olive oil
1 1/2 c. fresh basil leaves
1 to 2 cloves of garlic
1/2 c. pine nuts
1 c. fresh sprigs of parsley
3/4 c. Romano cheese, grated
1 tsp. salt
1 pkg. vermicelli, cooked, drained

Combine first 6 ingredients in blender container. Process until smooth. Add salt. Process to blend. Combine with hot vermicelli in serving dish; mix well. Yield: 6 servings.

Mrs. Calvine F. Johnson

PILAF EXTRAORDINAIRE

2 c. long grain rice
1/2 c. butter, melted
1 tsp. salt
1/4 tsp. saffron
Freshly ground pepper
3 cans consomme
2 med. onions, thinly sliced
1 c. raisins

Saute rice in 1/4 cup butter in Dutch oven until golden brown. Stir in seasonings and consomme. Bake, covered, at 325 degrees for 1 1/2 hours. Saute onions in 1/4 cup butter in skillet until tender. Stir raisins into rice. Let stand for 5 minutes before serving. Mound rice on serving platter. Garnish with onion rings.

Photograph for this recipe on page 53.

RICE CONSOMME

1/2 c. rice
1 can consomme soup
1 tbsp. butter

Place rice and consomme in baking dish. Bake, covered, in 350-degree oven for 40 minutes or until rice has absorbed all liquid. Add butter. Onion soup may be used for consomme.

Mrs. Floyd Standage

RICE-MUSHROOM MEDLEY

1 6-oz. package long grain and wild
    rice mix
3/4 c. beef bouillon
1 sm. onion, chopped
1/2 c. chopped celery
4 tbsp. butter
1 3-oz. can sliced mushrooms, drained

Prepare rice according to package directions using bouillon and 1 1/4 cups water. Saute onion and celery in butter in skillet until tender. Stir onion mixture and mushrooms into rice 5 minutes before end of cooking time. Cook until all liquid is absorbed.

Barbara Logan

WONDERFUL WILD RICE CASSEROLE

1 pkg. wild rice mix
1/2 c. chopped onion
1/2 c. margarine
3 c. chopped cooked chicken
1 c. cream of chicken soup
1 6-oz. can sliced mushrooms
1/4 c. chopped pimento
1 tsp. salt
1/4 tsp. pepper
1/2 c. chopped pecans

Cook rice using package directions. Saute onion in margarine. Add rice and remaining ingredients; mix well. Pour into buttered 2-quart casserole. Bake at 350 degrees for 25 to 30 minutes. Freezes well.

Claudine Arrasmith

Breads
for
All Seasons

CARAMEL ORANGE RING

1/2 c. orange marmalade
1 tbsp. butter
2 tbsp. chopped nuts
1 c. packed brown sugar
1/2 tsp. cinnamon
2 10-oz. cans flaky buttermilk
　　refrigerator biscuits, separated
1/2 c. butter, melted

Spoon marmalade over bottom of 12-cup bundt pan greased with 1 tablespoon butter. Sprinkle nuts over marmalade. Mix brown sugar and cinnamon in small bowl. Dip biscuits in melted butter then in brown sugar mixture. Arrange biscuits evenly, standing on edge, in prepared pan. Sprinkle with remaining brown sugar mixture. Drizzle with remaining butter. Bake at 350 degrees for 30 minutes or until golden brown. Cool for 5 minutes; invert on serving plate. Yield: 8 servings.

Mrs. C. S. Fabrigar

STREUSEL-FILLED COFFEE CAKE

1/4 c. shortening
3/4 c. sugar
1 egg, beaten
1 1/2 c. sifted flour
2 tsp. baking powder
1/2 tsp. salt
3/4 c. milk
1/2 c. packed brown sugar
2 tsp. cinnamon
1/2 c. finely chopped nuts
2 tbsp. margarine, melted

Cream shortening and sugar in large bowl. Add egg; mix well. Combine flour, baking powder and salt in bowl. Add to creamed mixture alternately with milk; mix until just moistened. Spread 1/2 of the batter in baking pan. Mix remaining 4 ingredients in small bowl. Sprinkle half the nut mixture over batter. Spread remaining batter on top; sprinkle remaining nut mixture over batter. Bake at 375 degrees for 25 to 30 minutes or until cake tests done. Yield: 9-12 servings.

Barbara Davis

RAISIN-MINCEMEAT COFFEE CAKE

2 1/2 c. biscuit mix
2/3 c. milk
Melted butter
1 c. seedless raisins
1 c. mincemeat
3/4 c. sifted confectioners' sugar
1/4 tsp. vanilla extract

Combine first 2 ingredients with 2 tablespoons butter in bowl; mix well. Roll to 8 x 18-inch rectangle on floured surface. Cut in half lengthwise. Combine raisins and mincemeat in bowl. Spoon down center of strips. Fold edges over, pinching together to enclose filling. Coil strips in buttered 9-inch cake pan, beginning at outer edge of pan and working towards center. Join ends of coil to form 1 continuous strip. Cut part way through strips at 2-inch intervals. Brush with melted butter. Bake at 400 degrees for 25 to 30 minutes or until browned. Mix confectioners' sugar with vanilla and 1 tablespoon warm water in medium bowl. Drizzle glaze over cake.

Mrs. James W. Osmar

ALMOND GINGER LOAF

1 c. sifted flour
3 tsp. baking powder
1/2 tsp. each salt, cinnamon
1 c. slivered almonds, chopped
1 1/2 c. crushed gingersnaps
1/2 c. packed brown sugar
1/2 c. butter
3 eggs
1/2 c. milk

Sift flour with baking powder, salt and cinnamon into bowl; add almonds, ginger crumbs and brown sugar. Cut in butter until crumbly. Beat eggs with milk in bowl. Pour into dry ingredients; mix well. Pour into greased and floured 4 x 8-inch glass loaf pan. Bake at 350 degrees for 40 minutes or until loaf tests done. Cool in pan for 10 minutes. Invert and cool on rack.

Photograph for this recipe on page 63.

ALMOND BUTTERSCOTCH BREAD

1 1/4 c. sugar
3/4 c. slivered almonds
1/2 c. butter, softened
2 eggs
1 1/2 tsp. vanilla extract
1 1/2 tsp. butter flavoring
1/2 tsp. maple flavoring
2 c. flour
2 tsp. baking powder
1/2 tsp. soda
3/4 tsp. salt
3/4 c. buttermilk

Caramelize 1/4 cup sugar with almonds in skillet over medium-low heat until almonds are coated and golden brown, stirring constantly. Remove immediately to foil. Cool thoroughly. Wrap in towel; break with hammer until coarsely crushed. Cream butter with 1 cup sugar in bowl. Add eggs and flavorings; beat well. Add sifted dry ingredients alternately with buttermilk, beating well after each addition. Fold in 2/3 of the almond mixture. Pour into greased and floured 9 x 5-inch loaf pan. Sprinkle remaining almond mixture over top. Bake at 300 degrees for 1 hour and 15 minutes or until bread tests done.

Photograph for this recipe on page 63.

BRAN CORN BREAD

1/2 c. sugar
1/2 c. shortening
2 eggs, beaten
1 1/2 c. All-Bran
1 c. milk
1 c. flour
1/2 c. yellow cornmeal
3 tsp. baking powder
1/2 tsp. salt

Cream sugar and shortening in bowl. Add eggs, mixing well. Stir in All-Bran and milk. Let stand for 5 minutes or longer. Add sifted dry ingredients, mixing well. Pour into greased 9 x 13-inch baking pan. Bake at 375 degrees until bread tests done. Yield: 8 servings.

Ada Westmoreland

CHEDDAR CHEESE BREAD

2 c. sifted flour
3/4 c. sugar
1 tbsp. baking powder
1/2 tsp. salt
1/2 c. grated sharp Cheddar cheese
1/2 c. chopped walnuts
1 c. drained crushed pineapple
2 tbsp. melted butter
1 egg, beaten

Sift flour, sugar, baking powder and salt into bowl. Add cheese and walnuts; toss to mix. Combine remaining 3 ingredients in bowl; mix well. Add to flour mixture; mix until just moistened. Pour into greased loaf pan. Bake at 350 degrees for 1 hour or until bread tests done. Cool; wrap well. Let stand overnight to improve flavor.

Mrs. J. Elmore Swenson

SPINACH BREAD

1 1/2 c. flour
1 tsp. salt
1 1/2 tsp. pepper
1/2 tsp. baking powder
6 tbsp. grated cheese
1/4 c. margarine
1/4 c. shortening
2 eggs
1 pkg. frozen spinach, thawed
Garlic salt to taste
Salt and pepper to taste
1 pkg. sliced pepperoni

Combine first 4 ingredients and 3 tablespoons cheese in large bowl. Cut in margarine and shortening until crumbly. Add 1 egg and enough water to make soft dough. Mix remaining egg and cheese in medium bowl. Add spinach, garlic salt, salt, pepper and pepperoni; mix well. Roll out dough on floured surface; spread spinach mixture over top. Roll as for jelly roll. Place on baking sheet. Bake at 350 degrees for 30 minutes. Slice into 1/2-inch slices.

Beth Allevato

QUICK BANANA BREAD

1 1/2 c. flour
3/4 c. sugar
1 1/2 tsp. baking powder
3/4 tsp. soda
1/2 tsp. salt
1 c. mashed ripe bananas
2 tbsp. lemon juice
1 egg, beaten
4 tbsp. oil
Nuts or cherries (opt.)

Sift dry ingredients into bowl. Add remaining ingredients. Mix until just moistened. Pour into greased and floured loaf pan. Bake at 350 degrees for 1 hour.

Patricia K. Rabago

MAUI MANGO BREAD

1 c. butter
2 c. sugar
4 eggs, beaten
3 c. flour
1 tsp. salt
2 tsp. soda
2 c. mango pulp
1 1/2 tsp. banana extract
1 c. nuts
1 c. coconut

Cream butter and sugar in large bowl. Add eggs, flour, salt and soda; stir until just moistened. Stir in remaining ingredients. Spoon into prepared loaf pan. Bake at 350 degrees for 50 minutes. Yield: 1 loaf.

Mrs. W. B. Monson, III

OATMEAL-APPLESAUCE BREAD

1 1/2 c. rolled oats
1/2 c. all-purpose flour
1/2 c. whole wheat flour
1/2 c. packed brown sugar
1/4 c. bran
1 tsp. each soda, baking powder
1 tsp. cinnamon
1/2 tsp. salt
1 c. applesauce
1/3 c. oil
2 eggs
1 c. raisins
1/2 c. chopped black walnuts

Combine first 9 ingredients in bowl. Add remaining ingredients except raisins and walnuts. mixing well. Stir in raisins and walnuts. Pour into greased and floured loaf pan. Bake at 350 degrees for 50 to 60 minutes or until loaf tests done. Cool for 10 minutes before removing from pan.

Lois Allison

RAISIN-BRAN BREAD

2 1/4 c. flour
1/3 c. unprocessed bran
4 tsp. baking powder
1 1/2 tsp. cinnamon
1 tsp. salt
Oats
1 c. packed brown sugar
2 eggs
1 1/4 c. milk
1/2 c. oil
1 to 1 1/2 c. raisins
1 tbsp. butter, melted

Combine first 5 ingredients with 3/4 cup oats and 3/4 cup brown sugar in bowl. Beat eggs, milk and oil in bowl. Add to dry ingredients. Stir until just mixed. Fold in raisins. Pour into greased loaf pan. Combine 1/3 cup oats, 1/4 cup brown sugar and butter in bowl. Sprinkle over batter. Bake at 325 degrees for 1 hour and 15 to 20 minutes or until bread tests done. Cool for 10 minutes; remove from pan. Cool completely on wire rack.

Evelyn Connors

JALAPENO CORN BREAD MUFFINS

2 c. cornmeal
1 c. flour
1 tsp. salt

6 tsp. baking powder
3 eggs, beaten
2 to 4 jalapenos, chopped
1 lg. onion, finely chopped
1/2 c. oil
1 1 1/2-lb. can cream-style corn
1 1/2 c. grated Cheddar cheese

Combine first 4 ingredients in large bowl; mix well. Add eggs, jalapenos, onion, oil and corn; mix well after each addition. Fold in cheese. Fill muffin cups 1/2 full. Bake at 350 degrees for 20 to 25 minutes or until muffins test done. Yield: 2 dozen.

Kitty Allen

SUPER-NATURAL BRAN MUFFINS

1 c. whole bran cereal
1/2 c. oil
1 1/4 c. packed brown sugar
1/4 c. honey
2 eggs
2 c. buttermilk
2 1/2 c. whole wheat flour
2 1/2 tsp. soda
1 tsp. salt
2 c. granola

Combine bran and 1 cup boiling water in 3-quart container. Let stand for 10 minutes or until water is absorbed. Combine oil, sugar, honey and eggs in large bowl; beat well. Mix in buttermilk. Add to bran mixture; mix well. Combine flour, soda, salt and granola. Blend slowly into bran mixture, mixing well. Refrigerate, covered, for several hours. Fill greased muffin cups 2/3 full. Bake at 400 degrees for 22 to 25 minutes or until well browned. May add chopped nuts, apples or raisins to batter before baking. Unused batter will keep up to 4 weeks.

Gail Allen

CHEESY APPLESAUCE BISCUITS

3 tbsp. shortening
2 c. self-rising flour, sifted
1 3-oz. package cream cheese, softened

1 c. grated sharp cheese
1 c. applesauce
2 eggs, slightly beaten

Cut shortening into flour in large bowl until crumbly. Combine remaining ingredients in bowl, mixing well. Add to flour mixture, mixing well. Knead on lightly floured surface. Roll and cut with biscuit cutter. Place on greased baking sheet. Bake at 375 degrees for 10 to 12 minutes or until brown. Yield: 20-25 servings.

Lunette Larson

BLUE CHEESE ROLLS

1 4-oz. package blue cheese
1 stick butter
1 pkg. refrigerator biscuits, separated
Paprika

Cream blue cheese and butter in bowl. Spread over biscuits. Sprinkle with paprika. Cut into 4 pieces. Place 1/2 inch apart on large baking sheet. Bake at 425 degrees for 8 minutes. Yield: 3 1/3 dozen.

Mrs. Milton A. Hintze, Jr.

BUTTER DIPS

2 1/4 c. sifted flour
1 tbsp. sugar
3 1/2 tsp. baking powder
1 1/2 tsp. salt
1 c. milk
1/3 c. butter, melted
1/2 clove of garlic, minced

Sift dry ingredients into bowl. Add milk, stirring until just moistened. Knead lightly about 10 times on floured surface. Roll into 8 x 12-inch rectangle; cut in half lengthwise. Cut crosswise into 16 strips. Mix butter and garlic in 9 x 13-inch baking pan. Coat each strip with butter mixture. Arrange in 2 rows in baking pan. Bake at 450 degrees for 15 to 20 minutes or until golden brown. Serve hot. Yield: 6-8 servings.

Mrs. James F. Prather

CHEESE BISCUITS

3 tbsp. shortening
2 c. sifted flour
4 tsp. baking powder
1 tsp. salt
3/4 c. milk
1/4 lb. butter
1 pkg. pimento cheese

Combine shortening with sifted dry ingredients in bowl; mix until crumbly. Add milk gradually; mix to make soft dough. Knead lightly on floured board. Roll out; cut with biscuit cutter. Place in baking pan. Melt butter and pimento cheese in saucepan; mix well. Pour over biscuits. Bake at 450 degrees for 12 minutes. Yield: 1 1/2 dozen.

Mrs. Emil D. Nichols

HERBED PINWHEELS

1 c. butter, softened
1/4 c. chopped parsley
1/2 tsp. oregano
1/4 tsp. tarragon
1/4 tsp. thyme
1/8 tsp. pepper
4 c. sifted flour
2 tbsp. baking powder
2 tsp. salt
2/3 c. shortening
1 1/2 c. milk
1 egg

Whip butter with parsley, oregano, tarragon, thyme and pepper in bowl. Let stand for 1 hour to blend flavors. Mix flour, baking powder and salt in bowl. Cut in shortening until crumbly. Stir in milk. Knead about 10 times on floured surface; divide in half. Roll into 10 x 12-inch rectangles. Spread half the butter mixture on each rectangle. Roll as for jelly roll; seal edge. Cut into 1/2-inch slices; place cut side down in muffin cups. Beat egg with 2 tablespoons water in bowl; brush over pinwheels. Bake at 425 degrees for 10 to 15 minutes or until golden brown.

Judi Mellow

ONION KUCHEN

2 med. onions, sliced, separated
into rings
3 tbsp. butter
1 pkg. refrigerator biscuits, separated
1 egg, beaten
1 8-oz. carton sour cream
1/2 tsp. salt
1 tsp. poppy seed

Saute onions in butter in skillet until tender. Arrange biscuits in single layer in 8-inch baking pan. Top with sauteed onions. Combine egg, sour cream and salt in bowl; spoon over onions. Sprinkle with poppy seed. Bake at 375 degrees for 30 minutes or until topping is set. Slice into wedges; serve warm. Yield: 6 servings.

Mrs. D. A. Panska

PARMESAN-WINE MUFFINS

2 c. biscuit mix
1 tbsp. sugar
1 tsp. instant minced onion
1/4 tsp. oregano
1/4 c. melted butter
1/4 c. white wine
1 egg, beaten
1/2 c. milk
1/4 c. Parmesan cheese

Combine first 4 ingredients in bowl; mix well. Add butter, wine, egg and milk; beat well. Fill paper-lined muffin cups 2/3 full. Sprinkle with cheese. Bake at 400 degrees for 10 minutes.

Beth Cousins

SOUR CREAM MINI ROLLS

1/4 c. butter
1 c. self-rising flour
1/2 c. sour cream

Cut butter into flour in bowl until crumbly. Stir in sour cream just until mixed. Fill muffin cups to rim. Bake at 450 degrees for 12 to 15 minutes or until golden brown. Yield: 1 dozen.

Mrs. Darrell I. Ritter

BEAUTIFUL BASIC DOUGH

2 pkg. dry yeast
1/4 c. sugar
1 tsp. salt
1/4 c. margarine, melted
1/2 c. milk, scalded
3 eggs
4 1/2 c. flour

Dissolve yeast in a small amount of warm water. Combine sugar, salt, margarine and milk in bowl. Cool to lukewarm. Add yeast mixture, eggs and half the flour; beat until smooth. Stir in enough flour to make soft dough. Knead on floured surface for 10 minutes or until smooth and elastic. Place in greased bowl, turning to grease surface. Let rise, covered, in warm place for 1 hour or until doubled in bulk. Punch dough down. Use for making rolls and bread.

Laurene Peterson

DILLY CASSEROLE BREAD

1 pkg. dry yeast
1 egg
Melted butter
1 c. creamed cottage cheese
2 tbsp. sugar
1 tbsp. instant minced onion
2 tsp. dillweed
1 tsp. salt
1/4 tsp. soda
2 1/2 c. flour

Dissolve yeast in 1/4 cup warm water. Add egg; mix well. Combine 1 tablespoon melted butter and next 6 ingredients in large bowl; mix well. Stir in yeast mixture. Beat in flour gradually. Knead on floured surface until smooth and elastic. Place in greased bowl, turning to grease surface. Let rise, covered, in warm place until doubled in bulk. Punch dough down. Knead several times. Place in well-greased 8-inch round baking pan. Let rise until doubled in bulk. Bake at 350 degrees for 40 to 45 minutes or until brown. Brush with melted butter.

Mrs. Royce A. Singleton

FAVORITE HERB BREAD

1/2 c. margarine
1/3 c. packed brown sugar
2 c. milk, scalded
1 tbsp. salt
1/2 tsp. thyme
1 tsp. each basil, caraway seed
2 pkg. dry yeast
7 1/2 to 8 c. sifted flour

Brown margarine in saucepan. Add next 6 ingredients; mix well. Cool to lukewarm. Dissolve yeast in 1/2 cup warm water in large bowl. Stir in milk mixture. Add enough flour gradually to make stiff dough; mix well. Knead on floured surface for 7 to 8 minutes or until smooth and elastic. Place in greased bowl, turning to grease surface. Let rise, covered, in warm place for 1 1/2 hours. Punch dough down. Let rise for 30 minutes. Shape dough into 2 loaves. Place in greased loaf pans. Let rise, covered, in warm place for 45 minutes. Bake at 375 degrees for 35 to 40 minutes or until bread tests done. Turn out on racks to cool. Yield: 2 loaves.

Mrs. William M. Morse

SWEDISH RYE BREAD

1 pkg. dry yeast
2 tbsp. lard
1/2 c. packed brown sugar
1/4 c. molasses
1 tbsp. salt
3 c. medium rye flour
3 c. flour

Dissolve yeast in a small amount of warm water. Combine lard, sugar, molasses and salt in large bowl. Pour in 2 cups very hot water; stir until sugar is dissolved. Cool to lukewarm. Stir in yeast mixture. Add rye flour and enough flour to make stiff dough; mix well after each addition. Knead remaining flour into dough on floured board. Let rise, covered, in warm place until doubled in bulk. Shape into 2 loaves; place in 2 pans. Let rise until doubled in bulk. Bake at 375 degrees for 45 to 60 minutes.

Mary Pat Thuma

GOURMET CHEESE BREAD

1 pkg. dry yeast
1 tbsp. instant minced onion
2 1/4 tsp. dillseed
2 tbsp. sugar
1 tsp. salt
1/4 tsp. soda
4 slices crisp-cooked bacon, crumbled
1 tbsp. warm bacon drippings
1 egg, beaten
1 c. warm cottage cheese
2 1/4 c. flour
Melted butter

Dissolve yeast in 1/4 cup warm water. Combine with next 9 ingredients in large bowl; mix well. Add enough flour to make stiff dough, beating well. Let rise, covered, in warm place for 1 hour or until doubled in bulk. Punch dough down. Place in well-greased 1 1/2-quart casserole. Let rise for 30 to 40 minutes or until doubled in bulk. Bake at 350 degrees for 40 to 45 minutes or until golden brown. Brush with butter; sprinkle with additional salt.

Mrs. John F. Smith

GOLDEN RAISIN BREAD

1 1/2 c. golden raisins
1/2 tsp. mace
2 tsp. grated orange rind
Sherry
1 pkg. dry yeast
2 c. warm milk
1/3 c. sugar
2 tsp. salt
Melted butter
5 to 6 c. flour
1 egg yolk
2 tbsp. cream

Soak raisins with mace and orange rind in Sherry to cover in bowl overnight. Dissolve yeast in 1/4 cup warm milk. Combine remaining 1 3/4 cups milk, sugar, salt and 3 tablespoons butter in large bowl; mix well. Stir in yeast mixture. Stir in enough flour to make stiff dough. Knead on floured surface for 10 minutes or until smooth and elastic. Place in greased bowl, turning to grease surface. Let rise, covered, in warm place until doubled in bulk. Punch dough down. Knead briefly. Let rise in bowl for 30 minutes. Roll dough into two 7 x 20-inch rectangles. Brush with melted butter. Sprinkle with drained raisin mixture. Roll as for jelly roll; pinch ends together. Place in 2 buttered 4 x 8-inch loaf pans. Let rise until dough is above rim. Mix egg yolk and cream in small bowl. Brush over loaves. Bake at 400 degrees for 10 minutes. Reduce temperature to 350 degrees. Bake for 20 to 30 minutes or until bread tests done.

Kathleen Carrington

OATMEAL-MOLASSES LOAVES

1 pkg. dry yeast
1/4 c. light molasses
4 to 4 1/2 c. flour
1 1/2 c. oatmeal
2 eggs
2 tbsp. margarine
1 tsp. salt
1 tbsp. milk

Dissolve yeast in 1 3/4 cups warm water in bowl. Stir in molasses. Mix 2 cups flour with oatmeal, 1 egg, margarine and salt in large bowl. Add dissolved yeast and enough remaining flour to make soft dough. Knead on floured surface for 8 to 10 minutes or until smooth and elastic. Place in greased bowl. Let rise, covered, in warm place for 1 to 1 1/2 hours or until doubled in bulk. Shape into 4 loaves. Place in greased loaf pans. Brush with mixture of milk and remaining egg. Let rise until doubled in bulk. Bake at 400 degrees for 20 minutes or until bread tests done.

Agnes Greene

HONEY-ORANGE BABA

1 pkg. Pillsbury Hot Roll Mix
1 tbsp. grated orange rind
1/2 c. butter

1 3/4 c. orange juice
2 eggs, beaten
1/3 c. raisins
1/3 c. chopped nuts
1/3 c. coconut
1/2 c. honey

Combine half the hot roll mix, yeast packet and orange rind in large mixer bowl. Heat 1/4 cup butter and 1 1/4 cups orange juice in saucepan until very warm, about 115 degrees. Add with eggs to roll mixture. Beat at low speed until moistened. Beat at medium speed for 2 minutes. Stir in raisins, nuts, coconut and remaining roll mix. Let rise, for 40 to 50 minutes or until doubled in bulk. Stir dough down. Spoon into greased 12-cup bundt pan. Let rise, covered, for 25 to 35 minutes or until doubled in bulk. Bake at 375 degrees for 30 to 40 minutes or until golden brown. Combine remaining 1/2 cup orange juice, honey and remaining 1/4 cup butter in saucepan. Boil for 3 minutes. Pour 3/4 of syrup over hot bread in pan. Let stand for 15 minutes. Invert onto serving platter. Brush remaining syrup over top and side. Garnish with mandarin oranges and coconut.

Photograph for this recipe above.

CROWN RING OF ROLLS

2 pkg. dry yeast
3/4 c. scalded milk
1/2 c. shortening
1 1/4 c. sugar
1 tsp. salt
2 eggs, well beaten
4 1/2 c. sifted flour
1 tsp. cinnamon
Melted butter
Chopped nuts (opt.)

Dissolve yeast in 1/4 cup warm water. Combine milk, shortening, 1/2 cup sugar and salt in bowl. Stir in yeast mixture and eggs. Blend in flour. Knead on floured surface until smooth and elastic. Place in greased bowl, turning to grease surface. Let rise, covered, in warm place until doubled in bulk. Punch dough down. Let rest for 10 minutes. Combine remaining 3/4 cup sugar and cinnamon in bowl; mix well. Shape dough into balls. Dip in butter; roll in cinnamon sugar. Arrange in greased 9-inch tube pan. Sprinkle with nuts. Let rise until doubled in bulk. Bake at 350 degrees for 40 minutes or until golden brown. Invert on serving platter. Serve warm.

Mrs. J. D. DeLoach

SWEET PETALS COFFEE CAKE

1 pkg. hot roll mix
3/4 c. sugar
1/4 c. packed brown sugar
2 tsp. cinnamon
3/4 c. chopped nuts
1/2 c. butter, melted
1/2 c. confectioners' sugar
1 to 2 tsp. milk

Prepare hot roll mix using package directions. Let dough rise until doubled in bulk. Combine next 4 ingredients on waxed paper; mix well. Pinch off small piece of dough; roll into 6-inch strip about 1/2 inch thick. Dip into melted butter; roll in sugar mixture. Shape into pinwheel in center of pizza pan. Repeat until all dough is used, placing each pinwheel to resemble flower petals around first pinwheel. Let rise, covered, until doubled in bulk. Bake at 350 degrees for 25 minutes or until brown. Combine confectioners' sugar with milk in bowl; drizzle over warm cake. Yield: 8 servings.

Doris Allen

EASY REFRIGERATOR ROLLS

1 pkg. dry yeast
1 c. warm milk
1 stick butter
1/4 c. sugar
2 eggs, well beaten
4 c. sifted flour
1 tsp. salt
Oil

Dissolve yeast in milk. Cream butter and sugar in bowl until fluffy. Add yeast mixture, eggs, flour and salt; mix well. Chill dough overnight. Remove dough from refrigerator 5 hours before serving time; divide into 3 portions. Roll on floured surface into 10-inch circles. Cut each circle into 12 wedges. Roll as for crescent rolls. Place rolls on baking pan. Brush with oil. Let rise in warm place until doubled in bulk. Bake at 400 degrees for 8 to 10 minutes. Yield: 3 1/2 dozen.

Mrs. Hal A. Kauffman

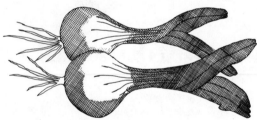

ONION-BEER ROLLS

2 pkg. dry yeast
1/2 c. packed brown sugar
1/4 tsp. salt
1/2 stick butter, melted
1 c. beer, at room temperature
1/2 pkg. dry onion soup mix
3 c. whole wheat flour
2 c. flour
1 egg, beaten

Dissolve yeast in warm water in large warm bowl. Mix in brown sugar, salt, butter and beer. Add dry ingredients gradually; mix well. Add egg; mix well. Knead on floured surface for 5 minutes. Place in greased bowl, turning to grease surface. Let rise, covered, in warm place for 1 hour or until doubled in bulk. Punch dough down. Let rise for 35 minutes. Divide dough into 4 portions. Roll into 12-inch squares. Roll up; cut each into 6 slices. Place cut side down in greased muffin cups. Cut deep cross through top of each roll. Cover. Let rise, covered, until doubled in bulk. Bake at 425 degrees for 10 to 12 minutes or until golden brown. Yield: 2 dozen.

Bee McWilliams

QUICK YEAST ROLLS

1 pkg. dry yeast
2 1/2 c. biscuit mix
1/4 c. (about) butter, melted

Dissolve yeast in 3/4 cup warm water in bowl. Add biscuit mix gradually, mixing well. Knead on floured surface until smooth and elastic. Let rest for 5 to 10 minutes. Shape as desired. Roll in melted butter. Arrange in 9-inch baking pan. Let rise, covered, until doubled in bulk. Bake at 400 degrees for 20 minutes or until golden brown. Yield: 1 1/2 dozen.

Mrs. J. E. Scanlon

SOUR CREAM AND CHIVE BUNS

3/4 c. sour cream
2 tbsp. sugar
1 tsp. salt
2 tbsp. shortening
1 pkg. dry yeast
2 1/4 c. flour
1 egg, slightly beaten
1 1/2 tbsp. chopped chives

Combine sour cream, sugar, salt and shortening in saucepan. Bring to boiling point. Cool to lukewarm. Dissolve yeast in 1/4 cup warm water in bowl. Add sour cream mixture and half the flour; beat until smooth. Add remaining flour, egg and chives; beat well. Let rise, covered, in warm place for about 1/2 hour or until doubled in bulk. Fill muffin cups 1/2 full. Let rise in warm place for 20 to 30 minutes or until dough reaches rim. Bake at 400 degrees for 15 to 20 minutes or until golden brown.

Mrs. Jolyon P. Girard

Microwave
Marvel

BACON AND DATE HORS D'OEUVRES

Pitted dates
Brandy
Bacon slices

Soak dates in enough Brandy to cover in bowl for 24 to 48 hours. Wrap bacon around each date; secure with toothpick. Place in glass dish. Microwave on High for 6 minutes; turn each date after 3 minutes.

Thalia Simmons

MICROWAVE BEEFY SPREAD

1   *2 1/2-oz. jar dried beef, chopped*
1/2 *c. Parmesan cheese*
1/2 *c. sour cream*
1/4 *c. chopped green onion*
1/4 *c. salad dressing*
1   *8-oz. package cream cheese, softened*
1 *tbsp. dried parsley flakes*

Combine dried beef with 1 cup water in 4-cup souffle dish. Microwave on High for 3 minutes; drain well. Stir in remaining ingredients, mixing well. Microwave on Roast for 2 minutes or until hot and well blended. Stir before serving. Serve with Melba toast. Yield: 3 cups.

Devon Ames

PIZZA FONDUE

1 *lb. ground round, crumbled*
2/3 *c. chopped onion*
3   *8-oz. cans pizza sauce with cheese*
1 *tbsp. cornstarch*
3/4 *tsp. oregano*
1/4 *tsp. garlic powder*
1 *c. shredded mozzarella cheese*
2   *5-oz. jars cheese spread*

Combine ground round and onion in 2-quart glass casserole. Microwave on High for 5 minutes or until cooked through; drain well. Blend sauce with cornstarch, oregano and garlic powder in bowl. Stir into ground beef mixture. Microwave on Roast for 13 to 15 minutes or

until heated through. Add cheeses, mixing well. Microwave on Roast for 6 to 7 minutes or until cheeses are melted. Serve hot with French bread cubes.

Francis Mackey

MICROWAVE HAM AND SWISS ROLL-UPS

2   *2-oz. slices Swiss cheese, cut in half*
4   *1-oz. slices boiled ham*
1/4 *c. sour cream*
Frozen potato nuggets, thawed

Place cheese on ham slices. Spread with sour cream. Top each slice with 3 nuggets. Roll to enclose filling, securing with toothpicks. Place on serving plate. Microwave, uncovered, for 2 minutes or until hot.

Corine Deller

MICROWAVE SPICED WALNUTS

1/2 *c. packed brown sugar*
1/2 *tsp. salt*
1/2 *tsp. cinnamon*
1/4 *tsp. allspice*
1/8 *tsp. each nutmeg, cloves*
1 1/2 *c. walnut halves*

Combine all ingredients except walnuts with 1 1/2 tablespoons water in 2-quart glass bowl. Microwave on High for 3 minutes, stirring occasionally. Stir in walnuts 1/2 cup at a time until well coated. Microwave on High for 5 minutes or until syrup hardens slightly. Spoon onto waxed paper; cool.

Patricia Lyles

MICROWAVE STUFFED MUSHROOMS

8 *oz. fresh mushrooms*
2 *tbsp. butter*
1/4 *c. chopped celery*
1/4 *c. chopped onion*

1/4 c. dry bread crumbs
1 tsp. Worcestershire sauce
1 tsp. parsley flakes
1/4 tsp. salt
1/8 tsp. oregano

Remove mushroom stems; chop stems and reserve caps. Combine stems, butter, celery and onion in glass bowl. Microwave on High for 1 1/2 to 2 minutes or until vegetables are tender-crisp. Stir in bread crumbs and seasonings. Spoon into mushroom caps. Arrange on paper towel-lined plate. Microwave on High for 1 1/2 to 3 minutes or until heated through, turning once.

Gail Butler

SHERRIED SHRIMP

1 lb. shrimp, deveined
1 stick margarine
1 clove of garlic, minced
2 tbsp. dry Sherry

Combine all ingredients in glass casserole. Microwave on High for 4 to 6 minutes or until shrimp are pink and tender, stirring occasionally. Serve with cocktail sauce.

Jeanne Anderson

SHRIMP-STUFFED CHERRY TOMATOES

1/3 c. sour cream
1/2 c. chopped shrimp, drained
1/4 tsp. onion salt
2 slices crisp-cooked bacon, crumbled
2 tbsp. mayonnaise
1 pt. cherry tomatoes

Combine sour cream, shrimp, onion salt, bacon and mayonnaise in bowl; mix well. Remove pulp from tomatoes; drain. Arrange on glass serving plate. Fill with sour cream mixture. Microwave on High for 1 1/2 minutes or until warm, rotating plate once. Garnish with parsley.

Mrs. C. Thomas Bell

BEEF AND NOODLES AVEC DEUX FROMAGES

2 tbsp. oil
3/4 c. chopped onion
2 cloves of garlic, crushed
1 1/2 lb. lean beef, chopped
2 tbsp. Sherry
1 tbsp. Worcestershire sauce
2 beef bouillon cubes
1 tsp. salt
1/4 tsp. pepper
2 c. grated Gouda cheese
2 c. hot cooked green noodles
1/4 c. butter
1/2 c. Parmesan cheese

Combine oil, onion and garlic in large glass casserole. Microwave on High for 3 minutes. Stir in beef. Microwave on High for 4 minutes, stirring once. Add next 5 ingredients and 1/2 cup water; mix well. Microwave on High for 3 minutes. Stir in 1 1/2 cups Gouda cheese. Combine noodles with butter and 1/4 cup Parmesan cheese in large glass baking dish; toss to mix. Spoon beef mixture over noodles. Microwave, covered, on High for 8 minutes. Sprinkle with remaining 1/2 cup Gouda and 1/4 cup Parmesan cheese. Microwave, uncovered, until bubbly. Yield: 6 servings.

Brenda Roberts

BEEF RAREBIT

1 lb. beef, finely chopped
1/2 c. chopped onion
1/4 c. chopped green pepper
3/4 c. beer
Dash of cayenne pepper
3 c. shredded Cheddar cheese
6 English muffins, split, toasted

Combine beef, onion and green pepper in glass bowl. Microwave on High for 5 to 6 minutes; drain. Add beer, cayenne pepper and cheese. Microwave on High for 3 1/2 minutes longer. Serve over English muffins.

Sylvia Webb

CHOPPED BEEF AND CHEDDAR

1 pkg. frozen broccoli
4 eggs, beaten
1 lb. round steak, chopped
1 tbsp. butter, melted
3 tbsp. flour
1/2 tsp. each dry mustard, salt,
  pepper, garlic powder
2 c. milk
6 oz. Cheddar cheese, shredded

Microwave broccoli in package using package directions on High for 6 minutes; drain. Microwave eggs, loosely covered, in glass bowl on High for 4 minutes, stirring twice. Brown steak in microwave browning dish for 2 minutes, stirring once. Microwave on High for 5 minutes longer; drain. Blend butter and flour in large glass baking dish. Microwave on High for 2 minutes. Stir in seasonings and milk. Microwave for 5 minutes, stirring twice. Add broccoli, eggs, cheese and steak; mix well. Microwave on Medium-High for 5 minutes or until cheese melts, stirring twice. Serve over toasted English muffins.

Susan Miller

ORIENTAL STEAK

2 tbsp. oil
1 1/2 lb. round steak, slivered
1 env. onion soup mix
2 tbsp. soy sauce
1/4 tsp. ground ginger
1 can water chestnuts, drained, sliced
1/2 green pepper, sliced
1 tomato, cut into wedges

Place oil in large glass casserole. Microwave on High for 1 1/2 minutes. Stir in steak. Microwave on High for 4 1/2 minutes, stirring once. Add soup mix, soy sauce, ginger and 1 cup water; mix well. Microwave, covered, on Low for 25 minutes or until tender. Stir in remaining ingredients. Microwave on High for 1 minute. Let stand for 10 minutes before serving. Garnish with toasted sesame seed. Serve with Chinese noodles. Yield: 4-5 servings.

Ruby Ford

CURRIED BEEF AND PINEAPPLE

1 lb. sirloin, cubed
1 med. onion, sliced
2 tsp. cornstarch
1 1/2 tsp. salt
1 to 2 tsp. curry powder
1/8 tsp. ginger
1 8-oz. can juice-pack pineapple chunks
2 c. hot cooked rice

Combine sirloin and onion in glass baking dish. Microwave, loosely covered, on High for 4 minutes, stirring once; drain. Sprinkle with cornstarch and seasonings; mix well. Add pineapple. Microwave, covered, on High for 5 minutes. Stir in rice. Microwave for 2 minutes longer, stirring once. Yield: 4 servings.

Marjorie Johnson

MICROWAVE BOEUF BOURGUIGNON

1 to 1 1/2 lb. round steak
3 tbsp. flour
2 tsp. instant beef bouillon
1 tbsp. onion flakes
1/2 tsp. salt
1/4 tsp. pepper
1/3 c. red wine
1 onion, sliced
1 can mushrooms, drained

Cut steak into serving-sized pieces. Combine flour, instant bouillon, onion flakes, salt and pepper in shallow dish; mix well. Coat steaks with flour mixture. Place in glass casserole. Add wine and 1/4 cup water. Microwave, covered, on High for 3 minutes. Turn steaks. Microwave on High for 2 minutes longer. Top with onion and mushrooms. Microwave, covered, on Low for 15 minutes or until tender.

Dorothy Helms

MICROWAVE BEEF STROGANOFF

1 1/2 lb. sirloin, slivered
1/4 c. flour
1/4 c. butter, melted

1 beef bouillon cube
1 sm. onion, chopped
1/4 lb. fresh mushrooms, sliced
2 tbsp. tomato paste
1 tsp. Worcestershire sauce
3/4 tsp. salt
1 c. sour cream

Coat sirloin lightly with flour. Stir into butter in large glass baking dish. Microwave on High for 5 minutes, stirring once. Add bouillon cube dissolved in 3/4 cup boiling water with remaining ingredients except sour cream; mix well. Microwave, covered, on High for 5 minutes. Let stand, covered, for 4 minutes. Stir in sour cream. Microwave, uncovered for 1 to 1 1/2 minutes or until heated through. Serve on poppy seed noodles.

Cathy Hicks

BEEFY QUICHE

4 eggs
1 c. cream
2 c. herb-seasoned stuffing mix
1/2 lb. ground chuck
1 tsp. Worcestershire sauce
1 tsp. salt
2 c. sliced green onions with tops
1 c. shredded Swiss cheese
Tabasco sauce to taste
Paprika to taste

Combine 1 beaten egg, 1/2 cup cream and stuffing mix in bowl; toss lightly to mix. Let stand for several minutes until liquid is absorbed. Add ground chuck, Worcestershire sauce, salt and 1/4 cup onions; mix lightly. Spoon into 9-inch glass pie plate. Press lightly over bottom and side to form crust. Sprinkle with remaining onions. Beat remaining eggs in bowl until foamy. Stir in remaining 1/2 cup cream, cheese and Tabasco sauce. Pour over onions. Sprinkle with paprika. Microwave on High for 10 to 13 minutes or until set turning twice. Let stand for 10 minutes before cutting.

Chris Thomas

LASAGNA CASSEROLE

1 lb. ground beef, crumbled
1/2 c. chopped onion
2 8-oz. cans tomato sauce
1/2 tsp. salt
1/2 tsp. basil
1/4 tsp. oregano
1 12-oz. carton cottage cheese
1 3-oz. package cream cheese, softened
1/4 c. sour cream
1/4 c. grated mozzarella cheese
2 c. egg noodles, cooked
Parmesan cheese

Place ground beef and onion in 1-quart glass casserole. Microwave on High for 3 to 4 minutes or until beef is brown; stir halfway through cooking time. Drain. Add tomato sauce, salt, basil and oregano; mix well. Combine remaining ingredients except noodles and Parmesan cheese in bowl; mix well. Spread 1/4 cup meat sauce over bottom of 2-quart casserole. Layer half the noodles, cheese mixture and meat sauce over top. Repeat layers using remaining ingredients. Sprinkle Parmesan cheese over top. Microwave on High for 8 to 10 minutes or until heated through.

Photograph for this recipe on page 73.

SOUP OLE

3/4 lb. lean ground beef
1/2 c. chopped onion
1 16-oz. can stewed tomatoes
1 16-oz. can kidney beans
1 sm. can tomato sauce
1 pkg. taco seasoning mix
1 avocado, chopped

Combine ground beef and onion in large glass casserole. Microwave on High for 3 minutes; drain. Mix in 1 1/4 cups water with remaining ingredients except avocado. Microwave on High for 5 minutes. Microwave, covered, on Medium for 10 minutes. Stir in avocado. Spoon into bowls. Garnish with shredded Cheddar cheese, corn chips and dollops of sour cream. Yield: 4-6 servings.

Polly Stephens

CHEDDARY BEEF FLORENTINE

1/2 lb. lean ground beef, crumbled
1/2 onion, chopped
1 clove of garlic, minced
1 pkg. frozen chopped spinach, cooked,
   drained
Dash of Tabasco sauce
1/2 tsp. each salt, oregano
Pepper to taste
1 can sliced mushrooms
1/2 c. sour cream
1 c. shredded Cheddar cheese

Combine first 3 ingredients in glass casserole. Microwave on High for 4 to 6 minutes or until ground beef is cooked and onions are tender; drain. Add remaining ingredients except cheese; mix well. Top with cheese. Microwave on High for 6 minutes.

Bonnie Amonette

ZESTY GLAZED HAM

1/3 c. orange marmalade
1 1/2 tbsp. Dijon mustard
1/8 tsp. ground cloves
1   1 1/2-lb. fully cooked ham

Blend marmalade, mustard and cloves in small bowl. Place ham in 7 x 11-inch glass baking dish. Brush half the marmalade mixture over top and sides. Microwave, lightly covered, on High for 4 minutes. Turn ham over; brush with remaining marmalade mixture. Microwave, uncovered, on High for 5 minutes. Let stand, covered, for 5 minutes. Yield: 4-6 servings.

Rhonda Patton

POLYNESIAN HAM

4 c. cooked rice
2 c. diced cooked ham
1 onion, sliced
1 tsp. dry mustard
1/2 tsp. salt·
1 c. coarsely chopped green pepper
1   20-oz. can pineapple chunks, drained
1 tbsp. brown sugar
1/4 tsp. pepper

Combine rice, ham, onion, mustard and salt in 7 x 12-inch glass casserole; mix well. Top with green pepper and pineapple chunks. Sprinkle with brown sugar and pepper. Microwave, loosely covered, on High for 10 to 15 minutes or until heated through.

Gladys Phelps

MARINATED LAMB CHOPS

1/2 c. dry red wine
2 tbsp. olive oil
2 sm. cloves of garlic, minced
1/2 tsp. salt
1 tsp. ground cumin
1/2 tsp. cinnamon
2 1/2 tbsp. instant minced onion
4 thick shoulder lamb chops

Combine first 7 ingredients in 7 x 11-inch glass baking dish; mix well. Place lamb chops in marinade. Refrigerate, covered, for 8 hours to overnight, turning occasionally. Drain chops. Microwave on High for 6 minutes, turning once. Let stand, covered, for 5 to 7 minutes before serving.

Linda Hayner

BAVARIAN PORK CHOPS

1   1-lb. can sauerkraut, drained
1/4 tsp. caraway seed
1 apple, peeled, grated
4 thick pork chops
Salt and pepper to taste

Combine first 3 ingredients in glass baking dish; toss lightly to mix. Arrange pork chops over mixture. Microwave, loosely covered, on Medium for 4 to 5 minutes. Turn chops. Microwave for 4 to 5 minutes longer. Season with salt and pepper.

Betty Langley

PORK CHOPS ITALIANO

1   8-oz. can mushrooms, drained
1 c. chopped green pepper
1 med. onion, sliced

1   16-oz. can tomatoes, drained
1 tsp. each oregano, salt
1/4 tsp. pepper
1/2 tsp. garlic powder
4 pork chops

Combine first 8 ingredients in 3-quart glass casserole; mix well. Arrange pork chops on top. Microwave, covered, on Roast for 10 to 15 minutes. Turn pork chops over. Microwave for 10 minutes longer.

Lois Knox

FRUITY SAUSAGE CREPES

1/2 lb. pork sausage, crumbled
1 lb. apples, peeled, sliced
Pancake syrup
1/4 c. raisins
2 tsp. cornstarch
1/2 tsp. ground cinnamon
Crepes

Place sausage between layers of paper towels in glass pie plate. Microwave on High for 2 to 3 minutes. Combine apples with 2 tablespoons syrup, raisins, cornstarch and cinnamon in glass bowl; mix well. Microwave, lightly covered, on High for 3 to 5 minutes or until apples are tender and sauce thickens. Stir in sausage. Spoon 1/4 cup mixture onto each crepe; roll to enclose filling. Place seam side down in glass baking dish. Drizzle 1/4 cup syrup over crepes. Microwave, tightly covered, for 3 to 4 minutes or until heated through.

Jill Rigsby

FIESTA CHICKEN KIEV

2 lg. chicken breasts, halved,
    boned, skinned
3 tbsp. butter, softened
2 tbsp. Old English sharp cheese
    spread, softened
2 tsp. instant minced onion
1 tsp. salt
1 tsp. monosodium glutamate
2 tbsp. chopped green chilies
2/3 c. butter, melted

1 1/2 c. crushed Cheddar cheese crackers
2 1/2 tbsp. taco seasoning mix

Pound chicken with meat mallet. Blend butter and cheese spread together in bowl. Stir in next 4 ingredients, mixing well. Spoon onto chicken pieces. Roll up to enclose filling; secure with toothpicks. Dip in butter; coat with cracker crumbs and taco mix. Place in glass 2-quart casserole. Microwave on High for 3 to 4 minutes; turn once. Microwave for 3 minutes longer.

Tally Robertson

MICROWAVE CHICKEN DIVAN

2   10-oz. packages frozen chopped
    broccoli
1 chicken, cooked, chopped
2 c. grated Cheddar cheese
1 can cream of chicken soup
1 can French-fried onion rings

Place broccoli in 9 x 13-inch baking dish. Microwave on High for 3 minutes. Arrange chicken on top. Sprinkle with cheese; cover with soup. Microwave, covered, on High for 15 minutes; turn once. Top with onion rings. Microwave for 1 minute longer. Yield: 4-6 servings.

Julie Thompson

CHICKEN IN WINE SAUCE

2 or 3 whole chicken breasts, split,
    boned, skinned
1   4-oz. can sliced mushrooms, drained
1/2 tsp. salt
Dash of pepper
1/3 c. white wine
1 can golden mushroom soup

Arrange chicken in 9 x 13-inch glass baking dish. Add mushrooms; season with salt and pepper. Drizzle with wine. Cover with soup. Microwave, covered, on High for 17 minutes, turning occasionally. Let stand, uncovered, for 5 minutes before serving.

Frances Hansen Gruver

MICROWAVE APRICOT CHICKEN

> 5 lb. chicken pieces
> 1 pkg. dry onion soup mix
> 1/4 c. mayonnaise
> 1/2 c. Russian dressing
> 1 c. apricot preserves

Place chicken in glass baking dish; cover with waxed paper. Microwave on High for 10 minutes; turn. Microwave on High for 10 minutes longer. Combine remaining ingredients in small bowl; blend well. Pour sauce over chicken. Microwave for 2 minutes longer. Serve over rice.

Marsha Wagoner

MICROWAVE CHICKEN CORDON BLEU

> 4 chicken breasts, boned
> 4 slices boiled ham
> 4 slices mozzarella cheese
> 1 egg white, beaten
> 1 c. fresh bread crumbs
> 1 stick butter, melted
> 1 tsp. salt
> 1/4 tsp. paprika

Pound chicken breasts with meat mallet until thin. Place 1 slice ham and cheese on each chicken breast. Roll up; secure with toothpicks. Dip in egg white; roll in crumbs. Place in buttered glass baking dish. Pour butter over top; sprinkle with remaining crumbs, salt and paprika. Microwave on Medium for 10 minutes. Microwave on High for 5 minutes; turn dish once. Yield: 4 servings.

Ilene Richards

MICROWAVE CHICKEN WITH WILD RICE

> 1 6-oz. package brown and wild
>   rice mix
> 1/4 lb. mushrooms, sliced
> 1/4 c. dry Sherry

> 2 lb. chicken breasts and thighs
> Paprika

Reserve 1 tablespoon rice seasoning mix. Combine remaining seasoning with rice, mushrooms, Sherry and 1 1/3 cups hot water in 7 x 11-inch glass baking dish. Microwave, covered, on High for 15 minutes; season chicken with reserved seasoning mix. Arrange chicken skin side up over rice; sprinkle with paprika. Microwave, covered, on High for 12 to 15 minutes or until chicken is no longer pink near bone, turning dish every 5 minutes. Let stand for 5 minutes before serving.

Rose Simms

TURKEY TETRAZZINI

> 2 tbsp. margarine, melted
> 1 med. onion, finely chopped
> 1 clove of garlic, minced
> 1 1-lb. can tomatoes, chopped
> 1 can mushroom pieces
> 1 1/2 c. chopped cooked turkey
> 1 tsp. salt
> 1/4 tsp. pepper
> 1/4 tsp. cayenne pepper
> 1 8-oz. package spaghetti, cooked
> 1/2 to 1 lb. Cheddar cheese, grated

Combine first 3 ingredients in large glass casserole. Microwave, covered, on High for 4 minutes. Stir in tomatoes, mushrooms, turkey and seasonings. Microwave, covered, on High for 8 to 10 minutes, stirring once. Add spaghetti; mix well. Top with cheese. Microwave, covered, on Medium for 4 to 6 minutes or until heated through.

Judy Morgan

TURKEY A LA KING WITH RICE RING

> 3 tbsp. margarine
> 1/4 c. flour
> 1/4 tsp. pepper
> 1 c. chopped onions

1 c. sliced celery
3 chicken-flavored bouillon cubes
2 c. milk
2 c. cubed cooked turkey
1/2 c. Hellmann's mayonnaise
1 3-oz. can sliced mushrooms,
    drained (opt.)
1 2-oz. jar diced pimentos, drained

Microwave margarine in 3-quart glass casserole on High until melted. Stir in next 5 ingredients. Stir in milk gradually. Microwave on High for 8 minutes until thickened, stirring twice. Add remaining ingredients; mix well. Microwave on High for 8 minutes or until of serving temperature.

Savory Rice Ring

2 tsp. instant chicken bouillon
3/4 tsp. salt
1 tbsp. instant minced onion
2 1/4 c. quick-cooking rice
1/4 c. butter, melted
1/8 tsp. saffron (opt.)
1 tbsp. parsley flakes
3/4 c. raisins

Combine first 2 ingredients with 2 1/4 cups hot water in 4-cup glass measuring cup. Microwave on High about 4 or 5 minutes or until mixture boils. Stir in onion and rice; let stand 7 minutes until water is absorbed. Microwave butter and saffron in glass container on High for 45 to 60 seconds or until butter melts. Stir into rice; add parsley flakes and raisins. Press rice into 8 1/2-inch ring mold. Turn onto serving dish. Spoon turkey mixture over ring. Garnish with almonds. Yield: 6 servings.

Photograph for this recipe above.

MICROWAVE FLOUNDER ROSEMARY

1 sm. onion, thinly sliced
1 tbsp. butter
1 clove of garlic, minced
1/4 tsp. rosemary
1/8 tsp. pepper
1 can Cheddar cheese soup
1/2 c. drained chopped canned tomatoes
1 lb. flounder fillets

Combine first 5 ingredients in glass casserole; mix well. Microwave on High for 3 minutes or until onion is tender. Add soup and tomatoes; blend well. Arrange flounder fillets in single layer in shallow glass baking dish. Pour sauce over flounder. Microwave on High for 15 minutes or until flounder flakes easily. Yield: 4 servings.

Kathy Bell

MICROWAVE SHRIMP JAMBALAYA

3 tbsp. oil
3 tbsp. flour
2 c. finely chopped onion
1/2 c. finely chopped green pepper
4 cloves of garlic, finely chopped
1 10-oz. can stewed tomatoes
2 c. shrimp, peeled
2 c. diced ham
3 c. cooked rice
1 tbsp. each chopped parsley, chopped
    green onion tops

Blend oil and flour in 3-quart glass casserole. Microwave on High for 5 to 6 minutes or until lightly browned. Add onion, green pepper and garlic; mix well. Microwave on High for 3 minutes. Add tomatoes, shrimp and 1 1/2 cups hot water; mix well. Microwave on High for 7 minutes or until shrimp are pink. Stir in ham and rice. Microwave, covered, on High for 3 minutes. Sprinkle parsley and onion tops over casserole. Yield: 6 servings.

Kitty Cardwell

MICROWAVE SALMON DUMPLINGS

1   7 1/2-oz. package refrigerator
    biscuits
1/2 lb. cooked salmon, flaked
1 can Cheddar cheese soup
1 c. milk
2 tbsp. flour
2 tbsp. chopped green pepper
1 tbsp. parsley

Arrange biscuits over bottom of 1 1/2-quart microwave casserole. Combine remaining ingredients in bowl, blending well. Spoon over biscuits. Microwave on High for 12 minutes, spooning sauce over biscuits after 6 minutes. Yield: 4 servings.

Julie Simpson

VEGETABLE MEDLEY

1 lg. bunch broccoli, cut into
    thin stalks
1 sm. head cauliflower, cut into
    flowerets
1 lg. zucchini, sliced
6 to 8 fresh mushrooms
1 red pepper, sliced into 1/8-in. rings
1 green pepper, sliced into 1/8-in.
    rings
1/4 c. butter
1/2 tsp. garlic salt
1/4 tsp. lemon-pepper marinade

Arrange first 3 vegetables in circles in glass baking dish in order given. Place mushrooms in center. Top with pepper rings. Melt butter in glass cup; stir in salt and lemon-pepper marinade. Drizzle over vegetables. Microwave, covered, on High for 8 to 10 minutes until tender-crisp. Yield: 8-10 servings.

Karen Brannam

BROCCOLI IN DILL SAUCE

1 lb. fresh broccoli
2 tbsp. margarine
1/4 c. chopped onion
1 can cream of chicken soup
2/3 c. milk
1/4 tsp. dried dillweed
Dash of pepper

Cut broccoli into serving-sized pieces, removing tough stem ends. Place in 2-quart glass casserole with 1/4 cup water. Microwave, loosely covered, on High for 8 to 10 minutes, or until tender; drain well. Place margarine and onion in glass bowl. Microwave, loosely covered, on High for 2 minutes or until onion is tender. Stir in soup, milk, dillweed and pepper. Pour over broccoli. Microwave on High for 4 minutes. Yield: 6 servings.

Martha White

MICROWAVE EGGPLANT CASSEROLE

1 med. eggplant, peeled, cubed
2 eggs, beaten
1/4 c. margarine, melted
1 c. bread crumbs
1/4 c. chopped pimentos
1 onion, chopped
2 c. cream-style corn
1 c. grated Colby cheese
Salt and pepper to taste
1/2 c. grated sharp Cheddar cheese

Place eggplant in 2-quart glass casserole. Microwave on High for 6 minutes or until tender; drain. Add next 7 ingredients and seasonings; mix well. Microwave, covered, on High for 7 to 9 minutes, turning once. Top with Cheddar cheese. Microwave on High for 1 minute longer or until cheese melts.

Margaret Shaver

MICROWAVE TASTY CAULIFLOWER

1/2 med. head cauliflower
1/4 c. mayonnaise
Salt and pepper to taste
1/2 tsp. onion, chopped
1/2 tsp. mustard
1/2 tsp. lemon juice
1/4 c. shredded Cheddar cheese

Place cauliflower in 1 1/2-quart glass casserole with 1 tablespoon water. Microwave, covered, on High for 4 to 5 minutes or until tender. Combine remaining ingredients except cheese in small bowl; blend well. Pour over cauliflower; top with cheese. Microwave on Medium for 1 1/2 to 2 minutes. Let stand for 2 minutes before serving. Yield: 5-6 servings.

Gail Sharpe

COMPANY BEAN MEDLEY

    8 slices bacon
    1 c. chopped onion
    1   1-lb. can each green beans, kidney
        beans, butter beans, lima
        beans, drained
    1   1-lb. can pork and beans
    1/2 tsp. each garlic salt, dry mustard

Place bacon in 3-quart glass casserole. Microwave for 4 to 5 minutes or until crisp. Remove bacon and add onion. Microwave on High for 3 minutes. Add remaining ingredients; mix lightly. Microwave, covered, on Medium for 1/2 hour, stirring once. Let stand for 5 to 10 minutes before serving. Crumble bacon over top.

Ruth Sisemore

MICROWAVE-BLENDER CARROT CAKE

    1 3/4 c. sifted flour
    1 tsp. each baking powder, soda
    1/2 tsp. each salt, cinnamon, nutmeg
    1 c. oil
    1 c. sliced carrots
    1 c. sugar
    2 eggs
    1/2 c. orange juice
    1 tsp. vanilla extract
    1/2 c. raisins

Sift first 6 dry ingredients together into large mixing bowl. Place oil and carrots in blender container. Process for 30 seconds until grated. Add sugar, eggs, orange juice and vanilla. Blend for 10 to 15 seconds. Add raisins. Process for 10 seconds. Stir blended mixture into dry ingredients. Pour into ungreased microwave tube pan. Microwave on Bake for 10 minutes, turn-

ing 1/4 turn every 3 minutes. Microwave on High for 3 minutes or until cake tests done. Frost with cream cheese icing if desired.

Sheila Davenport

MICROWAVE GERMAN CHOCOLATE CAKE

    1 pkg. German chocolate pudding cake mix
    1 c. sour cream
    3 eggs
    1/3 c. milk
    1/4 c. margarine
    1 pkg. coconut-pecan frosting mix

Combine first 3 ingredients with 1 cup water in bowl; mix well. Combine milk and margarine in glass bowl. Microwave on High for 1 minute. Blend in frosting mix. Pour cake batter into lightly greased glass tube pan. Spoon frosting into ring over batter. Do not allow frosting to touch sides of pan. Microwave on Simmer for 10 minutes. Microwave on High for 6 minutes. Let stand for 15 minutes or longer before turning out on serving plate.

Kelley Poston

LEMON BUNDT CAKE

    1 pkg. lemon supreme cake mix
    1 pkg. lemon instant pudding mix
    2 tbsp. oil
    4 lg. eggs
    1 6-oz. can frozen lemonade, thawed
    1 c. confectioners' sugar

Combine first 4 ingredients with 3/4 cup water in bowl; mix well. Pour into microwave bundt pan. Let stand for 15 minutes. Microwave on Medium for 12 to 14 minutes or until completely risen, turning 1/4 turn every 4 minutes. Microwave on High for 1 to 2 minutes or until cake tests done. Let stand for 5 to 10 minutes. Turn out onto serving plate. Combine lemonade and confectioners' sugar in glass bowl; blend well. Microwave on High for 2 minutes or until heated through. Pour over hot cake.

Fran Pryor

MICROWAVE CHERRY CRUNCH

1 can cherry pie filling
1 can crushed pineapple
1   1-layer yellow cake mix
1/2 to 3/4 c. chopped pecans
1/2 c. melted butter

Mix pie filling and pineapple in square glass baking dish. Layer cake mix and pecans evenly over top. Drizzle butter over pecans. Microwave on High for 15 minutes, turning occasionally.

Louise Rucker

CREME DE MENTHE PIE

30 marshmallows
1/2 c. milk
2 c. chocolate wafer crumbs
2 tbsp. sugar
6 tbsp. margarine
1/4 to 1/2 c. Creme de Menthe
2 or 3 drops of mint flavoring
1/2 pt. whipping cream, whipped

Place marshmallows and milk in 2-quart glass casserole. Microwave on High until melted; stir to blend. Chill until partially set. Combine crumbs, sugar and margarine in 9-inch glass pie plate. Microwave on High until margarine melts; mix well. Press over bottom and side of pie plate. Microwave on High for 1 1/2 minutes longer. Stir Creme de Menthe and flavoring into marshmallow mixture. Fold in whipped cream. Pour into cooled crust. Chill for several hours.

Donna Russel

SOUR CREAM-APPLE PIE

1 c. sour cream
3/4 c. sugar
1/4 tsp. salt
1 tsp. vanilla extract
1 egg
Flour
4 c. peeled sliced apples
1 baked 9-in. pie shell

1/2 c. packed brown sugar
3 tbsp. butter

Combine first 5 ingredients with 2 tablespoons flour in bowl; beat until sugar is dissolved. Fold in apples. Pour into pastry shell. Microwave on Medium for 5 minutes. Stir filling gently. Microwave on Low for 10 to 12 minutes or until set. Combine brown sugar and 1/3 cup flour in bowl. Cut in butter until crumbly. Sprinkle over pie. Microwave on Low for 8 to 10 minutes longer or until bubbly.

Stephanie Rule

ALMOND BUTTER TOFFEE

1   4-oz. package sliced almonds
1/4 lb. butter
1 c. sugar
1/4 tsp. salt
8 oz. milk chocolate bar, melted

Arrange almonds over greased baking sheet. Butter top inside edge of 2-quart glass bowl. Place butter in bowl; pour sugar over butter. Add salt and 1/4 cup water. Do not stir. Microwave on High for 7 minutes. Microwave at 30 second intervals for 2 to 6 minutes longer or until mixture is the color of brown sugar. Do not stir. Pour over almonds; cool. Drizzle with melted chocolate.

Karen Brannam

MICROWAVE PECAN BRITTLE

1 c. sugar
1/2 c. light corn syrup
1 c. pecans, frozen
1 tsp. vanilla extract
1 tbsp. butter
1 tsp. soda

Combine sugar and syrup in glass bowl; mix well. Microwave on High for 4 minutes. Stir in pecans. Microwave for 3 minutes longer. Stir in vanilla and butter. Microwave for 2 minutes longer. Stir in soda. Pour into buttered pan.

Ada Rutherford

Naturally Nutritious Dishes

CHEESE-SPINACH SOUP

3 tbsp. butter, melted
3 tbsp. flour
4 c. beef bouillon
1/2 lb. Velveeta cheese, cubed
1 pkg. frozen chopped spinach, thawed
Salt and pepper to taste
Paprika or nutmeg to taste

Blend butter and flour in large saucepan. Cook until bubbly, stirring constantly. Add beef bouillon; mix well. Cook until thick, stirring constantly. Mix in cheese. Cook until cheese is melted, stirring constantly. Add spinach and seasonings; mix well. Heat to serving temperature. Yield: 6 servings.

Bunny Waddell

GAZPACHO SOUP

8 or 9 tomatoes, peeled, chopped
1 clove of garlic, minced
2 med. cucumbers, peeled, finely chopped
1/2 c. minced green pepper
3/4 c. minced onion
2 c. tomato juice, chilled
1/4 c. oil
3 tbsp. wine vinegar
Salt and pepper to taste
Dash of Tabasco sauce

Combine first 5 ingredients in bowl. Blend tomato juice, oil, vinegar, salt, pepper and Tabasco in medium bowl. Pour over vegetables; mix well. Chill thoroughly before serving. Yield: 6 servings.

JoAnn Clark

HEARTY TOMATO SOUP

1 onion, chopped
1 clove of garlic, minced
1 stalk celery, chopped
1 carrot, chopped
3/4 c. rice
2 tbsp. whole wheat flour
1 28-oz. can tomatoes, mashed
2 tsp. salt

4 white peppercorns
1 tbsp. sugar
1 tsp. each oregano, basil
3 c. hot milk
1 tbsp. butter

Saute onion, garlic, celery and carrot in a small amount of oil in stock pot, stirring constantly. Stir in rice and flour. Cook until rice is golden brown, stirring frequently. Add next 6 ingredients; mix well. Cook for 45 minutes or until rice is tender. Remove from heat. Add milk and butter; mix well. Heat to serving temperature. Do not boil. Yield: 6 servings.

Patty Emge

AVOCADO VEGETABLE SALAD

3 tbsp. green olive oil
1 1/2 tbsp. vinegar
Dash of lemon juice
3 sm. green onions, finely chopped
Oregano, garlic salt, salt,
    chives to taste
Iceberg lettuce, chopped
1/2 cucumber, sliced
1 avocado, sliced
3 green onions, chopped
3 stalks celery, finely chopped
1 tbsp. chopped green pepper
Radishes, sliced

Combine first 4 ingredients with seasonings in bowl; mix well. Place lettuce and remaining vegetables in serving bowl; toss until mixed. Add dressing; toss gently to coat.

Shirley Morgan

HOT BRUSSELS SPROUTS SALAD

1 10-oz. package frozen Brussels sprouts,
    partially thawed, quartered
1 med. carrot, thinly sliced
Salt
1 tbsp. wine vinegar
1 tsp. sugar
Dash of pepper

Combine Brussels sprouts, carrot and 1/2 teaspoon salt in 1 inch boiling water in medium saucepan. Cook, covered, for 10 minutes or until tender-crisp; drain. Add vinegar, sugar, 1/4 teaspoon salt and pepper; toss to mix. Serve immediately. Yield: 4 servings.

Mrs. John P. Potthoff

FOOD-PROCESSOR COLESLAW

1/4 c. oil
1/4 c. vinegar
1/4 c. sugar
1/2 tsp. salt
1/4 tsp. celery seed
1 head cabbage, cut up
1 onion, quartered
1 carrot, peeled

Combine oil, vinegar, sugar, salt and celery seed in bowl. Process cabbage and onion, using slicing disc in food processor. Process cabbage core and carrot, using grating disc, packing tightly into tube. Combine dressing mixture with processed vegetables in large bowl; toss to mix. Garnish with parsley and paprika.

Abigail Brentham

WATERCRESS-ORANGE SALAD

2 bunches watercress
3 heads Belgian endive, cut into
    1/4-in. slices
2 oranges, peeled, sectioned
2 shallots, finely chopped
1/3 c. olive oil
2 tbsp. lemon juice
Salt and pepper to taste

Wash, trim and cut watercress into small pieces. Place in large bowl. Add endive and orange sections. Combine remaining ingredients in bowl; mix well. Pour over salad; toss gently. Yield: 6-8 servings.

Mrs. W. J. L. Parker

TANGERINE SALAD

4 tangerines, peeled, sectioned
1 grapefruit, peeled, sectioned
1 unpeeled apple, chopped

6 maraschino cherries, quartered
2 tbsp. cherry juice
2 tbsp. sugar
1 c. yogurt
1 lg. banana, sliced

Combine first 4 fruits in bowl; mix well. Blend cherry juice with sugar and yogurt in small bowl. Fold into fruit mixture. Chill for 1 hour. Add banana just before serving; mix well. Serve in lettuce-lined bowl. Garnish with toasted almonds.

Carolyn Hindman

MARINATED SHRIMP AND MUSHROOMS

2 c. thinly sliced fresh mushrooms
1/2 clove of garlic, minced
1/2 c. wine vinegar
1/2 tsp. pepper
1/4 c. lemon juice
1 lb. cooked shrimp, shelled
1 1/4 tsp. salt

Combine mushrooms, garlic, vinegar, pepper and lemon juice in bowl. Marinate in refrigerator for 1 hour; turn frequently. Add shrimp and salt. Chill for 30 minutes. Serve on lettuce leaves. Yield: 4 servings.

Winona Risley

PRETTY AND EASY SALAD

1 16-oz. can sliced diet apricots,
   drained
1 16-oz. can sliced diet peaches,
   drained
1 sm. can mandarin oranges, drained
1 sm. can unsweetened crushed pineapple,
   drained
1 pkg. strawberry gelatin
1 9-oz. carton whipped topping
1 8-oz. carton cottage cheese

Combine fruits in bowl. Sprinkle gelatin over top. Fold in whipped topping and cottage cheese. Chill for several hours.

Karen Gravelle

EGGPLANT SALAD

1 lg. eggplant
3 tomatoes, peeled, chopped
1 onion, peeled, chopped
2 tbsp. chopped fresh parsley
3 tbsp. olive oil
3 tbsp. cider vinegar
1 tsp. salt
1/2 tsp. pepper

Place eggplant in baking dish; prick deeply in several places. Bake at 350 degrees for 1/2 hour; cool. Peel and coarsely chop. Combine with tomatoes in bowl; mix well. Combine next 6 ingredients in covered container; shake to mix. Add to eggplant mixture; toss gently to coat. Serve on lettuce; garnish with tomato slices and ripe olives. Yield: 6-8 servings.

Lillian Inman

SPINACH AND STRAWBERRY SALAD

1/2 c. sugar
2 tbsp. sesame seed
1 tbsp. poppy seed
1 1/2 tsp. minced onion
1/4 tsp. Worcestershire sauce
1/4 tsp. paprika
1/2 c. oil
1/4 c. cider vinegar
2 bunches fresh spinach, washed, dried
1 pt. fresh strawberries

Combine first 6 ingredients in blender container. Process until well blended. Add oil and vinegar in a slow steady stream, processing constantly. Arrange spinach and strawberries on salad plates; drizzle with dressing. Dressing may be kept for several days in refrigerator. Yield: 8-10 servings.

Marjorie T. Pastino

TROPICAL SALAD DRESSING

1/2 c. unsweetened pineapple juice
1 tbsp. soy sauce
1 tbsp. Champagne vinegar
1/4 tsp. coconut extract
1/2 tsp. sugar
1/2 c. oil

Combine all ingredients except oil in jar; cover and shake well. Stir in oil slowly; cover and shake for 30 seconds. Chill in refrigerator. Use on fruit salads, green salads, chicken or fish salads.

Lacey Dalton

EASY EGG AND CHEESE SOUFFLE

3 c. croutons
1 1/2 c. shredded Cheddar cheese
6 eggs, slightly beaten
3 c. milk
3/4 tsp. salt
1/4 tsp. onion salt
Dash of pepper
4 slices crisp-cooked bacon, crumbled

Combine croutons and cheese in 6 x 10-inch baking dish; mix well. Mix remaining ingredients except bacon in bowl; pour over cheese mixture. Chill, covered, overnight. Sprinkle bacon over top. Bake at 325 degrees for 50 to 60 minutes or until set. Yield: 8-9 servings.

Kathleen Carrington

HOLIDAY EGGS MORNAY

Butter
3/4 c. flour
1 1/2 tsp. salt
3 c. cream
2 oz. Swiss cheese, grated
6 tbsp. Parmesan cheese
12 hard-boiled eggs
1/2 lb. mushrooms, minced
2 tbsp. finely chopped parsley
1/2 tsp. tarragon
1 c. fresh bread crumbs

Melt 3/4 cup butter in saucepan over low heat. Add flour and salt; blend until smooth. Cook for about 1 minute. Do not brown. Remove from heat. Add cream gradually, stirring con-

stantly. Cook until just bubbly, stirring constantly. Add Swiss cheese and 4 tablespoons
Parmesan cheese. Cook until cheese is melted.
Remove from heat. Cover; set aside. Slice eggs
in half lengthwise; separate yolks. Mash in small
bowl. Saute mushrooms in a small amount of
butter in skillet. Add parsley and tarragon.
Combine mushroom mixture, egg yolks and 1/2
cup cream sauce; mix well. Fill egg white cav-
ities with mushroom mixture. Arrange in 9 x
13-inch buttered casserole. Spoon remaining
sauce over eggs. Toss bread crumbs with 2
tablespoons melted butter and 2 tablespoons
Parmesan cheese in bowl; sprinkle over top.
Bake at 350 degrees for 30 minutes. May be
made ahead and refrigerated. Yield: 12 servings.

Stella Knight

HEALTH NUT OMELET

3 soft corn tortillas, cut up
Butter
1 sm. onion, finely chopped
6 eggs, beaten
1/2 green pepper, chopped
1/4 c. grated cheese
1 tomato, chopped
1 tbsp. sunflower seed
1 tbsp. bacon bits
2 tbsp. alfalfa sprouts

Brown tortillas in a small amount of butter in
skillet. Add onion. Saute until tender-crisp.
Pour eggs over top. Sprinkle with green pepper
and cheese. Cook over low heat until partially
set. Top with remaining ingredients. Cook until
set.

Jane Oleksy

ROQUEFORT AND APPLE OMELET

2 tart apples, peeled, cut into
    1/4-in. slices
3 tbsp. unsalted butter
5 eggs, lightly beaten
2 tbsp. milk
Salt and pepper to taste
1/2 c. crumbled Roquefort cheese

Saute apples in 2 tablespoons butter in skillet
until tender; remove. Beat eggs, milk, salt and
pepper in bowl. Heat remaining tablespoon butter in skillet. Add egg mixture. Cook over low
heat until set. Sprinkle cheese over half the
omelet. Spoon half the apple slices over cheese.
Fold omelet in half to enclose filling. Transfer
to warm plate. Top with remaining apple slices.
Yield: 2 servings.

Mary M. Brown

QUICHE LORRAINE

12 slices crisp-fried bacon, crumbled
1 c. shredded Swiss cheese
1/3 c. finely chopped onion
1 unbaked 9-in. pie shell
4 eggs, beaten
2 c. half and half
3/4 tsp. salt
1/4 tsp. pepper
1/8 tsp. cayenne pepper

Sprinkle bacon, cheese and onion in pie shell.
Combine eggs and remaining ingredients in
bowl; beat well. Pour into pie shell. Bake at 425
degrees for 15 minutes. Reduce temperature to
300 degrees. Bake for 30 minutes longer or until quiche tests done. Let stand for 10 minutes
before cutting. Yield: 6 servings.

Betty Dean

DAY-BEFORE FRENCH TOAST

6 to 10 slices French bread, 1 in. thick
4 or 5 eggs
1 c. milk
3 to 4 tbsp. sugar
1/4 tsp. salt
1 tsp. vanilla extract

Arrange bread in single layer in 9 x 13-inch
baking pan. Combine remaining ingredients in
bowl; beat well. Pour over bread; turn to coat
evenly. Chill overnight. Brown on griddle over
low heat. Serve with butter and jam. Yield: 3-4
servings.

Lee Charles

DUTCH CHEESE TART

10 oz. Gouda cheese, shredded
Butter, melted
1 c. soft bread crumbs
3 med. tomatoes, sliced
6 to 8 mushroom caps

Combine 1/3 of the cheese, 1/4 cup butter and bread crumbs in bowl; mix well. Press over bottom and side of greased 9-inch pie plate. Sprinkle remaining cheese over crust. Top with tomato slices and mushroom caps. Brush with 1 tablespoon butter. Bake at 350 degrees for 18 minutes. Broil for 2 minutes. Serve with French bread and salad. Yield: 4 servings.

Mary M. Brown

FOOD PROCESSOR CHEESE SOUFFLE

6 eggs
1/2 c. heavy cream
1/4 c. grated Parmesan cheese
1/2 tsp. prepared mustard
1/2 tsp. salt
1/4 tsp. pepper
1/2 lb. sharp Cheddar cheese, shredded
11 oz. cream cheese, cubed

Attach steel blade to food processor. Combine eggs, cream, Parmesan cheese, mustard, salt and pepper in processor container; process until smooth. Add Cheddar cheese and cream cheese while processor is running. Process until cheeses are incorporated, then for 5 seconds longer. Pour into buttered souffle dish. Bake at 375 degrees for 45 to 50 minutes.

Ellen Young

SPAGHETTI WITH STIR-FRIED FALL VEGETABLES

2 c. thinly sliced cabbage
2 c. broccoli flowerets
1 c. sliced carrots
1 c. thinly sliced onion rings
2 tbsp. butter
Salt and pepper to taste
8 oz. spaghetti, cooked, drained

Stir-fry vegetables in butter in large skillet over low heat until tender-crisp. Season with salt and pepper. Serve over hot spaghetti. Yield: 4 servings.

Photograph for this recipe above.

VEGETARIAN AVOCADO HALF SHELLS

1 c. sliced mushrooms
1 tbsp. chopped scallions
2 tbsp. oil
1 c. brown rice, steamed
2 tbsp. finely chopped parsley
6 ripe avocado halves

Saute mushrooms and scallions in oil in skillet until tender. Stir in rice and parsley. Spoon into avocado halves. Garnish with orange slices. Yield: 6 servings.

Delia Carruthers

VEGETARIAN LASAGNA

1/2 to 3/4 lb. mushrooms, sliced
3 tbsp. olive oil
2 med. onions, chopped
4 cloves of garlic, minced
2 c. tomato sauce
2 tsp. oregano

1 tsp. basil
1/4 c. parsley
Salt to taste
3/4 c. dry red beans, cooked
8 oz. lasagna noodles, cooked
2 c. ricotta cheese
3/4 lb. mozzarella cheese, thinly sliced
1/2 c. Parmesan cheese

Saute mushrooms in olive oil in skillet; remove mushrooms. Add onions and garlic. Saute until tender. Stir in tomato sauce and seasonings; mix well. Cook for 30 minutes or until thick, stirring frequently. Stir in beans and mushrooms. Layer noodles, tomato sauce, ricotta cheese, mozzarella and Parmesan in shallow baking dish. Repeat layers until all ingredients are used, ending with Parmesan cheese. Bake at 375 degrees for 20 minutes.

Pat Emge

SESAME ASPARAGUS

1 lb. fresh asparagus, cut diagonally
   into bite-sized pieces
1/4 c. unsalted butter
2 tbsp. lemon juice
2 tbsp. toasted sesame seed
2 tsp. sesame oil
Salt and pepper to taste

Cook asparagus in boiling salted water in saucepan for 3 to 4 minutes or until tender-crisp; drain. Rinse under cold water; pat dry. Melt butter in large skillet over medium heat. Stir in remaining ingredients. Add asparagus; toss to coat. Pour into heated serving dish.

Sarah Molten

ORIENTAL BEAN CASSEROLE

2 pkg. French-style green beans
1 can bean sprouts
1 can water chestnuts, sliced
1/2 c. Parmesan cheese
1 c. slivered almonds
6 tbsp. butter, melted
2 tbsp. flour
1 1/4 tsp. salt

1/4 tsp. pepper
1/4 tsp. Worcestershire sauce
1 pt. heavy cream

Combine first 5 ingredients in casserole; mix well. Combine butter and remaining ingredients in bowl; mix well. Pour over casserole; toss gently to mix. Bake at 425 degrees for 20 minutes or until bubbly. Yield: 8 servings.

Dana Lee Walker

PARTY CAULIFLOWER

1 head cauliflower, separated into
   flowerets
1/2 c. grated Swiss cheese
1/2 c. mayonnaise
1 egg white, stiffly beaten
1 tsp. lemon juice
1 tbsp. grated Parmesan cheese

Blanch cauliflower for 10 minutes; drain. Place in shallow baking dish. Combine Swiss cheese and mayonnaise in bowl. Fold in egg white and lemon juice. Spread over cauliflower. Sprinkle with Parmesan cheese. Broil 6 inches from heat source for 5 to 10 minutes or until golden brown.

Jill Wiegand

MARINATED MUSHROOMS

2/3 c. wine vinegar
1/2 c. oil
1 med. clove of garlic, minced
1 tbsp. sugar
1 1/2 tsp. salt
Dash of pepper
Several drops of Tabasco sauce
1 med. onion, sliced, separated
   into rings
3 cartons fresh mushrooms

Combine first 7 ingredients and 2 tablespoons water in wide-mouthed jar; shake well. Add onion and mushrooms. Chill, tightly covered, for 24 to 36 hours; shake to mix occasionally. Drain; serve with toothpicks. Yield: 10-15 servings.

Mickie Franklin

SPINACH-ARTICHOKE CASSEROLE

1 8-oz. package cream cheese, softened
1/2 c. skim milk
4 10-oz. packages chopped spinach,
   thawed
1 4-oz. can water chestnuts, sliced
1 6-oz. package frozen artichoke
   hearts, thawed
Salt and pepper to taste
Seasoned bread crumbs

Combine cream cheese and milk in bowl; blend
well. Alternate layers of spinach, cream cheese
mixture, water chestnuts and artichoke hearts
in greased baking dish, sprinkling layers with
salt and pepper. Top with bread crumbs. Bake
at 350 degrees for 30 minutes. Yield: 8
servings.

Mrs. Lacey Stevenson

RATATOUILLE SAVANNAH

2 lg. cloves of garlic, minced
1/3 c. olive oil
1/2 tsp. marjoram
1/2 tsp. oregano
1/4 tsp. dillweed
2 tsp. salt
1/8 tsp. pepper
Dash of Tabasco sauce
2 10-oz. packages frozen sliced yellow
   summer squash, partially thawed
1 med. eggplant, peeled, cubed
1 c. thinly sliced Bermuda onion
2 green peppers, slivered
4 med. firm tomatoes, peeled, sliced
Freshly ground pepper

Combine first 8 ingredients in bowl; mix well.
Let stand to blend flavors. Arrange vegetables
in layers in buttered 2 1/2 or 3-quart casserole,
beginning and ending with squash; sprinkle each
layer with seasoning mixture. Bake, covered, at
350 degrees for 1 hour. Uncover; sprinkle with
pepper. Bake for 15 minutes longer. Serve hot
or cold. Yield: 6 servings.

Susan O'Connor

VEGETABLE POTPOURRI

1 10-oz. package frozen peas
1 8-oz. can water chestnuts, sliced
2 tbsp. instant chicken bouillon
1 tbsp. cornstarch
1/2 tsp. seasoned salt
1/4 tsp. garlic powder
2 tbsp. margarine
1 c. halved cherry tomatoes

Combine peas and water chestnuts in 1 1/2-
quart casserole. Mix bouillon, cornstarch, seasoned salt and garlic powder in small bowl.
Sprinkle over vegetables; toss to coat. Add 1/2
cup water. Dot with margarine. Bake, covered,
at 400 degrees for 20 minutes. Stir in tomatoes.
Cook for 5 minutes longer. Yield: 3-4 servings.

Mary Lee Hart

GOLDEN RICE BAKE

2 c. cooked rice
4 c. grated carrots
3 eggs, beaten
1 tsp. salt
2 tbsp. minced onions
1/2 c. milk
1 lb. American cheese, grated

Combine all ingredients in well-greased baking
pan, reserving half the cheese. Bake at 350 degrees for 15 to 25 minutes. Sprinkle remaining
cheese over top. Bake for 10 minutes longer.

Mrs. Burnette S. Harrison

SHERRIED MELANGE

3 sm. onions, diced
1 lg. green pepper, diced
5 sm. hot peppers, finely chopped
1/4 tsp. thyme, oregano, coarsely
   ground pepper
2 cloves of garlic, finely chopped
1 bay leaf
2 cans Italian-style tomatoes, drained
4 cans pigeon peas, drained
1 c. Sherry
3 c. rice

Combine all ingredients except rice in skillet. Cook until well blended, stirring occasionally. Rinse and drain rice. Stir rice into tomato mixture. Cook over medium heat until liquid is absorbed. Reduce heat to very low. Cook, tightly covered, for 30 to 45 minutes. Do not uncover.

Roberta Green

SPIRITED WILD RICE

1 c. wild rice, rinsed, drained
1/2 c. dry white wine
1 tbsp. instant chicken bouillon
1/2 c. chopped celery
1/4 c. minced shallots
1/4 c. chopped parsley
1/4 c. butter
1 can water chestnuts, sliced
Salt to taste
1/8 tsp. pepper
Toasted almonds

Combine rice, 1 3/4 cups water, wine and bouillon in saucepan. Bring to a boil; reduce heat. Simmer, covered, for 30 minutes. Do not drain. Saute celery, shallots and parsley in butter in skillet until just tender; add water chestnuts, salt and pepper. Stir into rice. Turn into 2-quart casserole. Bake, covered, at 325 degrees for 45 to 60 minutes. Sprinkle with almonds. Bake, uncovered, for 5 to 10 minutes longer. Casserole may be refrigerated or frozen before baking.

Annette Kling

DEVILED SWISS STEAK

1 1/2 tsp. each salt, dry mustard
1/4 tsp. pepper
1   3-lb. beef round steak
2 tbsp. oil
1   6-oz. can mushrooms
1 tbsp. Worcestershire sauce

Combine salt, mustard and pepper. Sprinkle over steak. Pound with mallet. Brown steak slowly on both sides in hot oil in heavy skillet;

drain. Drain mushrooms, reserving 1/2 cup liquid. Add mushroom liquid and Worcestershire sauce to skillet. Cook, tightly covered, over low heat for 1 1/2 to 2 hours or until tender. Add mushrooms. Cook until heated through. Yield: 8 servings.

Roberta Risdale

GLAZED MEAT LOAF

2 eggs, beaten
2/3 c. milk
2 tsp. salt
1/4 tsp. pepper
3 slices bread, cubed
2/3 c. finely chopped onion
2/3 c. shredded carrots
1 1/2 c. shredded Cheddar cheese
2 lb. ground beef
1/4 c. packed brown sugar
1/4 c. catsup
1 tbsp. prepared mustard

Combine first 9 ingredients in bowl; mix well. Press into loaf pan. Bake, covered, at 350 degrees for 1 hour. Combine remaining ingredients in bowl; mix well. Pour over meat loaf. Bake, uncovered, for 15 minutes longer.

Retha Harrington

SAUCY CALF LIVER

Calf liver, sliced
Butter
1/2 c. tomato juice
1/3 c. milk
1/4 green pepper, minced
1 tbsp. onion flakes
Salt and pepper to taste
Dash each of Worcestershire sauce,
*   Tabasco sauce*

Brown liver in a small amount of butter in skillet. Add a small amount of water. Simmer for several minutes; drain. Combine remaining ingredients in small bowl; mix well. Pour over liver. Cook, covered, until liver is tender and sauce is thickened.

Pamela Easton

FAR EAST CURRIED BEEF

1 onion, finely chopped
2 cloves of garlic, minced
2 tart cooking apples, chopped
3 tbsp. oil
1 to 2 tbsp. curry powder
1 tsp. paprika
1/2 tsp. ginger
1/4 tsp. sugar
Salt to taste
1 lb. lean beef, cubed
1 tbsp. soy sauce
1 c. milk
1/2 c. (about) flour

Saute onion, garlic and apples in oil in skillet until golden brown. Add next 5 ingredients; mix well. Cook until dark brown, stirring constantly. Add beef. Cook until browned. Add enough hot water to cover. Simmer, covered, for 2 hours. Blend soy sauce, milk and flour in bowl. Add to beef mixture. Cook until thick, stirring constantly. Serve over rice with crisp crumbled bacon, peanuts, chopped egg yolks, chopped onion, chutney and chopped dill pickles.

Mrs. Wayne Duncan

SUKIYAKI

1 lb. boneless beef tenderloin,
*   very thinly sliced cross grain*
2 tbsp. oil
2 tbsp. sugar
1/2 c. beef stock
1/3 c. soy sauce
2 c. diagonally sliced green onions
2 c. diagonally sliced celery
1 c. small spinach leaves
1 16-oz. can bean sprouts, drained
1 c. thinly sliced fresh mushrooms
1 5-oz. can sliced water chestnuts,
*   drained*

Stir-fry beef in oil in wok for 1 to 2 minutes or until brown. Sprinkle with sugar. Mix beef stock and soy sauce in bowl. Pour over beef; push beef to side of wok. Stir-fry green onions

and celery for 1 minute; move to side. Stir-fry remaining ingredients 1 at a time for 1 minute each; move ingredients to side as each is cooked. Serve with rice.

Jennifer Hayes

CRISPY CHICKEN

3/4 c. crushed Grape Nuts
2 tsp. garlic salt
1/8 tsp. pepper
1 2-lb. fryer, cut up
2 tbsp. oil

Combine Grape Nuts, garlic salt and pepper in bowl; mix well. Moisten chicken with water; dip in Grape Nuts mixture. Place in ungreased baking pan. Sprinkle with oil. Bake at 400 degrees for 40 to 50 minutes.

Brenda Keckler

FRENCH-BAKED CHICKEN

1 fryer, cut up
1 tsp. each salt, pepper, onion salt
1/3 c. low-calorie French dressing

Sprinkle chicken with salt, pepper and onion salt; place in single layer in shallow baking pan. Coat chicken with dressing. Bake, covered, at 350 degrees for 30 minutes. Baste with French dressing. Bake, uncovered, for 15 minutes longer or until slightly browned. Yield: 4-5 servings.

Flora Montgomery

MEAL-IN-ONE BAKE

3 chicken bouillon cubes
3 cooked chicken breasts, chopped
1 10-oz. package frozen broccoli,
*   thawed*
1 c. coarsely shredded cabbage
1/2 c. shredded carrots
1/4 sm. red onion, finely chopped
1/2 c. skim milk

Dissolve bouillon cubes in 1/4 cup hot water. Combine with remaining ingredients in bowl; mix well. Spoon into lightly greased casserole. Bake, covered, at 325 degrees for 30 minutes.

Jessie Campbell

NUTRITIOUS STIR-FRY CHICKEN

> 12 oz. chicken breasts, cut into
>   2-in. strips
> 1 tbsp. soy sauce
> 1/2 c. chopped onion
> 2 sm. cloves of garlic, minced
> 4 tsp. sugar
> 1/2 green pepper, cut in strips
> 1 c. diagonally sliced celery
> 1 c. frozen snow peas
> 1 c. drained bean sprouts
> 1/2 c. sliced mushrooms
> 1/2 c. bamboo shoots
> 2 pkg. instant chicken broth

Combine first 4 ingredients with 1 cup water in skillet. Cook until chicken is tender, stirring frequently. Add sugar and next 3 vegetables. Cook for 3 to 5 minutes or until vegetables are tender-crisp. Add remaining ingredients. Heat to serving temperature. Serve over rice.

Kristin Overton

CHICKEN AND WILD RICE

> 1 c. cooked wild rice
> 1 pkg. frozen broccoli, cooked
> 4 chicken breasts, cooked, chopped
> 1 can cream of chicken soup
> 1 sm. can sliced mushrooms
> 1 tsp. lemon juice
> 1/2 tsp. curry powder
> 1 c. shredded sharp cheese

Place rice in casserole; arrange broccoli over rice. Spread chicken over broccoli. Combine soup with mushrooms, lemon juice and curry powder in bowl; mix well. Pour over chicken. Sprinkle cheese over top. Bake, covered, at 375 degrees for 30 minutes. Serve hot.

Freda Warley

TOMATO-BROCCOLI CHICKEN

> 2 lg. chicken breasts, boned
> Salt and pepper
> 1/4 c. chopped onion
> 2 tbsp. butter
> 1   10-oz. package frozen chopped
>   broccoli, thawed
> 1 tsp. lemon juice
> 1/4 tsp. thyme
> 3 med. tomatoes, cut into wedges

Sprinkle chicken lightly with salt and pepper; cut into 1/2-inch wide strips. Saute chicken and onion in butter in skillet until tender. Stir in broccoli, lemon juice, 3/4 teaspoon salt, 1/8 teaspoon pepper and thyme. Simmer, covered, for 6 minutes. Add tomatoes. Simmer, covered, for 3 to 4 minutes longer. Yield: 4 servings.

Leona Pinkerton

AUNT PEARL'S FAVORITE FISH

> 1/4 c. butter, melted
> 1 c. sour cream
> 4 oz. Parmesan cheese
> Dash each of onion salt and pepper
> 2 lb. fresh haddock fillets
> Herb-seasoned stuffing mix

Combine butter, sour cream, Parmesan cheese, onion salt and pepper in bowl; mix well. Place haddock in baking dish; cover with sour cream mixture. Sprinkle with stuffing mix. Bake at 400 degrees for 30 minutes. Yield: 4-6 servings.

Carol Anne Shoesmith

SPICY BROILED FISH

> 4   5-oz. turbot fish pieces
> 1 tsp. seasoned salt
> 1 tbsp. lemon juice
> 1 pkg. ranch dressing mix

Place fish pieces on rack in broiler pan; sprinkle with seasoned salt, lemon juice and dry dressing mix. Broil for 6 minutes on each side. Yield: 4 servings.

Betty Fancher

JOHNNY'S GREEK HALIBUT ROAST

1   3 to 4-lb. halibut roast
Salt and pepper
2 onions, thinly sliced
1 c. chopped celery
3 carrots, finely diced
1 clove of garlic, minced
1/3 c. oil
1/4 c. chopped parsley
1 c. white wine
1   8-oz. can tomato sauce

Sprinkle halibut generously with salt and pepper. Saute onions, celery, carrots and garlic in oil in skillet. Add parsley, wine and tomato sauce. Season to taste with salt and pepper. Simmer for 15 minutes. Cover bottom of baking dish with sauce. Arrange halibut on top; cover with remaining sauce. Bake, covered, at 350 degrees for 1 hour or until halibut flakes easily. Yield: 6-8 servings.

Dianne Vasilou

SNAPPER SUPREME

2 lb. red snapper fillets
1/2 c. frozen orange juice concentrate, thawed
2 tbsp. margarine, melted
1 tbsp. soy sauce
1 tsp. salt
Dash of pepper

Cut fillets into 4 pieces. Combine remaining ingredients in small bowl. Spoon 2 tablespoons orange mixture into 9 x 13-inch baking dish. Top with fillets; pour remaining sauce over fillets. Bake at 375 degrees for 15 to 20 minutes or until fish flakes easily. Serve with sauce. Garnish with orange rind and parsely sprigs.

Carolyn Packwood

DELICIOUS SHRIMP CASSEROLE

1 pkg. long grain and wild rice mix
1 lg. green pepper, chopped
1 lg. onion, chopped

3 cloves of garlic
1 lb. mushrooms, sliced
1 stick butter
1/2 tbsp. cornstarch
1/2 c. Sherry
3/4 c. chicken bouillon
Salt and pepper
1 lb. cooked shrimp

Cook rice using package directions. Place in casserole. Saute next 4 ingredients in butter in skillet. Remove garlic. Stir cornstarch into Sherry until dissolved. Add to mushroom mixture with bouillon. Season to taste. Add shrimp. Simmer for about 10 minutes. Pour over rice. Bake, covered, at 375 degrees for 1/2 hour.

Margaret L. Knee

ALL-RYE QUICK BREAD

2 c. rye flour
1/2 tsp. salt
2 tsp. baking powder
2/3 c. instant nonfat dry milk powder
1 tbsp. honey
2 tbsp. oil

Combine flour, salt, baking powder and milk in bowl. Combine honey, 1 cup water and oil in small bowl; mix well. Add to flour mixture; mix well. Spoon into oiled and floured 10-inch cast iron skillet. Press to 1/2-inch thickness. Prick dough with fork. Bake at 350 degrees for 10 minutes or until well browned.

Polly Harrison

SPICY HEALTH BREAD

1/2 c. shortening
1/2 c. packed brown sugar
1/2 c. honey
2 eggs
1 c. cottage cheese
1/4 c. unsweetened apple butter
1/2 tsp. ginger
1/4 tsp. cinnamon
1/4 tsp. salt
3/4 tsp. soda
2 c. flour

2 tsp. baking powder
1/2 c. raisins

Combine first 3 ingredients in bowl; beat until creamy. Beat in eggs, cottage cheese and apple butter. Add remaining ingredients except raisins; mix until smooth. Stir in raisins. Pour into greased casserole. Bake at 375 degrees for 45 minutes or until loaf tests done. Yield: 12 servings.

Dinah Pickens

PROTEIN-PLUS MUFFINS

1 1/4 c. soy flour
2/3 c. dry milk powder
2 tsp. baking powder
1/2 tsp. salt
2 eggs, beaten
1 tsp. grated orange rind
3/4 c. orange juice
2 tbsp. honey
2 tbsp. oil
1/2 c. chopped pitted dates
1/4 c. chopped nuts

Combine flour, milk powder, baking powder and salt in bowl. Combine eggs, orange rind, juice, honey and oil in small bowl. Add to dry ingredients; stir until just moistened. Fold in dates and nuts. Fill greased muffin cups 2/3 full. Bake at 350 degrees for 30 minutes or until brown. Yield: 12 muffins.

Selma Butler

LINDA'S NO-SUGAR BRAN MUFFINS

1 c. whole wheat flour
1 c. bran
3 tsp. baking powder
1/2 tsp. salt
2 tbsp. honey
1 egg, beaten
1/3 c. milk
1 c. unsweetened applesauce
1/4 c. oil
1 tsp. grated lemon rind

Combine first 4 ingredients in bowl. Mix honey, egg, milk, applesauce, oil and lemon rind in large bowl. Stir in dry ingredients until just moistened. Fill greased muffin cups 2/3 full. Bake at 375 degrees for 20 minutes.

Linda Touzin

OATMEAL PANCAKES

1/2 c. oats
1 c. buttermilk
1/2 c. flour
1 1/4 tsp. salt
1/4 tsp. soda
2 tsp. baking powder
2 tsp. sugar
2 tbsp. oil
1 egg, beaten

Combine oats and 1/2 cup buttermilk in bowl; mix well. Chill overnight. Add sifted dry ingredients; mix well. Stir in oil, egg and remaining 1/2 cup buttermilk to make thin batter; beat well. Pour batter onto hot greased skillet. Bake on both sides until golden brown.

Carol W. Padalino

CALIFORNIA-STYLE GRANOLA AND STRAWBERRIES

1 c. oats
1 c. wheat germ
1/2 c. graham cracker crumbs
1/2 c. flaked coconut
1/2 c. slivered blanched almonds
1 to 2 tbsp. light brown sugar
1 tsp. vanilla extract
Milk
3 pt. California strawberries

Combine oats, wheat germ, cracker crumbs, coconut, almonds, brown sugar and vanilla in shallow baking pan; mix well. Bake at 275 degrees for 1 hour, stirring occasionally. Cool. Store granola in tightly covered container in refrigerator. Combine 1/2 cup granola, 1/2 cup milk and 3/4 cup whole strawberries for each serving.

Bonita Bracken

FRESH STRAWBERRY PARFAITS

2 pt. fresh strawberries, halved
1/2 c. sifted confectioners' sugar
2 c. yogurt
3/4 tsp. almond extract

Combine strawberries and confectioners' sugar in bowl; mix well. Chill for several hours. Mix yogurt and almond extract in bowl. Place strawberries in parfait glasses. Top with yogurt. Garnish with mint leaves.

Sandy Conley

DANISH COLD FRUIT SOUP

1 1/2 c. dried California apricots
1 c. pitted prunes
1 c. sugar
1/4 c. dark seedless raisins
1/2 lemon, sliced
1 cinnamon stick
1/2 tsp. whole cloves
1 c. Chablis
3 tbsp. cornstarch

Combine first 7 ingredients with 5 cups water in saucepan. Simmer for 5 minutes, stirring occasionally. Blend Chablis and cornstarch in small bowl. Stir into fruit mixture. Cook until slightly thickened, stirring frequently. Remove cloves, cinnamon and lemon. Refrigerate until well chilled. Serve in soup bowls. Garnish with lemon wedges. Yield: 8 cups.

Photograph for this recipe on page 85.

PEACHES IN SPICED WINE

1/4 c. dry Sauterne
2 tbsp. sugar
1 tbsp. lemon juice
Dash each of cinnamon, cloves
2 c. peeled sliced peaches

Combine Sauterne, sugar and lemon juice in small saucepan. Cook until sugar is dissolved. Do not boil. Stir in cinnamon and cloves. Pour hot wine mixture over peaches in deep bowl. Chill thoroughly. Yield: 4 servings.

Lana Rosenberg

APRICOT WHIP

2   8-oz. cans unsweetened apricot
  halves, finely chopped
1 pkg. orange gelatin
1 tbsp. lemon juice (opt.)

Drain apricots, reserving juice; add enough water to juice to measure 1 cup. Dissolve gelatin in 1 cup boiling water; add apricot liquid and lemon juice. Place bowl of gelatin in larger bowl of ice and water; stir until thickened. Whip with electric mixer until fluffy and thick and almost doubled in bulk. Fold in apricots. Pour into dessert dishes. Chill for 2 hours or until firm. Garnish with mint sprigs. Yield: 8 servings.

Marilyn Fields

YOGURT AMBROSIA

2 lg. ripe bananas, sliced
1 red Delicious apple, chopped
1 pear, peeled, chopped
Lemon juice
2 navel oranges, sectioned
1 1/3 c. flaked coconut
1 c. pineapple yogurt

Dip bananas, apple and pear in lemon juice; drain. Combine with orange sections in glass bowl. Chill for 1 hour. Fold in coconut and yogurt

Diane Treadway

PATIO WATERMELON ICE

1/2 lg. watermelon
Juice of 4 oranges
Juice of 2 lemons
1 c. sugar
1 egg white, stiffly beaten

Scoop pulp from watermelon; reserve rind. Place pulp in cloth bag. Squeeze juice into bowl. Add citrus juices and sugar; mix well. Pour into 1-gallon freezer container. Freeze until partially set. Fold in egg white. Freeze until firm. Serve in watermelon rind. Garnish with melon balls. Yield: 24 servings.

Denise Jones

Desserts
&
Beverages

Cakes

SPICED APPLE CAKE

1   2-layer pkg. spice cake mix
2 cans apple pie filling
1 tbsp. lemon juice

Sprinkle half the dry cake mix over bottom of 9 x 13-inch cake pan. Spoon pie filling over cake mix. Sprinkle remaining cake mix over apples. Pour mixture of 1 cup water and lemon juice over top. Bake at 350 degrees for 1 hour. Serve warm with ice cream.

Bobbie Williams

CHOCOLATE-FILLED ANGEL CAKE

2 tbsp. sugar
1 1/2 c. semisweet chocolate chips
4 eggs, separated
1 tsp. vanilla extract
1 angel food cake
2 c. whipping cream, whipped

Combine sugar, chocolate chips and 2 tablespoons water in double boiler. Heat until chocolate melts, stirring to blend well. Stir a small amount of chocolate mixture into beaten egg yolks. Stir egg yolks into chocolate mixture. Cook for 2 minutes, stirring constantly; cool. Fold in stiffly beaten egg whites and vanilla. Loosen cake from side of pan. Invert onto cake plate. Slice top 1/3 from cake. Scoop out center evenly to within 1 inch of side and bottom. Combine cake pieces and chocolate mixture; spoon into cake. Replace top layer. Flavor whipped cream as desired. Spread over cake. Chill for several hours. Yield: 16 servings.

Nancy Youden

BLUEBERRY AND CREAM CHEESE CAKE

3 eggs
8 oz. cream cheese, softened
1   2-layer pkg. butter cake mix
1/2 c. oil
1 can blueberries, drained
2 tbsp. confectioners' sugar

Beat eggs and cream cheese in bowl until light and fluffy. Add cake mix and oil; mix well. Add 1 cup water; mix well. Fold in blueberries gently. Pour into greased and floured 9 x 13-inch cake pan. Bake at 350 degrees for 30 to 40 minutes or until cake tests done. Dust cooled cake with confectioners' sugar. Yield: 16 sevings.

Reysa Yeager

BUTTERSCOTCH CAKE

1   3-oz. package butterscotch
    pudding and pie filling mix
2 c. milk
1   2-layer pkg. yellow cake mix
6 oz. butterscotch chips
3/4 c. chopped pecans

Cook pudding mix with milk according to package directions. Add hot pudding to cake mix in bowl; mix well. Pour into greased and floured 9 x 13-inch pan. Sprinkle with butterscotch chips and pecans. Bake at 350 degrees for 30 minutes or until cake tests done. Yield: 12 servings.

Bunny Cooper

BUTTERSCOTCH-RUM RIPPLE CAKE

1 c. butter, softened
2 c. sugar
1 c. sour cream
3 c. flour
1 tsp. each soda, salt
1 tsp. vanilla extract
1 tsp. rum extract
6 eggs
1 sm. package butterscotch
    instant pudding mix
3/4 c. butterscotch ice
    cream topping

Combine first 8 ingredients and 5 eggs in mixer bowl. Beat for 3 minutes. Mix 2 cups prepared batter, pudding mix, ice cream topping and remaining 1 egg in small mixer bowl. Beat for 1 minute. Spoon half the cake batter into greased and floured bundt pan. Add half the butterscotch batter. Cut with knife to marbleize. Repeat with remaining batters. Bake at 350 degrees for 1 hour and 15 minutes or until cake tests done. Cool in pan for 10 to 15 minutes. Remove to serving plate. Garnish with rum-flavored confectioners' sugar glaze. Yield: 12 servings.

Ruth Bartlett

RAISIN AND WALNUT CARROT CAKE

    2 c. sugar
    4 eggs
    1 c. oil
    3 sm. jars strained baby food carrots
    1 c. drained crushed pineapple
    2 c. flour
    2 tsp. soda
    2 tsp. cinnamon
    1 tsp. vanilla extract
    1 c. chopped walnuts
    1 c. boiled raisins

Combine first 5 ingredients in bowl; mix well. Add flour, soda and cinnamon; mix well. Add vanilla. Fold in walnuts and raisins. Pour into greased and floured 9 x 13-inch cake pan. Bake at 375 degrees for 40 to 45 minutes or until cake tests done. Cool.

Rose Noviello

CREAM CHEESE FROSTED CARROT CAKE

    4 eggs
    2 c. sugar
    1 1/4 c. oil
    2 c. finely grated carrots
    2 tsp. vanilla extract
    2 c. sifted flour
    1/2 tsp. salt
    1 tsp. soda
    2 tsp. cinnamon
    1 1/2 c. chopped pecans

    1 8-oz. package cream cheese, softened
    1 stick butter, softened
    1 box confectioners' sugar
    1 c. flaked coconut

Beat eggs in bowl; add sugar gradually. Add oil; mix well. Stir in carrots and 1 teaspoon vanilla. Sift flour, salt, soda and cinnamon together. Add to carrot mixture; beat well. Stir in 1 cup pecans. Pour into ungreased tube pan. Bake at 350 degrees for 1 hour and 15 minutes. Combine cream cheese, butter, confectioners' sugar, remaining 1 teaspoon vanilla, coconut and remaining 1/2 cup pecans in bowl; mix well. Frost cooled cake.

Frances Hansen Gruver

BLACK FOREST TORTE

    1 2-layer pkg. devil's food
       cake mix
    8 oz. whipped topping
    1 21-oz. can cherry pie filling

Prepare cake mix according to package directions. Pour into greased and floured 10-inch tube pan. Bake at 350 degrees using package directions. Cool. Split cake into 3 layers. Spread 1/3 of the whipped topping and 1/3 of the pie filling between each layer and on top. Chill until set. Yield: 12-15 servings.

Jean F. Reavis

FAST FIXING CHOCOLATE CAKE

    1/4 c. oil
    1 2-layer pkg. devil's food
       cake mix
    2 eggs
    6 oz. chocolate chips
    1 sm. package chocolate
       instant pudding

Pour oil into 9 x 13-inch cake pan. Add remaining ingredients and 1 1/4 cups water to pan; mix with fork until blended. Bake at 350 degrees for 35 to 45 minutes or until cake tests done. Cool. Sprinkle with confectioners' sugar.

Sharon Vollmer

TRIPLE-THREAT CHOCOLATE CAKE

  1 *2-layer pkg. sour cream*
      chocolate cake mix
  1 *sm. package chocolate instant*
      pudding mix
  4 *eggs*
  1 *c. sour cream*
1/2 c. oil
  1 *tsp. vanilla extract*
12 oz. chocolate chips

Combine 1/2 cup water and all ingredients except chocolate chips in large mixer bowl. Beat for 4 minutes or until smooth. Stir in chocolate chips. Pour into greased and floured bundt pan. Bake at 350 degrees for 50 to 60 minutes. Cool for 15 minutes. Turn onto serving platter. Garnish with sprinkle of confectioners' sugar and strawberries. Yield: 12 servings.

Cyndy Talmant

CREAM OF COCONUT CAKE

  1 *2-layer pkg. white cake mix*
  1 *15-oz. can cream of coconut*
  1 *15-oz. can sweetened*
      condensed milk
  8 *oz. whipped topping*
  1 *c. toasted coconut*
1/2 c. nuts

Prepare and bake cake mix according to package directions using 9 x 13-inch baking pan. Cool for 15 minutes. Punch holes in cake using knife handle. Drizzle mixture of cream of coconut and condensed milk over cake. Cool for 15 minutes longer. Spread whipped topping over top. Sprinkle with coconut and nuts.

Betty F. Wiley

COCONUT-BLUEBERRY CAKE

1 3/4 c. sugar
  1 *c. margarine, softened*
  4 *eggs*
  3 *c. flour*
1/2 tsp. salt
  1 *tsp. each baking powder, soda*
      and cinnamon
  1 *c. milk*
  1 *tsp. vanilla extract*
  2 *c. blueberries*
  2 *tbsp. butter, softened*
1 1/2 c. coconut

Cream 1 cup sugar and margarine in bowl until light. Beat in 3 eggs. Add mixture of flour, salt, baking powder, soda and cinnamon alternately with milk and vanilla, mixing well after each addition. Stir in blueberries. Pour into greased and floured 9 x 13-inch cake pan. Mix butter, remaining 3/4 cup sugar and 1 egg in bowl. Stir in coconut. Spread over batter. Bake at 350 degrees for 45 to 50 minutes or until cake tests done. Cool in pan. Yield: 16 servings.

Jacquelyn M. Gabor

HONEY GINGERBREAD

2 3/4 c. sifted flour
  1 *tsp. each soda, salt*
  2 *tsp. baking powder*
  1 *tsp. each ginger, cinnamon*
  1 *egg, beaten*
  1 *c. oil*
3/4 c. honey
3/4 c. molasses
  1 *c. buttermilk*

Sift flour, soda, salt, baking powder and spices together. Cream egg and oil together in bowl until light. Add honey in a fine stream, beating constantly. Add molasses in a fine stream, beating constantly. Add sifted flour alternately with buttermilk, beating until smooth after each addition. Pour into greased 9 x 13-inch baking pan. Bake at 325 degrees for 40 minutes or until gingerbread tests done. Cool in pan for 5 minutes. Invert onto wire rack to cool completely. Serve with whipped cream. Yield: 12 servings.

Patricia Malone

LEMON MERINGUE CAKE

2 eggs, separated
1/2 c. sugar
1 1-layer pkg. yellow cake mix
1 tsp. lemon extract
1/4 c. sliced almonds

Beat egg whites in mixer bowl until soft peaks form. Add sugar gradually, beating until stiff and glossy. Combine cake mix, 1/2 cup water, egg yolks and flavoring in mixer bowl. Beat at low speed for 2 minutes. Pour into greased and floured 8-inch round cake pan. Spoon meringue over batter to within 1 inch of side; smooth with spatula. Sprinkle with almonds. Bake at 350 degrees for 30 minutes or until cake pulls from side of pan. Cool on wire rack. Yield: 6 servings.

Helen Heath

ORANGE-ALMOND CAKE

2 lg. navel oranges
6 eggs, beaten
1 1/2 c. ground almonds
Pinch of salt
1 c. sugar
1 tsp. baking powder

Boil unpeeled oranges in water to cover in saucepan for 15 to 30 minutes or until soft; drain. Cool. Cut into quarters; remove seed. Place in food processor container. Process until smooth. Beat eggs in large bowl. Add ground oranges and remaining ingredients; beat until smooth. Pour into buttered and floured 9-inch cake pan. Bake at 400 degrees for 1 hour or until cake tests done. Cool on wire rack. Invert onto serving platter. Serve with whipped cream or raspberries. Yield: 10-12 servings.

Sally Bice

ORANGE JUICE CAKE

1 2-layer pkg. yellow cake mix
1 pkg. instant coconut pudding mix
1/2 c. coconut
3/4 c. oil

4 eggs
2 c. confectioners' sugar
1/2 c. orange juice
2 tbsp. melted butter

Beat first 5 ingredients and 3/4 cup water in mixer bowl for 8 minutes. Pour into greased and floured 9 x 12-inch pan. Bake at 350 degrees for 30 to 40 minutes. Pierce with fork. Pour mixture of remaining ingredients over hot cake. Yield: 12 servings.

Christine Anders

DELICIOUS ORANGE AND PINEAPPLE CAKE

1 2-layer pkg. yellow cake mix
1 11-oz. can mandarin oranges
4 eggs
1 8-oz. container whipped topping
1 10-oz. can juice-pack crushed pineapple
1 pkg. instant vanilla pudding mix

Combine first 3 ingredients in large bowl; mix well. Pour into 3 prepared 9-inch round cake pans. Bake at 350 degrees for 30 to 35 minutes or until cake tests done. Combine whipped topping, pineapple and pudding mix in bowl; mix well. Frost cooled cake.

Lee Charles

PISTACHIO MARBLE CAKE

1 2-layer pkg. white cake mix
1 pkg. pistachio instant pudding mix
4 eggs
1/2 c. oil
1 c. orange juice
3/4 c. chocolate syrup

Mix first 5 ingredients in bowl. Pour 2/3 of the batter into greased and floured bundt pan. Add chocolate syrup to remaining batter; mix well. Spoon over white batter; swirl to marbleize. Bake at 350 degrees for 50 to 60 minutes or until cake tests done. Cool in pan. Invert onto serving plate. Garnish with confectioners' sugar. Yield: 16 servings.

Barbara Curtis

PEANUT BUTTER CAKE

1 2-layer pkg. German chocolate
   cake mix
1 c. peanut butter
1 can ready-to-spread
   chocolate frosting

Prepare and bake cake mix according to package directions using 9 x 13-inch baking pan. Spread peanut butter over hot cake. Cool completely. Frost with chocolate frosting.

Ann Kline

POPPY SEED CAKE

1 2-layer pkg. yellow cake mix
2 3-oz. packages butterscotch
   instant pudding mix
3/4 c. oil
4 eggs
1/2 c. poppy seed

Mix first 4 ingredients and 1 cup water in bowl. Add poppy seed; mix well. Pour into greased and floured tube pan. Bake at 350 degrees for 1 hour. Cool in pan. Remove to serving plate. Yield: 16 servings.

Violet Duffy

AUNT BETTY'S RASPBERRY CAKE

1 3-oz. package raspberry gelatin
1 2-layer pkg. white cake mix
5 eggs
2/3 c. oil
1 10-oz. package frozen
   raspberries, thawed
2 tsp. raspberry flavoring

Combine gelatin and cake mix in large mixer bowl; mix well. Add eggs and oil. Beat at medium speed until well blended. Fold in raspberries and flavoring. Pour into greased and floured 9 x 13-inch baking pan. Bake at 325 degrees for 50 minutes. Top with favorite frosting. Yield: 16 servings.

Paula D. Younkin

SEVEN-UP CAKE

3 sticks butter, softened
3 c. sugar
6 eggs
3 c. flour
2 tbsp. lemon extract
3/4 c. 7-Up

Cream butter and sugar in large mixer bowl for 20 minutes or until very light and fluffy. Add eggs 1 at a time, beating well after each addition. Mix in flour. Beat in lemon extract and 7-Up. Pour into large greased and floured fluted pan. Bake at 325 degrees for 1 hour and 15 minutes. Cool. Invert onto serving plate. Yield: 20 servings.

Ann Hoffman

STRAWBERRY SHORTCUT CAKE

2 c. sweetened strawberries
1 sm. package strawberry gelatin
1/2 c. shortening
1 1/2 c. sugar
3 eggs
2 1/4 c. flour
1/2 tsp. salt
1 tbsp. baking powder
1 c. milk
1 tsp. vanilla extract
1 to 2 c. miniature marshmallows

Mix strawberries and gelatin in bowl. Let stand for several minutes. Cream shortening and sugar in mixer bowl until fluffy. Beat in eggs. Add mixture of dry ingredients alternately with milk and vanilla, mixing well after each addition. Sprinkle marshmallows in greased 9 x 13-inch cake pan. Pour batter over marshmallows. Spoon strawberry mixture over top. Bake at 350 degrees for 40 minutes or until golden. Cool. Cut into squares. Invert squares onto dessert plates. Strawberries will sink to bottom and marshmallows melt and rise to top. Yield: 12 servings.

Catherine Bradley

UGLY DUCKLING PUDDING CAKE

1   *2-layer pkg. yellow cake mix*
1 *sm. package lemon instant*
    pudding mix
1   *16-oz. can fruit cocktail*
4 eggs
2 1/3 c. flaked coconut
1/2 c. packed brown sugar
1/2 c. chopped nuts
1/2 c. butter
1/2 c. sugar
1/2 c. evaporated milk

Combine first 4 ingredients and 1 cup coconut in large mixer bowl. Beat at medium speed for 4 minutes. Pour into greased and floured 9 x 13-inch baking pan. Sprinkle with brown sugar and nuts. Bake at 325 degrees for 45 minutes or until cake tests done. Cool in pan for 15 minutes. Combine butter, sugar and evaporated milk in saucepan. Boil for 2 minutes, stirring constantly. Stir in remaining 1 1/3 cups coconut. Spoon over warm cake.

Mary Ann Larzelere

WALNUT CAKE

5 eggs, separated
Sugar
1/4 c. fine dry bread crumbs
Angostura aromatic bitters
1 c. finely ground walnuts
Juice of 1/2 lemon

Beat egg yolks and 6 tablestoons sugar in bowl until thick and lemon-colored. Stir in bread crumbs, 1 teaspoon angostura bitters and walnuts. Fold in stiffly beaten egg whites. Pour into greased and floured 8-inch fluted baking pan. Bake at 350 degrees for 1 hour. Invert on wire rack. Cool. Combine 1 1/2 cups sugar, 1/2 cup water, lemon juice and 2 tablespoons angostura bitters in saucepan. Bring to a boil. Boil for 2 minutes. Place cake on serving platter. Spoon hot syrup over cake slowly. Serve with sweetened whipped cream and walnut halves.

Photograph for this recipe on page 99.

CUPCAKE CONES

1   *2-layer pkg. chocolate cake mix*
24 *2 to 3-in. high flat-bottom*
    ice cream cones
2   *16 1/2-oz. cans prepared*
    chocolate frosting
M and M's chocolate candies,
    sprinkles, gumdrops, toasted
    coconut, chopped nuts

Prepare cake mix batter according to package directions. Spoon 3 tablespoons into each cone. Place 3 inches apart on ungreased baking sheet. Bake at 350 degrees for 30 to 35 minutes. Cool on wire rack. Frost and decorate with candies, coconut or nuts. Yield: 2 dozen.

Lynnette Carmichael

POP-TOP ORANGE CUPCAKES

1 *2-layer pkg. orange cake mix*
1 *c. whipping cream*
1 *tsp. grated orange rind*
1 *tsp. grated lemon rind*
6 *tbsp. honey*

Prepare cake mix according to package directions. Fill greased and floured miniature muffin cups half full. Bake at 375 degrees for 15 minutes. Cool in pans. Cover cupcakes with towel to keep moist. Whip cream in bowl until soft peaks form. Stir in rinds and honey. Cut out centers of each cupcake. Fill with honey-cream, mounding slightly. Replace tops. Garnish as desired. Yield: 4 dozen.

Joyce Taylor

FAST FROSTING

1 stick margarine
1 c. sugar
1/4 c. milk
1/2 c. chocolate, butterscotch or
    peanut butter chips

Combine margarine, sugar and milk in saucepan. Boil for 1 minute; remove from heat. Add chips. Beat until smooth. Spread over cooled cake. Yield: Enough for 9 x 13-inch cake.

Elaine Rowett

Candies

ALMOND BARK DELIGHTS

1 3/4 c. almond bark
1 c. crunchy peanut butter
2 c. dry roasted peanuts
3 c. crisp rice cereal
2 c. miniature marshmallows

Melt almond bark and peanut butter in baking dish in 200-degree oven; blend well. Stir in peanuts, cereal and marshmallows. Drop by teaspoonfuls onto waxed paper. Cool. Store in cool place. Yield: 7 1/2 dozen.

Rhonda Rydell

ALMOND ROCA

1 lb. butter
2 1/3 c. sugar
1 1/2 c. slivered almonds
1 c. chocolate chips
1/4 c. ground walnuts

Mix butter and sugar in heavy skillet. Cook over medium-high heat for 8 minutes, stirring frequently. Add almonds. Cook for 8 minutes longer, stirring constantly. Pour into 9 x 13-inch pan lined with buttered foil. Sprinkle chocolate chips over top. Spread evenly when melted. Top with walnuts. Break into pieces when cool. Yield: 3 pounds.

Dawn Moudy

APRICOT BALLS

1 8-oz. package dried apricots,
   finely chopped
2 1/2 c. flaked coconut
3/4 c. sweetened condensed milk
2/3 c. chopped pecans
Pecan meal

Combine apricots, coconut, condensed milk and pecans in bowl; mix well. Shape into 1-inch balls. Roll in pecan meal; place in paper bonbon cups. Let stand for 2 hours or until firm. Yield: 4 dozen.

Margaret Hunter

BUCKEYES

2 c. chunky peanut butter
1/2 c. margarine, softened
2 c. confectioners' sugar
3 c. crispy rice cereal
6 oz. chocolate chips
1 to 1 1/2 tbsp. melted paraffin

Combine first 4 ingredients in large bowl; mix well. Chill until firm. Shape into walnut-sized balls. Melt chocolate chips in saucepan over low heat. Blend in paraffin. Dip each ball into chocolate, leaving small portion uncoated to represent eye. Place in paper bonbon cups. Store in airtight container in freezer. Yield: 2 pounds.

Cindy Fischer

CARAMELS

2 c. sugar
1 c. light corn syrup
1/2 c. butter
1 can sweetened condensed milk

Combine sugar and corn syrup in heavy saucepan. Bring to a boil. Stir in butter. Add condensed milk gradually, stirring constantly. Cook for 15 minutes or to 230 degrees on candy thermometer, stirring constantly. Pour into buttered 8-inch square dish. Let stand until firm. Cut into squares. Yield: 2 pounds.

Gordon Gee

FUDGY CARAMELS

3 sq. unsweetened chocolate, melted
2 c. sugar
1 c. packed brown sugar
1/2 c. butter
1/8 tsp. salt
1 c. corn syrup
1 c. cream
1 tsp. vanilla extract

Combine first 7 ingredients in saucepan. Bring to the boiling point. Cook, covered, for 5 minutes. Cook, uncovered, to 240 to 248 degrees on candy thermometer, firm-ball stage, stirring constantly. Remove from heat. Stir in vanilla. Pour into buttered 6 x 10-inch dish; do not scrape bottom or side of pan. Let stand until firm. Cut into 3/4-inch squares. Yield: 3 pounds.

Lois Smith

FANTASY FUDGE

3 c. sugar
3/4 c. margarine
2/3 c. evaporated milk
1 c. chopped nuts
12 oz. semisweet chocolate chips
1 7-oz. jar marshmallow creme
1 tsp. vanilla extract

Combine sugar, margarine and evaporated milk in saucepan. Bring to the boiling point, stirring constantly to dissolve sugar completely. Cook, covered, for 2 to 3 minutes or until steam washes sugar crystals from side of pan. Cook, uncovered, over medium heat for 5 minutes. Remove from heat. Add remaining ingredients. Beat until mixture thickens and loses its luster. Pour into buttered 9 x 13-inch dish. Let stand until firm. Cut into squares. Yield: 3 1/2 pounds.

Kim Rubbino

VELVETY CHEESE FUDGE

4 lb. confectioners'
   sugar, sifted
1 c. baking cocoa, sifted
1 lb. margarine
1 lb. Velveeta cheese, cubed
1 tsp. vanilla extract

Sift confectioners' sugar and cocoa together into bowl. Melt margarine and cheese in double boiler; stir to blend well. Stir into dry ingredients; mix well. Add vanilla. Pour into greased 9 x 13-inch pan. Let stand until firm. Cut into squares. Yield: 6 1/2 pounds.

Constance M. Orell

ONE-BOWL PEANUT BUTTER FUDGE

3/4 c. peanut butter
1 c. ground peanuts
1/2 c. corn syrup
1/2 c. butter, softened
4 c. confectioners' sugar

Combine all ingredients in large bowl; knead until well mixed. Pat into buttered 8-inch square dish. Chill until firm. Cut into 1-inch squares. Yield: 2 pounds.

Patricia Taylor

QUICK PENUCHE FUDGE

1/2 c. melted margarine
1 c. packed brown sugar
1/4 c. milk
1 2/3 to 2 c. confectioners' sugar

Combine margarine and brown sugar in saucepan. Cook until sugar dissolves, stirring constantly. Add milk; blend well. Cook for 1 minute, stirring constantly. Remove from heat. Cool. Stir in enough confectioners' sugar gradually to make of desired consistency. Pour into buttered 8 x 8-inch dish. Chill until firm. Cut into squares. Yield: 1 pound.

Diane Norbury

FOREVER AMBERS

1 14-oz. package candy orange
   slices, chopped
1 can sweetened condensed milk
1 can flaked coconut
1 c. chopped pecans
1 tsp. orange extract
2 c. confectioners' sugar

Combine orange slices, condensed milk, coconut, pecans and orange extract in baking dish; mix well. Bake at 300 degrees until bubbly. Stir in confectioners' sugar. Drop by spoonfuls onto waxed paper. Let stand until firm. Yield: 2 dozen.

Dee Ann Williams

MILLIONAIRES

1 c. sugar
1 c. packed brown sugar
1 c. margarine
1 tsp. vanilla extract
2 c. evaporated milk
1 lb. pecan halves
12 oz. sweet chocolate, melted
2 tbsp. melted paraffin

Combine sugar, brown sugar, margarine, vanilla and 1 cup evaporated milk in saucepan; mix well. Bring to a boil, stirring constantly. Add remaining milk gradually. Cook to 234 to 240 degrees on candy thermometer, soft-ball stage. Stir in pecans. Pour into large buttered pan. Chill overnight. Cut into squares. Place on waxed paper. Blend melted chocolate and paraffin in bowl. Spoon carefully over squares. Yield: 5 pounds.

Annelle Salyer

CRUNCHY CRITTERS

6 oz. semisweet chocolate chips
2/3 c. sweetened condensed milk
1 tsp. vanilla extract
1 1/2 c. salted Spanish peanuts

Melt chocolate chips in top of double boiler over hot water; remove from heat. Add condensed milk, vanilla and peanuts; mix well. Drop by teaspoonfuls onto waxed paper. Cool. Yield: 1 1/2 dozen.

Megan Martin

PEANUT CLUSTERS

12 oz. milk chocolate chips
12 oz. butterscotch chips
1/4 c. peanut butter
4 c. unsalted dry roasted peanuts

Melt chocolate chips, butterscotch chips and peanut butter in double boiler; stir to blend well. Add peanuts; mix well. Drop by spoonfuls onto lightly greased baking sheet. Chill until firm. Yield: 5 dozen.

Kaye Dame

PEANUT BUTTER BALLS

1 c. butter, softened
2 c. graham cracker crumbs
1 tsp. vanilla extract
1 c. finely shredded coconut
1 lb. confectioners' sugar
1 c. crunchy peanut butter
12 oz. semisweet chocolate chips
1 to 2 tbsp. grated paraffin

Beat butter in large mixer bowl until creamy. Add next 5 ingredients; mix well. Shape into 1-inch balls; place on baking sheet. Freeze for 15 minutes. Melt chocolate and paraffin in top of double boiler. Insert pick in candy and dip in chocolate. Let stand on waxed paper until firm. Store in refrigerator or freezer. Yield: 8 dozen.

Mrs. Thomas B. Haywood

SKILLET PEANUT BRITTLE

3 c. sugar
1/2 c. corn syrup
1/4 c. butter
1 c. peanuts
1 tsp. soda
1 tsp. vanilla extract

Combine sugar, corn syrup and 1 cup water in heavy skillet. Cook to 300 to 310 degrees on candy thermometer, hard-crack stage. Stir in butter and peanuts. Cook over low heat to 300 degrees, stirring occasionally. Stir in soda and vanilla. Spread on 2 buttered baking sheets. Stretch as thin as possible as mixture cools. Break into pieces when completely cooled. Yield: 2 pounds.

Blossom E. Snively

EASY PRALINES

1 c. sugar
1/2 c. packed brown sugar
1/2 c. evaporated milk
1 tbsp. margarine
1 sm. package butterscotch
*   pudding and pie filling mix*
1 c. chopped pecans

Bring all ingredients except pecans to a boil in saucepan over low heat; stir to blend well. Cook for 5 minutes, stirring constantly. Stir in pecans. Beat until thick. Drop by teaspoonfuls onto waxed paper. Cool until firm. Yield: 2 dozen.

Jolene Broussard

QUICK CHOCOLATE TURTLES

 144 sm. pecan halves
 36 light caramels
 2/3 c. chocolate chips
 2/3 c. chopped white chocolate

Arrange pecans in groups of 4 on greased baking sheet. Place caramel on each cluster. Bake at 325 degrees for 6 to 8 minutes. Do not let caramels melt completely. Flatten caramels over pecans with well-buttered spatula. Place on waxed paper. Melt chocolate chips and white chocolate in top of double boiler. Swirl over turtles. Let stand until set. Yield: 3 dozen.

Marie Fredricks

Cookies

APPLE-FILLED CRESCENTS

 1/2 c. margarine, softened
 3 oz. cream cheese, softened
 1 c. sifted flour
 1/8 tsp. salt
 1 can apple pie filling
 1 egg white
 1 tbsp. cinnamon
 1/2 c. sugar

Beat margarine and cream cheese in bowl. Blend in flour and salt. Chill for 2 hours to overnight. Roll dough on floured surface. Cut with biscuit cutter. Spoon apple pie filling onto each circle. Fold to enclose filling; seal edge with fork. Place on baking sheet. Mix egg white and 1 tablespoon water. Brush over crescents. Sprinkle with mixture of cinnamon and sugar. Bake at 350 degrees for 15 minutes. Yield: 3 dozen.

Annabelle Hall

BANANA BARS

 10 tbsp. margarine, softened
 1 1/2 c. sugar
 2 eggs
 1 1/2 c. milk
 4 bananas, mashed
 2 c. flour
 1 tsp. baking powder
 1/2 tsp. soda
 1 1/2 tsp. cinnamon
 1 tsp. salt
 2 c. confectioners' sugar
 1 tsp. vanilla extract

Cream 1/2 cup margarine and sugar in mixer bowl until light and fluffy. Add eggs, milk and bananas; mix well. Add mixture of flour, baking powder, soda, cinnamon and salt; mix well. Spread into greased and floured 10 x 15-inch baking pan. Bake at 350 degrees for 20 minutes. Combine confectioners' sugar, vanilla, remaining 2 tablespoons margarine and 2 tablespoons hot water in bowl; mix well. Spread over warm layer. Cool. Cut into bars. Yield: 2-3 dozen.

Gina Mondi

BLACKBERRY BARS

 2 1/4 c. quick-cooking oats
 2 1/4 c. flour
 1 c. packed brown sugar
 1 1/2 tsp. baking powder
 1 1/3 c. margarine
 1 can blackberry pie filling

Combine oats, flour, brown sugar, baking powder and margarine in bowl. Mix with fingers until crumbly. Press 2/3 of the mixture into 9 x 13-inch baking pan. Spread with pie filling. Sprinkle with remaining crumb mixture. Bake at 350 degrees for 12 minutes. Cool on wire rack. Cut into bars. Yield: 3 dozen.

Heather Nolan

BUTTERSCOTCH REFRIGERATOR COOKIES

1 c. butter, softened
2 c. packed brown sugar
2 eggs
1 tbsp. vanilla extract
3 1/2 c. flour
1 tsp. cream of tartar
1 tsp. soda
1/8 tsp. salt

Cream butter and brown sugar in mixer bowl until light and fluffy. Beat in eggs. Add remaining ingredients; mix well. Shape into 2 rolls. Chill, wrapped in waxed paper, for 4 hours to overnight. Slice 1/4 inch thick. Place on cookie sheet. Bake at 350 degrees for 10 to 12 minutes or until brown. Cool on wire rack. Yield: 3 dozen.

Jean Hamrick

BUTTERSCOTCH BROWNIES

1/4 c. butter
1 c. packed light brown sugar
1 egg, slightly beaten
1/2 c. sifted flour
1 tsp. baking powder
1/4 tsp. salt
1/2 tsp. vanilla extract
1/2 c. chopped walnuts

Melt butter in saucepan over low heat; remove from heat. Add brown sugar. Stir until blended; cool. Add egg. Sift in flour, baking powder and salt; mix well. Add vanilla and walnuts. Spread in greased and floured 8 x 8-inch baking pan. Bake at 350 degrees for 20 to 25 minutes. Cool to lukewarm. Cut into squares.

Marlene A. Fasel

CARAMEL BROWNIES

2 c. packed brown sugar
10 tbsp. oil
2 eggs
1 tsp. vanilla extract
1 c. flour
2 tsp. baking powder
1 tsp. salt
1 c. flaked coconut
1 c. chopped pecans

Combine brown sugar, oil, eggs and vanilla in bowl. Add mixture of flour, baking powder and salt; mix well. Stir in coconut and pecans. Pour into greased and floured 9 x 13-inch baking pan. Bake at 350 degrees for 30 minutes. Cut into squares. Yield: 3 dozen.

Martha Plunkett

HOMEMADE BROWNIE MIX

4 c. flour
4 tsp. salt
4 tsp. baking powder
2 1/2 c. baking cocoa
8 c. sugar
2 c. shortening
2 eggs

Combine first 5 ingredients in large bowl. Cut in shortening until crumbly. Store in airtight container. Mix 2 cups Brownie Mix and 2 eggs in bowl, blending well. Pour into greased 8-inch square baking pan. Bake at 350 degrees for 30 minutes. Cool. Cut into squares.

Sue Glen

BROWNIES SUPREME

Butter, softened
2 1/3 c. sugar
1/8 tsp. salt
4 eggs, well beaten
1   16-oz. can chocolate syrup
1 c. flour
1/2 tsp. baking powder
1 1/2 tsp. vanilla extract
1/2 c. chopped nuts
6 tbsp. milk
1/2 c. chocolate chips

Cream 1/2 cup butter, 1 cup sugar and salt in bowl. Add next 4 ingredients, 1 teaspoon vanilla and nuts; mix well. Pour into greased and floured jelly roll pan. Bake at 350 degrees for 25 minutes. Combine milk with remaining 1 1/3 cups sugar and 6 tablespoons butter in saucepan. Boil for 3 minutes. Remove from heat; add chocolate chips and remaining 1/2 teaspoon vanilla. Beat until creamy. Spread over brownies.

Dianne Vasilou

PEANUT BUTTER-CHOCOLATE CHIP BROWNIES

1/3 c. butter, softened
1/2 c. peanut butter
1 c. sugar
1/4 c. packed brown sugar
2 eggs
1 c. flour
1 tsp. baking powder
1/4 tsp. salt
1 tsp. vanilla extract
1/2 c. semisweet chocolate chips

Cream butter and peanut butter in bowl until fluffy. Add sugars gradually, beating constantly. Add eggs 1 at a time, beating well after each addition. Blend in dry ingredients and vanilla. Fold in chocolate chips. Pour into greased 9-inch square baking dish. Bake at 350 degrees for 30 minutes or until brownies test done. Cool. Cut into squares. Yield: 1 dozen.

Janice Sechrist

CASHEW COOKIES

1 c. butter, softened
1 c. packed brown sugar
1 egg, beaten
3/4 tsp. vanilla extract
2 c. sifted flour
3/4 tsp. baking powder
3/4 tsp. soda
1/4 tsp. salt
1/3 c. sour cream
1 3/4 c. salted cashews
1 tbsp. coffee cream
2 c. confectioners' sugar

Cream 1/2 cup butter, brown sugar, egg and 1/2 teaspoon vanilla in bowl. Add next 4 dry ingredients with sour cream; mix well. Fold in nuts. Drop by teaspoonfuls on cookie sheet. Bake at 375 degrees for 10 minutes. Cool. Combine 1/2 cup butter, coffee cream, 1/4 teaspoon vanilla and 2 cups confectioners' sugar in bowl; mix well. Frost cookies.

Mrs. Francis Adamo

CHESS SQUARES

1 2-layer pkg. butter-recipe yellow cake mix
2 eggs
1 stick margarine, softened
2 eggs
1 lb. confectioners' sugar
1 stick margarine, softened
8 oz. cream cheese, softened

Combine cake mix, 2 eggs and 1 stick margarine in bowl; mix well. Spread in 9 x 13-inch cake pan. Batter will be very thick. Combine 2 eggs, confectioners' sugar, 1 stick margarine and cream cheese in bowl; blend well. Spread over cake mix layer. Bake at 350 degrees for 50 to 60 minutes. Cool. Cut into squares. Yield: 3 dozen.

Paula C. Middleton

CRACKLES

1 2-layer pkg. favorite flavor cake mix
2 eggs, lightly beaten
1/2 c. shortening
3/4 c. confectioners' sugar

Combine cake mix, eggs, shortening and 1 tablespoon water in bowl; mix with spoon. Chill for 1 hour or longer. Shape into walnut-sized balls; roll in confectioners' sugar. Place on greased cookie sheet. Bake at 375 degrees for 8 to 10 minutes or until browned. Yield: 4 dozen.

Dorothy P. Ferrell

CINNAMON EGG KICHELS

3 eggs
1 1/2 tbsp. sugar
Dash of salt
1 1/2 tsp. vanilla extract
1/2 c. oil
1 c. flour
1/2 tsp. baking powder
Cinnamon sugar

Beat first 5 ingredients at high speed in mixer bowl for 12 minutes. Reduce speed; add flour and baking powder gradually until well blended. Beat on high for 3 minutes. Drop by teaspoonfuls 1 inch apart onto greased cookie sheet. Add a small amount of additional flour if dough spreads when dropped. Sprinkle with cinnamon sugar. Bake at 350 degrees for 20 minutes or until lightly browned. Yield: 3-4 dozen.

Roberta Chang

DANISH CONE COOKIES

3 egg whites
1/2 c. sugar
1/8 tsp. salt
1 tsp. vanilla extract
1/3 c. butter, melted
Whipped cream

Beat egg whites in bowl until soft peaks form; add sugar, salt and vanilla gradually, beating until stiff. Fold in butter. Drop by teaspoonfuls 2 inches apart onto buttered and floured cookie sheet. Bake at 370 degrees for 10 minutes or until lightly browned. Shape into cones while' warm. Cool. Fill with whipped cream. Reheat cookies slightly if too brittle to form cone. Yield: 1 dozen.

Mrs. Ralph I. Kretzer

HARVEST BARS

1/4 c. melted shortening
1 c. packed brown sugar
2 eggs
2/3 c. pumpkin
3/4 c. self-rising flour
1/2 tsp. each cinnamon,
   nutmeg, ginger
1/2 tsp. vanilla extract
1 c. chopped dates
1/2 c. chopped nuts
Confectioners' sugar

Combine melted shortening, brown sugar, eggs and pumpkin in mixer bowl. Add flour, spices and vanilla; mix well. Stir in dates and nuts. Spoon into greased 9 x 13-inch baking pan. Bake at 350 degrees for 25 to 30 minutes or until brown. Sprinkle confectioners' sugar over top. Cool. Cut into bars. Yield: 2 dozen.

Gayle Manson

HONEY DROPS

1 c. sugar
2 eggs
1 c. flour
1 tsp. soda
1 c. chopped nuts
1/4 c. honey

Mix first 5 ingredients in bowl; mix well. Add honey in a fine stream, stirring constantly. Drop by spoonfuls onto greased cookie sheet. Bake at 350 degrees until light brown. Cool on wire rack. Yield: 3 dozen.

Falisia Williams

WALNUT HONEY COOKIES

3 1/2 c. sifted flour
2 tsp. baking powder
1/2 tsp. salt
1 c. butter, melted
1/4 c. cooking oil
1/4 c. sugar
1/4 c. orange juice
2 c. chopped walnuts
1 c. honey
1   3-in. cinnamon stick
1 tsp. grated orange rind

face. Cut into small circles. Place on cookie sheet. Spoon 1/2 teaspoon preserves onto each cookie. Bake at 350 degrees for 20 minutes or until golden on bottom. Sprinkle with confectioners' sugar. Cool on wire rack. Yield: 2 dozen.

Carla Warnock

LEMON SQUARES

> 1 c. margarine, softened
> 1/2 c. confectioners' sugar
> 1/2 tsp. salt
> 2 c. plus 6 tbsp. flour
> 4 eggs
> 1/2 tsp. vanilla extract
> 2 c. sugar
> 2 tbsp. lemon juice

Combine margarine, confectioners' sugar and salt with 2 cups flour in bowl; mix until crumbly. Pat into buttered 8 x 8-inch baking dish. Bake at 350 degrees for 25 minutes. Combine eggs, vanilla, sugar, lemon juice and remaining 6 tablespoons flour in bowl. Beat for 1 minute. Pour over baked layer. Bake for 30 minutes longer. Cut into squares. Sprinkle with additional confectioners' sugar. Yield: 16 squares.

Marleen Thomas

1 tsp. grated lemon rind
1 tsp. cinnamon

Sift flour with baking powder and salt. Blend butter, oil, sugar and orange juice in bowl. Add sifted flour, baking powder and salt; blend well. Stir in 1 cup walnuts. Shape dough into 22 ovals. Place on ungreased cookie sheet. Bake at 350 degrees for 20 to 25 minutes or until very lightly browned. Combine honey, cinnamon stick, rinds and 1/2 cup water in saucepan. Simmer for 10 minutes. Toss 1 cup walnuts with cinnamon. Dip warm cookies one at a time into the honey mixture; place in fluted cupcake liner. Sprinkle tops with walnut mixture. Yield: 22 cookies.

Photograph for this recipe on this page.

ICE CREAM KOLACHES

> 4 c. flour
> 1 lb. butter, softened
> 1 pt. vanilla ice cream, softened
> Strawberry preserves
> Confectioners' sugar

Combine flour, butter and ice cream in bowl; mix well. Roll 1/8 inch thick on floured sur-

MALT DROPS

> 2 c. flour
> 1 pkg. coconut-pecan frosting mix
> 1 c. crushed malted milk balls
> 1 c. butter, softened
> 1/2 tsp. soda
> 2 eggs, beaten

Combine first 5 ingredients in bowl; mix well. Add eggs; mix well. Drop by teaspoonfuls onto greased cookie sheet. Bake at 375 degrees for 8 minutes or until golden brown. Cool on wire rack. Yield: 4-5 dozen.

Barbara Roader

OATMEAL CARAMELITAS

1 14-oz. package caramels
1/2 c. evaporated milk
2 c. flour
2 c. quick-cooking oats
1 1/2 c. packed brown sugar
1 tsp. soda
1/2 tsp. salt
1 c. melted margarine
6 oz. semisweet chocolate chips
1 c. chopped pecans

Melt caramels in evaporated milk in heavy saucepan over low heat. Cool slightly. Combine next 6 ingredients in large bowl; mix well. Press half the crumb mixture over bottom of greased 9 x 13-inch baking pan. Bake at 350 degrees for 10 minutes. Sprinkle with chocolate chips and pecans. Spread with caramel mixture. Sprinkle remaining crumb mixture on top. Chill until firm. Cut into bars. Yield: 3 dozen.

Frances Tharpe

OATMEAL NIBBLES

1 c. butter
1 1/3 c. packed dark brown sugar
2/3 c. honey
3 c. quick-cooking oats
2 c. chopped raisins
1 c. shredded coconut
1 c. chopped almonds
1 c. wheat germ

Microwave butter in 2-quart glass baking dish on High for 1 minute or until melted. Blend in brown sugar and honey. Add remaining ingredients; mix well. Spread evenly in dish. Microwave on High for 6 minutes or until firm but moist, stirring once. Cool slightly. Shape into bite-sized balls; place in paper bonbon cups. Store in airtight container. Yield: 8 dozen.

Donae Parker

PEACH DROPS

Margarine, softened
3 oz. cream cheese, softened
1/4 c. packed brown sugar
3/4 c. peach preserves
1 1/4 c. flour
1 1/2 tsp. baking powder
1 tsp. cinnamon
1/4 tsp. salt
1/2 c. walnuts
1 c. confectioners' sugar

Cream 1/2 cup margarine, cream cheese and brown sugar in bowl until fluffy. Beat in 1/2 cup preserves. Combine next 4 ingredients, mixing well. Add to creamed mixture; mix well. Stir in walnuts. Drop by spoonfuls on greased baking sheet. Bake at 350 degrees for 12 minutes. Blend confectioners' sugar, 1 tablespoon margarine and 1/4 cup preserves in bowl. Frost cooled cookies.

Helen Harris

MIRACLE PEANUT BUTTER COOKIES

1 c. peanut butter
1 c. sugar
1 egg, beaten
1 tsp. vanilla extract

Blend peanut butter and sugar in bowl. Add egg and vanilla; mix well. Shape into 3/4-inch balls. Place on ungreased cookie sheet; flatten with floured fork. Bake at 350 degrees for 10 minutes. Cool in pan. Yield: 4 dozen.

Jane Koehn

CREAMY PEANUT BUTTER SQUARES

1 c. melted margarine
2/3 c. graham cracker crumbs
1 12-oz. jar creamy peanut butter
1 lb. confectioners' sugar
12 oz. chocolate chips, melted

Mix margarine and graham cracker crumbs in bowl. Add peanut butter; mix well. Add confectioners' sugar; mix well. Spread in 9 x 13-

inch dish. Chill until firm. Spread chocolate over peanut butter layer. Chill until firm. Cut into squares. Yield: 5 dozen.

Gayle Bosman

PEANUT BUTTER AND JELLY BARS

3 c. flour
1 c. sugar
1 1/2 tsp. baking powder
1/2 c. butter, softened
1/2 c. peanut butter
2 eggs, slightly beaten
1 c. grape jelly

Stir flour, sugar and baking powder together in bowl. Cut in butter and peanut butter until crumbly. Stir in eggs. Press half the mixture into 9 x 13-inch baking pan. Spread jelly over top. Crumble remaining dough over jelly. Bake at 375 degrees for 30 minutes or until light brown. Cool. Cut into bars. Yield: 2 dozen.

Irene Reppard

PECAN DREAM BARS

1 2-layer pkg. pudding-recipe
  yellow cake mix
1/3 c. margarine, softened
2 eggs
1 14-oz. can sweetened
  condensed milk
1 tsp. vanilla extract
1 c. chopped pecans
1/2 c. almond brickle baking chips

Combine cake mix, margarine and 1 egg in mixer bowl. Beat at high speed until crumbly. Press into greased 9 x 13-inch baking pan. Beat 1 egg, condensed milk and vanilla in bowl until blended. Stir in pecans and almond brickle chips. Spread evenly over top. Bake at 350 degrees for 25 to 35 minutes or until golden brown. Cut into bars when cool. Yield: 2 dozen.

Mrs. Earl Nicholson

PECAN-FILLED GOODIES

1 c. margarine, softened
1 c. cream-style cottage cheese
2 c. sifted flour
1 c. finely ground pecans
1/2 c. dark corn syrup
36 pecan halves

Cream margarine and cottage cheese in bowl until light and fluffy. Add flour; mix well. Chill for 1 hour to overnight. Divide into 3 portions. Roll each portion 1/8 inch thick on lightly floured surface. Cut into 3-inch squares. Mix ground pecans and corn syrup in bowl. Place 1 teaspoon pecan mixture on each square. Fold corners to center; press to seal. Top each with pecan half dipped in additional corn syrup. Place on ungreased cookie sheet. Bake at 350 degrees for 25 minutes or until light brown. Cool on wire rack. Yield: 3 dozen.

Patsy Reynolds

TOFFEE-PECAN BARS

1 1/2 c. sifted flour
2 1/4 c. packed brown sugar
3/4 c. butter, softened
1 1/2 tsp. vanilla extract
2 eggs, well beaten
3 tbsp. flour
1 1/2 tsp. baking powder
3/4 tsp. salt
1 1/2 c. each coconut, chopped pecans

Combine sifted flour, 3/4 cup brown sugar and butter in bowl; mix well. Press into 9 x 13-inch baking pan. Bake at 350 degrees for 15 minutes. Stir remaining 1 1/2 cups brown sugar and vanilla into eggs in large bowl. Mix next 3 ingredients together; stir into egg mixture. Fold in coconut and pecans. Spread over baked layer. Bake for 30 minutes longer or until topping is brown. Cool slightly; cut into bars.

Mrs. A. G. Kouts

EASY PEPPERMINT BARS

1 roll any flavor refrigerator
   cookie dough
2 egg whites
1/2 c. sugar
1/8 tsp. peppermint flavoring
2 tbsp. crushed peppermint
   stick candy

Slice cookie dough 1/4 inch thick. Place overlapping slices in greased 9-inch square baking pan. Bake at 350 degrees for 15 minutes. Cookie layer will be puffy. Beat egg whites in bowl until foamy. Add sugar gradually, beating until stiff peaks form. Stir in flavoring. Spread over baked layer. Sprinkle with candy. Bake for 10 minutes longer. Cool. Cut into bars.

Cara Sue Smith

BLUEBERRY PIZZA

1 2-layer pkg. white cake mix
1 1/4 c. quick-cooking oats
1/2 c. butter, softened
1 egg
1 can blueberry pie filling
1/2 c. chopped nuts
1/4 c. packed brown sugar
1/2 tsp. cinnamon

Combine cake mix, 1 cup oats and 6 tablespoons butter in mixer bowl; mix until crumbly. Reserve 1 cup crumbs. Blend remaining crumb mixture with egg. Press into 2 greased 10-inch pizza pans. Bake at 350 degrees for 12 minutes. Cool slightly. Spread pie filling over baked layers. Combine reserved crumb mixture, remaining 1/4 cup oats and 2 tablespoons butter, nuts, brown sugar and cinnamon; mix well. Sprinkle over pie filling. Bake at 350 degrees for 15 minutes or until golden. Cool. Cut into wedges. Yield: 2 dozen.

Cynthia Kolberg

RAISIN COOKIES

1 15-oz. package raisins
1/3 c. margarine
2 c. flour
1 tsp. each baking powder, soda
1/2 tsp. salt
1/4 c. sugar
1/2 tsp. nutmeg
2 tbsp. cinnamon
2 eggs
1/2 c. coconut

Combine raisins, margarine and 1 1/4 cups water in saucepan. Bring to a boil. Boil for 3 minutes. Cool. Combine flour, baking powder, soda, salt, sugar and spices in bowl. Add eggs, coconut and raisin mixture; mix well. Drop by teaspoonfuls onto greased cookie sheet. Flatten with fork dipped in water. Bake at 350 degrees for 15 minutes. Cool on wire rack. Yield: 5 dozen.

Thelma Brammer

ROCKY ROAD BARS

1/2 c. flour
1/2 tsp. baking powder
1/4 tsp. salt
2/3 c. packed brown sugar
2 eggs
2 tbsp. butter, softened
1 tsp. vanilla extract
1 c. chopped walnuts
1 c. miniature marshmallows
1 c. semisweet chocolate chips

Sift flour, baking powder and salt into mixer bowl. Add brown sugar, eggs, butter and vanilla; beat until smooth. Stir in 1/2 cup walnuts. Pour into greased 9-inch square pan. Bake at 350 degrees for 15 minutes or until top is lightly browned and cake tests done. Sprinkle marshmallows, remaining 1/2 cup walnuts and chocolate chips over hot cake. Bake for 2 minutes or until chocolate has softened. Swirl chocolate over marshmallows and walnuts. Cool until chocolate is set. Cut into bars. Yield: 1 1/2 dozen.

Laura Murphy

BUTTERSCOTCH SHORTBREAD

1/2 c. butter, softened
1 tsp. vanilla extract
1/2 c. packed brown sugar
1 1/4 c. sifted flour
1/4 tsp. baking powder
1/8 tsp. salt
6 oz. butterscotch chips
1 c. finely chopped toasted almonds
1 tsp. grated orange rind

Cream butter and vanilla in bowl. Beat in brown sugar gradually. Sift flour, baking powder and salt into creamed mixture; mix well. Add butterscotch chips, almonds and orange rind to dough; mix well. Spread in ungreased 8-inch square pan. Bake at 350 degrees for 30 minutes. Cut into bars while warm. Yield: 2 1/2 dozen.

Shauna Devlan

HAZELNUT SHORTBREAD

1 1/4 c. butter, softened
1/2 c. sugar
2 c. flour
1 c. cornstarch
1/3 c. ground hazelnuts

Beat butter and sugar in mixer bowl until light. Add mixture of flour, cornstarch and hazelnuts; mix well. Divide into 6 portions. Roll each portion into 6-inch circle on ungreased cookie sheet. Smooth edges with fingers. Score each circle into 8 wedges with spatula. Press edges with fork. Bake at 325 degrees for 35 minutes or until light brown. Cool on cookie sheet on wire rack. Break into wedges. Store in airtight container. Yield: 4 dozen.

Lisa Wilcox

STRAWBERRY BARS

1 c. butter, softened
1 c. sugar
2 egg yolks
2 c. flour

1 c. chopped walnuts
1/2 c. strawberry jam

Cream butter in bowl until smooth. Add sugar gradually, creaming until light and fluffy. Beat in egg yolks. Mix in flour gradually. Fold in walnuts. Spread half the batter in greased 8-inch square baking pan. Top with jam. Cover with remaining batter. Bake at 325 degrees for 1 hour or until light brown. Cool. Cut into bars. Yield: 1 1/2 dozen.

Peggy Cutlip

SUPER-EASY STRAWBERRY COOKIES

1   2-layer pkg. strawberry cake mix
2 c. whipped topping
2 eggs
Confectioners' sugar

Combine cake mix, whipped topping and eggs in bowl; mix well. Shape by teaspoonfuls into balls. Roll in confectioners' sugar. Place on greased cookie sheet. Bake at 350 degrees for 10 minutes. Cool on wire rack. Yield: 3 1/2 dozen.

Gloria Carrier

SOUR CREAM-NUT CRESCENTS

1 pt. sour cream
1 lb. margarine, softened
2 egg yolks
4 c. sifted flour
1 1/2 c. ground nuts
1 1/2 c. sugar
2 tsp. cinnamon
Confectioners' sugar

Combine first 4 ingredients in bowl; mix well. Chill, covered, for 24 hours. Roll out small portions of dough. Cut into triangles. Combine nuts, sugar and cinnamon in small bowl; sprinkle over triangles. Roll up from wide end. Bake at 350 degrees for 20 minutes. Cool. Dust with confectioners' sugar. Yield: 4 dozen.

Mrs. Louis K. Pall

SOUR CREAM SUGAR COOKIES

2 c. sugar
1 c. shortening
1 tsp. salt
1 tsp. vanilla extract
1 c. sour cream
1/4 c. buttermilk
3 eggs
1 tsp. grated orange rind
3 c. (about) flour
2 tsp. baking powder
1 tsp. soda
Juice of 1 orange

Cream sugar, shortening, salt and vanilla in bowl until fluffy. Combine sour cream, buttermilk, eggs and orange rind in mixer bowl; mix well. Add to sugar mixture; mix well. Sift flour, baking powder and soda together. Add to sugar mixture alternately with orange juice, mixing well after each addition. Add additional flour if necessary to make stiff batter. Drop by teaspoonfuls onto greased cookie sheet. Flatten with bottom of glass dipped in additional flour. Sprinkle with additional sugar. Bake at 375 degrees for 7 to 8 minutes or just until cookies begin to brown. Yield: 4 dozen.

Paula J. Thomas

Pies

ALMOND SILK PIE

1/3 c. butter, softened
1/2 c. sugar
1 tsp. vanilla extract
3 tbsp. baking cocoa
2 eggs
2/3 c. chopped toasted almonds
1 baked 9-in. pie shell
2 c. (or more) whipped cream

Cream butter and sugar in mixer bowl. Add vanilla and cocoa; mix well. Add eggs 1 at a time. Beat for 5 minutes after each addition. Reserve several almonds for topping. Fold remaining almonds gently into chocolate mixture. Pour into pie shell. Top with generous layer of whipped cream and reserved almonds. Chill until serving time.

Rebecca Olson

HOT BUTTERED RUM-APPLE PIE

1/4 c. margarine
1/2 c. packed brown sugar
1/4 c. light rum
1 tsp. grated lemon rind
1 tbsp. lemon juice
1 tsp. nutmeg
8 c. sliced peeled apples
1 unbaked 9-in. pie shell
1/2 c. flour
1/2 c. sugar
1/4 c. margarine
1/4 c. sliced almonds

Melt 1/4 cup margarine and brown sugar in large skillet. Stir in rum, lemon rind and juice and nutmeg. Add apples; mix well. Simmer, covered, for 10 minutes or until apples are tender. Cool slightly. Spoon into pie shell. Mix flour and sugar in bowl. Cut in 1/4 cup margarine until crumbly. Mix in almonds. Sprinkle over apples. Bake at 375 degrees for 35 minutes.

Kathy Lindsey

APPLESAUCE CUSTARD PIE

1 c. sugar
2 eggs
1/4 c. butter
1 can applesauce
1/4 tsp. vanilla extract
1 unbaked 9-in. pie shell
Cinnamon

Cream sugar, eggs and butter in mixer bowl. Add applesauce and vanilla; mix well. Pour into pie shell. Sprinkle with cinnamon. Bake at 425 degrees for 30 to 40 minutes or until set.

Fay Shaw

BANANA-COCONUT MERINGUE PIE

5 egg whites
Dash of salt
Sugar
1 9-in. graham cracker pie shell
1 c. flaked coconut
1 c. whipping cream, whipped
2 lg. bananas, sliced

Beat egg whites and salt in bowl until soft peaks form. Add 1 cup sugar gradually, beating until stiff. Spread evenly in pie shell. Bake at 200 degrees for 1 hour. Cool. Add coconut and sugar to taste to whipped cream; mix well. Alternate layers of bananas and whipped cream mixture over meringue.

Judie Silvasy

BANANA SPLIT PIE

2 1/4 c. milk
1 c. sugar
1 tsp. salt
1/2 c. cornstarch
1 tbsp. butter
1 20-oz. can crushed pineapple
1 baked 9-in. pie shell
Pineapple slices
Bananas, sliced
Maraschino cherries, chopped

Bring 2 cups milk, 1/2 cup sugar and 1/2 teaspoon salt to a boil in saucepan. Add 1/4 cup cornstarch dissolved in remaining 1/4 cup milk. Cook over medium heat until thickened, stirring constantly. Remove from heat. Stir in butter. Cool. Combine pineapple, remaining 1/2 cup sugar and 1/2 teaspoon salt in saucepan. Bring to a boil. Add remaining 1/4 cup cornstarch dissolved in 1/4 cup cold water. Cook over medium heat until thickened and clear, stirring constantly. Remove from heat. Cool. Pour cream filling into pie shell. Top with pineapple filling. Arrange pineapple, bananas and maraschino cherries over filling. Chill until serving time. Garnish with whipped cream. Yield: 6 servings.

Anita Bender

BROWNIE PIE

1 c. sugar
1 stick margarine, melted
2 eggs
1/4 c. flour
3 tbsp. baking cocoa
1 tsp. vanilla extract
1/2 c. chopped pecans

Combine sugar and margarine in bowl; mix well. Add eggs, flour, cocoa and vanilla; mix well after each addition. Stir in pecans. Pour into 8-inch pie pan. Bake at 350 degrees for 20 to 25 minutes or until set. Cool. Serve with ice cream. Yield: 8 servings.

Vera Cooper

FRENCH SILK PIE

1 c. butter, softened
1 1/3 c. sugar
2 1/2 sq. unsweetened chocolate, melted
1 1/2 tsp. vanilla extract
4 eggs
1 baked 9-in. pie shell

Cream butter in mixer bowl. Add sugar gradually; cream well. Mix in cooled chocolate. Stir in vanilla. Add eggs 1 at a time, beating for 5 minutes after each addition. Pour into pie shell. Chill for several hours. Yield: 8 servings.

Liz Wallin

BUTTER BRICKLE ICE CREAM PIE

1 c. chopped pecans
1 c. graham cracker crumbs
1 c. sugar
1 tsp. baking powder
3 egg whites, stiffly beaten
1 qt. butter brickle ice cream, softened
1 Heath bar, crushed

Combine first 4 ingredients in bowl; mix well. Fold into egg whites. Spread over bottom and side of buttered pie plate. Bake at 325 degrees for 20 minutes. Fill cooled shell with ice cream. Sprinkle Heath bar over top. Freeze until firm.

Valerie Adams

BAKED ALASKA PIE

1 qt. coffee ice cream, softened
1 baked 9-in. pie shell
3 egg whites
1/4 c. sugar
1/4 c. toasted slivered almonds
2 1/4 c. packed brown sugar
1 1/3 c. light corn syrup
1/2 c. butter
1 1/2 c. evaporated milk

Spread ice cream over bottom of pie shell. Beat egg whites until soft peaks form; add sugar gradually, beating until stiff. Cover ice cream with meringue, sealing to edge. Sprinkle with almonds. Bake at 450 degrees until lightly browned. Boil brown sugar and corn syrup in saucepan for 3 minutes. Add butter. Cool slightly. Stir in evaporated milk. Serve warm over pie. Yield: 8 servings.

Mrs. Arthur J. Lacouture, Jr.

CANDY CRUST ICE CREAM PIE

2/3 c. semisweet chocolate chips
1/4 c. butter
1/4 c. milk
2   3 1/2-oz. cans flaked coconut
1 qt. cherry vanilla ice
*   cream, softened*
Sweetened whipped cream

Combine chocolate, butter and milk in small saucepan. Place over low heat; stir until chocolate is melted. Remove from heat; blend in coconut. Spread over bottom and side of buttered 9-inch pie plate. Chill until firm. Fill pie shell with ice cream. Freeze until firm. Place in refrigerator 20 minutes before serving time for easier slicing. Garnish with whipped cream.

Dody Freeman

QUICKIE STRAWBERRY PIE

1 1/4 c. graham cracker crumbs
1/4 c. melted butter

3/4 c. crushed strawberries
2 tbsp. sugar
1 tbsp. lemon juice
1 pt. vanilla ice cream, softened
8 oz. whipped topping

Combine graham cracker crumbs and butter in bowl; mix well. Press over bottom and side of 9-inch pie plate. Chill for 1 hour. Combine strawberries, sugar and lemon juice in bowl; mix well. Stir in ice cream. Fold in whipped topping. Spoon into crust. Freeze for 4 hours or longer.

Geri Logeais

TURTLE PIE

20 Oreo cookies, crushed
1/4 c. butter, melted
1 pt. caramel ice cream, softened
1 c. chopped pecans
1 jar caramel ice cream topping
12 oz. whipped topping
1/2 c. instant chocolate drink mix

Combine first 2 ingredients in bowl; mix well. Press over bottom and side of 9-inch pie plate. Bake at 375 degrees for 8 to 10 minutes. Cool on wire rack. Combine ice cream and 3/4 cup pecans in bowl; mix well. Spread over cooled crust. Pour caramel topping over ice cream. Cover with half the whipped topping. Mix remaining whipped topping with chocolate drink mix. Pipe around edge of pie. Sprinkle with remaining 1/4 cup pecans. Freeze until ready to serve.

Kathy Beinecke

FRUIT-A-PLENTY PIE

1   30-oz. can apricot halves
1   12-oz. package frozen
*   pineapple chunks, thawed*
2 tbsp. butter
8 oz. cream cheese, softened

LEMON CHESS PIE

  2 c. sugar
  4 eggs, beaten
  1 tbsp. flour
  1 tbsp. cornmeal
  1/4 c. milk
  1/4 c. melted butter
  1/4 c. lemon juice
  3 tbsp. grated lemon rind
  1 unbaked 9-in. pie shell

Beat sugar, eggs, flour and cornmeal in bowl until blended. Add next 4 ingredients; mix well. Pour into pie shell. Bake at 400 degrees for 10 minutes. Reduce temperature to 300 degrees. Bake for 30 minutes longer or until set. Yield: 8 servings.

Denise Welchel

1 c. buttermilk baking mix
1/2 c. sugar
1/4 tsp. grated lemon rind
2 tbsp. cornstarch
1/4 tsp. salt
1/4 c. lemon juice
2 c. strawberry halves
1 sm. bunch fresh seedless grapes

Drain apricots; reserve syrup. Drain pineapple; reserve syrup. Cut butter and 3 ounces cream cheese into baking mix in bowl until crumbly. Shape into ball. Pat out on lightly greased pizza pan to form very thin crust; flute edges. Bake at 425 degrees for about 8 minutes or until lightly browned. Cool. Combine remaining 5 ounces cream cheese, 2 tablespoons reserved apricot syrup, 1/4 cup sugar and lemon rind in bowl; mix well. Spread over cooled crust. Combine remaining sugar, cornstarch, salt, 1 cup reserved apricot syrup, 1/2 cup reserved pineapple syrup and lemon juice in saucepan. Simmer for 1 minute or until thickened, stirring constantly. Arrange fruit in circles over cream cheese mixture. Garnish center with apricot halves. Brush fruit with glaze. Cut into wedges; serve with remaining glaze. Yield: 10-12 servings.

Photograph for this recipe above.

SOUR CREAM LEMON PIE

  1 c. sugar
  3 tbsp. cornstarch
  1/4 c. butter, softened
  1 tbsp. grated lemon rind
  6 tbsp. lemon juice
  1 c. milk
  3 egg yolks
  1 c. sour cream
  1 baked 9-in. pie shell

Mix sugar, cornstarch, butter, lemon rind and juice in saucepan; blend well. Stir in milk gradually. Bring to a boil over low heat, stirring constantly. Stir a small amount of hot mixture into beaten egg yolks; stir egg yolks into hot mixture. Cook for 1 minute, stirring constantly. Cool. Fold in sour cream. Pour into pie shell. Chill in refrigerator. Garnish with whipped cream and unpeeled lemon slices. Yield: 6-8 servings.

Catherine Repass

MOCK KEY LIME PIE

1 can sweetened condensed milk
8 oz. whipped topping
1   6-oz. can frozen limeade
   concentrate, thawed
1 graham cracker pie shell

Combine first 3 ingredients in bowl; blend well. Pour into pie shell. Chill for 3 hours or longer. Garnish with chopped nuts.

Cheryl Hug

MACADAMIA-MOCHA PIE

1/2 c. chopped macadamia nuts
1   9-in. chocolate crumb pie shell
1/4 c. coffee
1   7-oz. jar marshmallow creme
12 oz. whipped topping

Sprinkle nuts into pie shell. Mix coffee, marshmallow creme and 2 tablespoons water in bowl. Fold in whipped topping. Pour into pie shell. Freeze until firm.

Violet S. Voges

PEANUT BUTTER REFRIGERATOR PIE

3/4 c. chunky peanut butter
3 oz. cream cheese, softened
1 c. confectioners' sugar, sifted
8 oz. whipped topping
1 baked pie shell

Whip peanut butter, cream cheese and confectioners' sugar in mixer bowl until light and fluffy. Fold in whipped topping. Spoon into pie shell. Chill until serving time.

Glenda White

PECAN FUDGE PIE

4 oz. sweet cooking chocolate
1/4 c. butter
1 can sweetened condensed milk
2 eggs, well beaten
1 tsp. vanilla extract
1/8 tsp. salt
1 1/4 c. pecan halves
1 unbaked 9-in. pie shell

Melt chocolate and butter in medium saucepan over low heat. Add condensed milk, 1/2 cup hot water and eggs; mix well. Remove from heat. Stir in vanilla, salt and pecans. Pour into pie shell. Bake at 350 degrees for 50 to 60 minutes or until center is set. Chill for 3 hours.

Zonell Cook

SPECIAL PECAN PIE

1 tbsp. butter
1 c. sugar
3 eggs, slightly beaten
1 c. light corn syrup
1 tsp. vanilla extract
1 c. chopped pecans
1 unbaked 10-in. pie shell
1 c. pecan halves

Cream butter and sugar in bowl. Add eggs; mix well. Stir in syrup, vanilla and chopped pecans. Pour into pie shell. Arrange pecan halves in symmetrical design over filling. Bake at 350 degrees for 40 to 50 minutes or until set.

Mary Bell Wicks

PUMPKIN-PECAN PIE

4 eggs, lightly beaten
2 c. mashed cooked pumpkin
1 c. sugar
1/2 c. dark corn syrup
1 tsp. vanilla extract
1/2 tsp. cinnamon
1/4 tsp. salt
1 unbaked 9-in. pie shell
1 c. chopped pecans

Mix eggs, pumpkin, sugar, corn syrup, vanilla, cinnamon and salt in bowl. Spoon into pie shell. Top with pecans. Bake at 350 degrees for 40 minutes or until set.

Yvette Winslow

STRAWBERRY CREAM PIE

> 1/2 c. butter, softened
> Sugar
> 1 c. flour
> 1 egg white
> 1 1/2 c. sliced strawberries
> 2 tsp. lemon juice
> 1/2 c. whipping cream, whipped

Cream butter with 2 tablespoons sugar in bowl. Cut in flour until crumbly. Sprinkle 1/4 cup crumbs into baking pan. Bake at 375 degrees until golden brown. Press remaining crumbs over bottom and side of 9-inch pie plate. Bake at 375 degrees for 12 to 15 minutes or until brown. Beat egg white in mixer bowl until soft peaks form; add 1/2 cup sugar, strawberries and lemon juice gradually, beating until stiff. Fold in whipped cream. Spoon into cooled pie shell. Sprinkle with crumbs. Freeze for 4 hours or longer.

Norma McDonald

STRAWBERRY LADYFINGER PIE

> 20 ladyfingers, split
> 1 sm. package vanilla instant
>   pudding mix
> 1 1/2 c. milk
> 1 pt. strawberries
> 6 tbsp. currant jelly, melted

Arrange enough ladyfingers soft side up to cover bottom of 9-inch pie plate. Cut remaining ladyfingers crosswise into halves; arrange around side of pie plate. Prepare pudding mix according to package directions using 1 1/2 cups milk. Spoon into prepared pie plate. Arrange strawberries in rings around edge of pie. Spoon jelly over strawberries. Chill until serving time.

Bettye Horne

STRAWBERRY DEVONSHIRE PIE

> 3 oz. cream cheese, softened
> 3 tbsp. sour cream

> 1 baked 9-in. pie shell
> 1 c. sugar
> 3 tbsp. cornstarch
> 1 to 1 1/2 qt. strawberries

Beat cream cheese in bowl until fluffy. Add sour cream; beat until smooth. Spread on bottom of pastry shell; chill. Mix sugar and cornstarch in saucepan. Add 1/2 cup plus 1 tablespoon water and 1 cup mashed strawberries; mix well. Cook over medium heat until thickened, stirring constantly. Boil for 1 minute. Cool. Arrange remaining strawberries over cream cheese mixture; spoon glaze over strawberries. Chill for 1 hour.

Annette Walton

EASY ELEGANT FRUIT TARTS

> Sugar
> 6 tbsp. frozen butter, cut
>   into 6 pieces
> 1 c. flour
> 1 egg yolk
> 1 tsp. grated lemon rind
> Salt
> 4 1/2 tsp. cornstarch
> 1 c. orange juice
> 2 tsp. grated orange rind
> 1 tbsp. orange liqueur
> Favorite fruit

Combine 2 tablespoons sugar, next 4 ingredients, 1/8 teaspoon salt and 1 tablespoon cold water in food processor container. Process with metal blade for 5 seconds, pulsing rapidly until mixture sticks to blade. Press over bottom and sides of 6 tart cups. Bake at 425 degrees for 10 minutes or until golden brown. Cool on wire rack. Combine 1/2 cup sugar, cornstarch and dash of salt in saucepan. Stir in orange juice gradually until smooth. Simmer for 1 minute, stirring constantly. Mix in orange rind. Cool, covered. Stir liqueur into cooled glaze. Place fruit in bottom of cooled tart shells. Cover fruit with glaze. Chill for several hours.

Janet L. LaGrassa

CHESS TARTLETS

3/4 c. butter, softened
2 c. sugar
6 eggs
1 tbsp. cream
2 tbsp. cornmeal
1 tbsp. vanilla extract
1 tbsp. vinegar
12 unbaked 3-in. tart shells

Cream butter and sugar in bowl. Add eggs 1 at a time, beating well after each addition. Add next 4 ingredients; mix well. Spoon into tart shells. Bake at 350 degrees until set. Yield: 1 dozen.

Melinda Pitts

TEATIME TASSIES

9 tbsp. margarine, softened
3 oz. cream cheese, softened
1 c. flour
1 egg
3/4 c. packed brown sugar
1 tbsp. vanilla extract
Dash of salt
2/3 c. chopped pecans

Cream 8 tablespoons margarine and cream cheese in mixer bowl until fluffy. Add flour; mix well. Chill for 1 hour. Shape into 1-inch balls. Press into miniature muffin cups. Combine next 4 ingredients and remaining 1 tablespoon margarine in bowl; mix well. Sprinkle half the pecans into pastry-lined muffin cups. Spoon brown sugar mixture over pecans. Sprinkle with remaining pecans. Bake at 325 degrees for 25 minutes or until set. Cool completely in pan. Yield: 2 dozen.

Dona M. McCloud

WALNUT TASSIES

1 c. margarine, softened
8 oz. cream cheese, softened
2 1/2 c. flour
1 c. chopped walnuts
4 eggs
1 lb. brown sugar

2 tbsp. melted margarine
1/2 tsp. vanilla extract

Combine first 3 ingredients in bowl; mix well. Chill for 1 hour. Shape into balls. Press into miniature muffin cups. Place 1 teaspoon chopped walnuts in each. Beat eggs into brown sugar in bowl 1 at a time. Add margarine and vanilla; mix well. Spoon into pastry-lined muffin cups. Bake at 350 degrees for 15 to 20 minutes or until set. Yield: 3-4 dozen.

Maryann Reibsome

Miscellaneous Desserts

INDIVIDUAL BAKED ALASKAS

6 individual sponge dessert shells
1 9-oz. can crushed
     pineapple, drained
6 scoops strawberry ice cream
6 egg whites
3/4 c. sugar

Place shells on baking sheet. Place 1 tablespoon pineapple and 1 scoop ice cream in each shell. Freeze until firm. Beat egg whites in mixer bowl until soft peaks form. Add sugar gradually, beating until stiff peaks form. Cover ice cream and shells completely with meringue. Bake at 500 degrees for 4 minutes. Serve immediately.

Evelyn Piper

ELEGANT RAINBOW ALASKA

1 17-oz. package pound cake mix
1 pt. strawberry ice cream, softened
1 pt. vanilla ice cream, softened
1 1/2 pt. pistachio ice
     cream, softened
5 egg whites
1/4 tsp. cream of tartar
1/2 tsp. vanilla extract

2/3 c. sugar
1/4 c. flaked coconut

Prepare pound cake batter using package directions. Pour into two 8-inch round cake pans. Bake according to directions. Cool. Line deep 1 1/2-quart bowl with foil allowing 1 inch to extend over edge of bowl. Spread strawberry ice cream in bottom of bowl; freeze until firm. Pack vanilla ice cream over strawberry; freeze until firm. Top with pistachio ice cream. Cover with foil; press to smooth top. Freeze until firm. Place one cake layer on baking sheet. Wrap remaining layer in foil; freeze for future use. Let bowl of ice cream stand at room temperature while preparing meringue. Combine egg whites with cream of tartar and vanilla in bowl; beat until soft peaks form. Add sugar gradually, beating until stiff peaks form. Remove foil from top of ice cream; invert onto cake layer. Spread meringue over ice cream and cake, covering completely. Sprinkle with coconut. Bake in preheated 500-degree oven for 3 minutes or until brown. Yield: 10 servings.

Alice Sturgess

AMBROSIA

2 bananas, sliced
1 apple, chopped
1 pear, chopped
1/4 c. lemon juice
2 oranges, sectioned
1 1/3 c. coconut
1 c. pineapple yogurt

Combine bananas, apple and pear with lemon juice in bowl; toss lightly. Combine with oranges in serving bowl; mix well. Chill until serving time. Fold in coconut and yogurt. Yield: 8 cups.

Paula Page

APPLE DUMPLINGS

1/2 c. red cinnamon candies
1/4 c. water

1/3 c. confectioners' sugar
1/4 tsp. nutmeg
1/3 c. chopped pecans
2 2/3 c. sifted flour
1 1/4 tsp. salt
1 c. shortening
6 1/2 tbsp. cold water
6 tart apples, peeled, cored
1/2 c. (about) cream
2 c. confectioners' sugar

Combine candies and 1/4 cup water in saucepan. Cook until candies dissolve, stirring constantly; remove from heat. Add 1/3 cup confectioners' sugar, nutmeg and pecans; mix well. Mix flour and salt in bowl. Cut in shortening until crumbly. Sprinkle with cold water; mix with fork until mixture forms ball. Divide into 6 portions. Roll each on lightly floured surface; cut into 7-inch square. Place apple in center; fill with pecan mixture. Moisten edges of pastry with cream. Fold pastry over apples, pressing edges to seal. Brush with cream. Place on ungreased baking sheet. Bake at 400 degrees for 35 minutes or until brown. Mix confectioners' sugar with just enough cream to moisten; beat until fluffy. Place hot dumplings on dessert plates. Add dollop of confectioners' sugar mixture. Garnish plates with cooked apple slices. Yield: 6 servings.

Photograph for this recipe on cover.

ORANGE-GLAZED APPLES

2 20-oz. cans sliced apples, drained
1/4 c. melted butter
1/4 c. flour
1 1/2 c. sugar
1/2 c. orange juice
2 tbsp. grated orange rind

Spread apples in 1 1/2-quart baking dish. Blend remaining ingredients in saucepan. Cook over medium heat until thickened, stirring constantly. Pour over apples. Bake at 375 degrees for 30 minutes. Yield: 8 servings.

Nita Mayr

FRESH APRICOT ICE CREAM

2 lb. fresh apricots
1 1/4 c. sugar
2 c. light cream
2 c. whipping cream
1 c. milk
1/8 tsp. salt
1 tsp. vanilla extract

Dip apricots in boiling water for 30 seconds. Plunge into cold water; peel. Cut into halves; remove pits. Puree in blender container. Combine with remaining ingredients in 1-gallon ice cream freezer container. Freeze using manufacturer's instructions. Yield: 8 servings.

Regina Madden

BANANA FRITTERS

3 lb. bananas
1 c. buttermilk baking mix
1/2 c. milk
1 egg
Hot oil for frying
Confectioners' sugar

Slice bananas into thirds; split lengthwise. Combine baking mix, milk and egg in bowl; mix well. Dip each banana piece in batter. Fry bananas in hot oil in skillet until brown on both sides. Remove from skillet; drain. Sprinkle with confectioners' sugar. Yield: 12 servings.

Inez Erickson

FROZEN BLACKBERRY CREAM

2 c. strained blackberry puree
16 lg. marshmallows
1 tbsp. lemon juice
1 c. sugar
3 c. whipped cream

Mix blackberry puree with marshmallows, lemon juice and sugar in double boiler. Cook until marshmallows are melted, stirring constantly. Chill in refrigerator. Fold in whipped cream. Spoon into mold. Freeze until firm. Unmold on serving plate. Yield: 4-6 servings.

Teresa Allen

BLACKBERRY COBBLER

1/4 c. shortening
1 c. sugar
1 1/4 c. sifted flour
2 tsp. baking powder
1/2 c. milk
2 c. blackberries
1 c. sugar
2 tbsp. butter

Beat shortening and 1 cup sugar in mixer bowl until light. Add flour and baking powder alternately with milk, mixing well after each addition. Pour into greased 9 x 13-inch baking pan. Sprinkle blackberries and remaining 1 cup sugar over batter. Dot with butter. Bake at 350 degrees for 1 hour. Yield: 10 servings.

Betty Stocking

EASY BLINTZES

4 oz. cream cheese, softened
1/2 c. confectioners' sugar
1/4 tsp. vanilla extract
1/2 c. whipped topping
12 slices bread, trimmed
Margarine, melted
Cinnamon-sugar to taste

Combine first 4 ingredients in bowl; mix well. Flatten bread. Spread with cream cheese mixture; roll as for jelly roll. Dip in margarine; roll in cinnamon-sugar. Place on baking sheet. Bake at 425 degrees for 10 minutes. Serve warm with whipped cream, sour cream or fruit filling. Yield: 12 servings.

Dean V. Bauer

BLUEBERRY SLUMP

2 c. blueberries
1/2 c. sugar
1 tsp. cinnamon
Pinch of salt
1 tbsp. sugar
1 c. flour
2 tsp. baking powder

1/4 tsp. salt
1/2 c. milk

Combine blueberries, 1 1/2 to 2 cups water to cover, 1/2 cup sugar, cinnamon and salt in 2-quart saucepan; mix well. Bring to a boil, stirring occasionally. Sift 1 tablespoon sugar and remaining dry ingredients into bowl. Add milk slowly, stirring until mixture leaves side of bowl. Drop dumpling batter by spoonfuls carefully onto boiling blueberries. Simmer, covered, for 10 to 25 minutes. Remove cover; cook for 10 minutes longer. Serve with whipped cream. Yield: 4-6 servings.

Joan M. Waal

PECAN BRICKLE DESSERT

1 c. melted margarine
2 c. flour
1/2 c. oats
1/2 c. packed brown sugar
1/2 c. chopped pecans
1 12-oz. jar caramel sauce
1/2 gal. ice cream, softened

Combine margarine, flour, oats, brown sugar and pecans in bowl; mix well. Press into baking sheet. Bake at 400 degrees for 10 to 12 minutes or until lightly browned. Cool. Crumble half the mixture into 9 x 13-inch dish. Drizzle half the sauce over crumbs. Spread ice cream over sauce. Layer remaining crumbs and sauce over ice cream. Freeze until firm. Yield: 10-12 servings.

Kathie Connor

BUTTERSCOTCH DELIGHT

2 sm. packages butterscotch
   pudding and pie filling mix
3 c. milk
1/2 c. margarine
1 c. flour
2 tbsp. sugar

1 c. chopped pecans
1 c. confectioners' sugar
8 oz. cream cheese, softened
16 oz. whipped topping

Combine pudding mix with milk in saucepan. Cook according to package directions. Cool. Combine margarine, flour, sugar and pecans in bowl; mix well. Press into 9 x 11-inch baking pan. Bake at 350 degrees for 20 minutes. Cool. Cream confectioners' sugar and cream cheese in bowl until light. Reserve 1/2 cup whipped topping. Blend remaining whipped topping into creamed mixture. Spread in prepared pan. Top with cooled pudding and reserved whipped topping. Chill. Yield: 12 servings.

Joan Hollingsworth

BLENDER CHEESECAKE

1 21-oz. can pie filling
1 3-oz. package lemon gelatin
2 c. cottage cheese
2 tbsp. lemon juice
1 8-oz. carton whipped topping

Spread pie filling in 8 x 8-inch pan. Combine next 3 ingredients and 1/2 cup boiling water in blender container. Process until smooth. Combine with whipped topping in bowl; mix well. Spoon over pie filling. Chill until firm. Cut into squares. Invert squares on serving plates. Yield: 12-16 servings.

Maryann Cotterill

ICE CREAM CHEESECAKE

1 recipe graham cracker crust
12 to 16 oz. cream cheese, softened
1 1/2 qt. vanilla ice cream, softened

Press graham cracker crust mixture into 9-inch springform pan. Combine cream cheese and ice cream in large mixer bowl; beat until smooth. Spoon into prepared pan. Freeze until firm. Yield: 10 servings.

Mary Jane Currier

LEMON CHEESECAKE

1/4 c. melted butter
3 c. graham cracker crumbs
1 sm. package lemon gelatin
1 c. sugar
8 oz. cream cheese, softened
1 tsp. vanilla extract
1 pt. whipping cream, whipped

Mix butter and crumbs in bowl. Press into 9 x 13-inch baking dish, reserving small amount for topping. Bake at 400 degrees for 5 minutes. Dissolve gelatin in 1 cup boiling water in bowl; cool. Cream sugar and cream cheese in mixer bowl until light and fluffy. Beat in vanilla. Add gelatin; mix well. Fold whipped cream gently into creamed mixture. Spoon into prepared dish. Chill in refrigerator. Yield: 20 servings.

Hilda Foster

FROZEN MOCHA CHEESECAKE

1 1/4 c. chocolate wafer crumbs
1/4 c. sugar
1/4 c. melted butter
8 oz. cream cheese, softened
2/3 c. chocolate syrup
1 14-oz. can sweetened
   condensed milk
2 tbsp. instant coffee granules
1 c. whipping cream, whipped

Combine cookie crumbs, sugar and butter in bowl. Press over bottom and side of 9-inch springform pan. Chill in refrigerator. Beat cream cheese in mixer bowl until fluffy. Add chocolate syrup and condensed milk; mix well. Stir in coffee dissolved in 1 teaspoon hot water. Fold in whipped cream. Pour into prepared crust. Freeze, covered, for 6 hours or until firm. Place on serving dish; remove side of pan. Garnish with additional cookie crumbs. Yield: 12-15 servings.

Jeannie Cox

CHERRY DUMP CAKE

1 lg. can crushed pineapple
1 can cherry pie filling
1 2-layer pkg. white cake mix
1 c. chopped walnuts
2 sticks butter, sliced

Layer pineapple, pie filling, cake mix and walnuts in 9 x 13-inch baking pan. Do not mix. Dot with butter. Bake at 350 degrees for 30 to 35 minutes or until golden brown. Yield: 6-8 servings.

Mary Bell Wicks

QUICK CHERRY BAKE

1 can cherry pie filling
2 sticks pie crust mix, crumbled
1/2 c. sugar
1/4 tsp. each cinnamon and nutmeg

Pour pie filling into greased 8 x 8-inch baking dish. Mix remaining ingredients in small bowl. Spread over filling. Bake at 375 degrees for 20 minutes or until brown. Yield: 6 servings.

Helen Cade

CHOCOLATE ICE CREAM

3 eggs, beaten
2 12-oz. cans evaporated milk
3 c. sugar
3 c. whipping cream
1 can chocolate syrup
1 6-oz. package chocolate
   instant pudding mix
2 1/2 c. milk
Dash of salt
2 tbsp. vanilla extract
1 c. chopped pecans
Milk

Combine first 3 ingredients in large bowl; mix well. Add cream and chocolate syrup. Combine pudding mix with 2 1/2 cups milk in bowl. Add to cream mixture. Add salt, vanilla and pecans; mix well. Pour into 1 1/2-gallon ice cream freezer container. Add milk to within 4 inches of top of container. Freeze using manufacturer's directions. Yield: 12 servings.

Sue Pew

CHOCOLATE COOKIES AND CREAM DESSERT

1   19-oz. package Oreo
      cookies, crushed
1/2 c. melted margarine
1/2 gal. vanilla ice cream,
      softened
2   8-oz. jars fudge sauce
1   16-oz. carton whipped topping

Combine cookie crumbs and melted margarine in 9 x 13-inch dish, reserving a small amount for topping. Press evenly over bottom of pan. Layer ice cream, fudge sauce, whipped topping and reserved crumbs over crust. Freeze until firm. Yield: 18 servings.

Carol Sassin

COCONUT FREEZE

2   c. sour cream
1   3-oz. package vanilla
      instant pudding mix
1 1/3 c. shredded coconut
1   7-oz. can crushed pineapple
1/2 c. chopped maraschino cherries

Mix sour cream with pudding mix in bowl. Add coconut, pineapple and cherries; mix well. Spoon into loaf pan. Freeze for 3 hours or until firm. Slice and serve. Yield: 12 servings.

Jo Anne M. Stringer

CRANAPPLE CRUNCH

3   c. chopped unpeeled apples
1   can whole cranberry sauce
1 1/2 c. quick-cooking oats
1/2 c. packed brown sugar
1/3 c. flour
1/3 c. chopped pecans
1/2 c. melted margarine

Combine apples and cranberry sauce in 2-quart casserole. Combine remaining ingredients in bowl; mix well. Spread over fruit. Bake at 350 degrees for 1 hour. Yield: 8 servings.

Frances H. Campbell

CRANBERRY FREEZE

2/3 c. graham cracker crumbs
2   tbsp. sugar
1/4 c. melted butter
8   oz. cream cheese, softened
1/4 c. sugar
1   pt. vanilla ice cream, softened
1   16-oz. can whole cranberry sauce

Combine graham cracker crumbs, 2 tablespoons sugar and butter in bowl; mix well. Press into bottom of 8-inch springform pan. Beat cream cheese with 1/4 cup sugar in bowl until fluffy. Add ice cream by tablespoonfuls, beating to blend quickly. Pour over crust. Stir cranberry sauce with fork. Drop by spoonfuls over ice cream mixture. Freeze, covered, for 4 hours or until firm. Yield: 8 servings.

Jessica Winkler

MINIATURE CREAM PUFFS

1/2 c. butter
1/4 tsp. salt
1   c. sifted flour
4   eggs

Mix 1 cup water, butter and salt in saucepan. Bring to a full rolling boil. Reduce heat. Stir in flour quickly, mixing vigorously with wooden spoon until mixture leaves side of pan. Remove from heat. Add eggs 1 at a time, beating after each addition until smooth. Drop by heaping teaspoonfuls onto greased baking sheet. Bake at 400 degrees for 20 minutes. Fill as desired. Yield: 3 dozen.

Nell Baker

EASY FRUIT TRIFLE

1   lg. angel food cake
1   15-oz. can crushed pineapple
1   6-oz. jar maraschino cherries,
      drained, chopped
1   12-oz. carton whipped topping
1   3-oz. can flaked coconut, toasted

Tear cake into bite-sized pieces. Layer cake, pineapple, cherries, whipped topping and coconut 1/2 at a time in 2-quart dish. Chill, covered, overnight. Yield: 12 servings.

Mary Gamble

FROZEN FRUIT CUPS

1 17-oz. can apricots
1 17-oz. can crushed pineapple
1/2 c. sugar
1 6-oz. can frozen orange
   juice concentrate
2 tbsp. lemon juice
3 10-oz. packages frozen
   strawberries, thawed
3 bananas, chopped

Drain apricots and crushed pineapple, reserving liquid; chop apricots. Add enough water to reserved liquid to measure 1 cup. Heat liquid and sugar in saucepan, stirring to dissolve sugar. Stir in orange juice concentrate, lemon juice and fruit. Spoon into paper-lined muffin cups. Freeze until firm. Remove from freezer 10 to 20 minutes before serving. Yield: 30 servings.

Dorothy Eckert

HOT FRUIT COMPOTE

2 apples, sliced
2 tbsp. butter
2 oranges, sectioned
2 peaches, sliced
2 bananas, sliced
3 tbsp. honey
2 c. sliced strawberries
1 c. blueberries

Saute apples in butter in skillet for 2 minutes. Add oranges and peaches. Saute for 5 minutes. Add bananas and honey. Saute for 2 minutes. Add strawberries and blueberries. Heat to serving temperature. Spoon into dessert dishes. Garnish with coconut and whipped cream. Yield: 8-10 servings.

Thelma Savale

GINGER PEACHY SUNDAE

1/2 c. finely chopped preserved ginger
1/4 c. syrup from ginger
3/4 c. chopped walnuts
4 ripe peaches
1 qt. vanilla ice cream

Combine ginger, syrup and walnuts in bowl. Peel peaches; slice thinly. Scoop ice cream into 8 dessert dishes. Arrange peach slices over ice cream. Spoon ginger sauce over top. Yield: 8 servings.

Photograph for this recipe on this page.

FIESTA FRUIT CUPS

6 flour tortillas
Oil for deep frying
6 scoops lime sherbet
1 c. sliced banana
1 c. fresh strawberries
2 c. sliced kiwifruit
1 c. fresh orange sections

Place tortillas 1 at a time in several inches deep hot oil in skillet. Form cup by pressing down in center with empty can with holes punched in bottom. Fry until crisp and golden; drain on paper towels. Store in airtight container. Place on serving plates. Fill with sherbet and fruit. Yield: 6 servings.

Donita Massey

CANTALOUPE
WITH BLUEBERRY SAUCE

1/2 c. sugar
1 tbsp. cornstarch

3 thin slices lemon
3/4 c. grape juice
1 1/2 to 2 c. blueberries
8 peeled cantaloupe rings
8 vanilla ice cream scoops

Combine sugar, cornstarch, lemon slices and grape juice in small saucepan. Simmer for 5 minutes or until clear. Remove lemon slices. Add blueberries. Chill well. Place cantaloupe rings on serving plates. Place scoop of ice cream in each ring. Top with chilled blueberry sauce. Yield: 8 servings.

Nonnie Coombs

WATERMELON ICE

1/2 lg. watermelon
Juice of 4 oranges
Juice of 2 lemons
1 c. sugar
1 egg white, stiffly beaten

Scoop pulp from watermelon; reserve rind. Place pulp in cloth bag. Squeeze juice into bowl. Add citrus juices and sugar; mix well. Pour into 1-gallon freezer container. Freeze until partially set. Fold in egg white. Freeze until firm. Spoon into watermelon rind. Garnish with melon balls. Yield: 24 servings.

Alice Brooks

MINTED MELON BALLS

1 c. sugar
4 mint leaves
1/4 c. lemon juice
1 c. cantaloupe balls
4 c. watermelon balls
1 c. honeydew melon balls

Bring 2 cups water, sugar and mint leaves to a boil in saucepan; mix well. Cook for 2 minutes. Remove from heat; strain. Mix with lemon juice in bowl. Chill syrup. Arrange melon balls in chilled dessert cups. Pour syrup over melon. Yield: 8 servings.

Nadine Collins

AVOCADO MOUSSE

1 avocado, chopped
2/3 c. lemon juice
1 can sweetened condensed milk

Combine avocado with lemon juice and condensed milk in blender container. Process until smooth. Spoon into dessert glasses. Chill until firm. Garnish with whipped cream. Yield: 4 servings.

Sheila Pendel

BOYSENBERRY MOUSSE

2 env. unflavored gelatin
1/4 c. sugar
3 eggs, separated
1 c. milk
2 c. boysenberry yogurt
1/4 c. sugar
1 c. whipping cream, whipped

Combine gelatin and 1/4 cup sugar in saucepan. Add mixture of egg yolks and milk. Cook until gelatin dissolves, stirring constantly. Cool slightly. Add yogurt. Chill until partially set. Beat egg whites until soft peaks form. Beat in remaining 1/4 cup sugar until stiff. Fold egg whites and whipped cream into boysenberry mixture. Spoon into 9-cup mold. Chill for several hours to overnight. Unmold onto serving plate. Yield: 10 servings.

Holly Zimmerman

ORANGE SHERBET

6 cans orange soda
1 can sweetened condensed milk
1 sm. can evaporated milk
1 7-oz. can crushed pineapple

Mix soda, condensed milk, evaporated milk and pineapple in ice cream freezer container. Chill for 20 minutes. Freeze using manufacturer's instructions. Yield: 2 quarts.

Kathy Graham

PEANUT BUTTER PARFAITS

1 c. packed brown sugar
1/3 c. milk
1/4 c. white corn syrup
1 tbsp. butter
1/4 c. peanut butter
Vanilla ice cream
Peanuts

Combine brown sugar, milk, corn syrup and butter in saucepan. Cook over medium heat until sugar dissolves and butter melts, stirring constantly; remove from heat. Add peanut butter; beat until smooth. Cool. Alternate layers of peanut butter sauce and ice cream in parfait glasses, beginning and ending with ice cream. Top with peanuts. Serve immediately. Yield: 4 servings.

Linda Andrews

STRAWBERRY AND RICE PARFAITS

1/2 c. strawberry yogurt
3/4 c. cooked rice, chilled
5 oz. frozen strawberries, thawed
Whipped topping

Stir yogurt and rice together in bowl. Chill, covered, in refrigerator. Layer rice and strawberries alternately in parfait glasses. Garnish with whipped topping. Yield: 2 servings.

Lynn Covington

PEACHES AND CREAM DESSERT

1   16-oz. can sliced peaches
3/4 c. flour
1 sm. package vanilla instant
    pudding mix
1 tsp. baking powder
1 egg, beaten
1/2 c. milk
3 tbsp. melted butter
8 oz. cream cheese, softened
1/2 c. plus 1 tbsp. sugar
1/2 tsp. cinnamon

Drain peaches, reserving 1/3 cup juice. Chop peaches. Combine next 3 ingredients in bowl. Stir in mixture of egg, milk and butter. Spread in greased 8-inch baking pan. Spoon peaches into prepared pan. Combine cream cheese, 1/2 cup sugar and peach juice in bowl; mix well. Pour over peaches. Sprinkle mixture of 1 tablespoon sugar and cinnamon over top. Bake at 350 degrees for 30 minutes. Cool. Yield: 9 servings.

Sally Waverman

PERSIAN PEACHES

4 c. sliced peaches
1 c. orange juice
6 tbsp. honey
1 tbsp. finely chopped candied
    ginger
Dash of salt

Mix all ingredients gently in bowl. Chill mixture, covered, in refrigerator. Spoon into chilled sherbet glasses. Yield: 5 servings.

Haley Sullivan

LAYERED PEACH DELIGHT

1 lg. package peach gelatin
1 can peach pie filling
1 sm. package peach gelatin
8 oz. whipped topping
8 oz. cream cheese, cubed, softened

Dissolve large package peach gelatin in 2 cups hot water in bowl; mix well. Stir in pie filling. Pour into 9 x 13-inch dish. Chill until firm. Dissolve small package peach gelatin in 1 cup hot water in mixer bowl. Add whipped topping and cream cheese; beat well. Pour over congealed bottom layer. Chill until firm. Yield: 15 servings.

Vera Cooper

POACHED PEARS

2 c. cranberry juice cocktail
1 c. strawberry preserves
2   4-in. long cinnamon sticks
12 whole cloves
6 lg. firm pears

Combine cranberry juice, strawberry preserves, cinnamon and cloves in large saucepan. Bring to a boil. Simmer, covered, for 15 minutes. Peel pears, leaving stems intact. Cut thin slice off bottom of each pear. Remove cinnamon sticks and cloves. Add pears. Cook over low heat for 35 to 45 minutes or until just tender, turning and basting occasionally. Remove from heat; cool on rack. Refrigerate pears in liquid, turning occasionally to color evenly. Transfer pears to serving dish using slotted spoon. Use leftover poaching liquid as marinade for chopped fresh fruit. Yield: 6 servings.

Marilee Burrus

PISTACHIO DESSERT

> 16 graham crackers, crushed
> 1/4 c. packed brown sugar
> 1/2 c. melted butter
> 1 qt. vanilla ice cream,
>   softened
> 1 1/2 c. milk
> 2 sm. packages pistachio instant
>   pudding mix
> 1 16-oz. carton whipped topping
> 4 Heath bars, crushed

Combine cracker crumbs, brown sugar and butter in bowl; mix well. Press into 9 x 13-inch baking dish. Bake at 350 degrees for 10 minutes. Cool. Mix ice cream, milk and pudding mix in bowl until smooth. Pour over crumb layer. Freeze until firm. Top with whipped topping and crushed candy. Freeze until serving time or store in refrigerator for softer consistency. Yield: 20 servings.

Mardele Toth

BROILED BUTTERSCOTCH RICE PUDDING

> 1/2 c. uncooked rice
> 1/4 tsp. salt
> 1 tsp. maple extract
> 1 3 1/4-oz. package butterscotch
>   pudding and pie filling mix
> 2 c. milk

> 1 tbsp. butter
> 1/3 c. maple syrup
> 2 tbsp. melted butter
> 1 c. shredded coconut

Combine rice, 1 cup water, salt and maple extract in saucepan. Bring to a boil over high heat; stir, cover and reduce heat. Simmer for 15 minutes. Blend pudding mix with milk and 1 tablespoon butter in saucepan. Cook over medium heat for about 5 minutes, stirring constantly. Fold in cooked rice. Spoon into ovenproof serving dishes. Chill until serving time. Mix maple syrup, 2 tablespoons butter and coconut in small bowl. Spread mixture over pudding. Broil for 2 to 3 minutes or until golden. Yield: 6 servings.

Photograph for this recipe on this page.

HONEY CUSTARD

> 3 eggs, beaten
> 1/4 c. honey
> 1/4 tsp. salt
> 2 c. milk
> Nutmeg

Beat eggs, honey and salt in bowl. Scald milk. Stir slowly into egg mixture. Pour into custard cups. Sprinkle with nutmeg. Set cups in pan of hot water. Bake at 325 degrees for 30 minutes or until knife inserted in mixture comes out clean. Yield: 6 servings.

Kate Malone

BLENDER COCONUT CUSTARD

2 c. milk
1/2 c. honey
1 c. coconut
4 eggs
1/2 c. flour
6 tbsp. butter
1/4 tsp. salt
1 tsp. vanilla extract

Combine all ingredients in blender container. Process until smooth. Pour into greased and lightly floured 9-inch pie plate. Bake at 325 degrees for 45 minutes. Yield: 6 servings.

Mary I. Grafton

CHOCOLATE BREAD PUDDING

1 1/2 oz. baking chocolate,
*   chopped*
3 c. milk
3 eggs, separated
1/3 c. sugar
1/4 c. packed brown sugar
2 tsp. vanilla extract
1/2 tsp. salt
2 to 2 1/2 c. stale bread cubes
1/4 tsp. cream of tartar
6 tbsp. sugar
1/2 tsp. vanilla extract

Combine chocolate and milk in saucepan. Cook over low heat until chocolate is melted, stirring constantly. Beat egg yolks slightly. Add 1/3 cup sugar, brown sugar, 2 teaspoons vanilla and salt; mix well. Stir chocolate mixture into egg yolk mixture. Arrange bread in buttered 8-inch square pan. Pour chocolate mixture over bread. Place in pan of hot water. Bake at 350 degrees for 1 hour or until set. Beat egg whites until frothy. Add cream of tartar and remaining 6 tablespoons sugar gradually, beating until stiff and glossy. Stir in remaining 1/2 teaspoon vanilla. Mound meringue over pudding. Bake for 10 minutes longer or until meringue is browned. Serve with cream. Yield: 8 servings.

Marie E. Dierks

EASY MOCHA PUDDING

1 env. whipped topping mix
1 sm. package chocolate instant
*   pudding mix*
1 tbsp. instant coffee powder
2 c. cold milk

Combine all ingredients in mixer bowl. Beat for 5 minutes at high speed or until thick. Spoon into dessert dishes. Garnish with chopped nuts. Chill in refrigerator. Yield: 6 servings.

June Graf

BROWNIE FUDGE PUDDING

1 17-oz. package brownie mix
1/2 c. chopped pecans
3/4 c. packed brown sugar
3/4 c. sugar
1/3 c. baking cocoa
1 1/4 c. cold coffee

Prepare brownie mix using package directions for cake-type brownies. Stir in pecans. Pour into greased 9 x 13-inch baking pan. Mix brown sugar, sugar and cocoa together in bowl. Sprinkle over brownie mixture. Drizzle coffee over top. Bake using package directions. Serve warm with ice cream. Yield: 12 servings.

Michelle Epps

HONEY-RICE PUDDING

2 c. cooked rice
3 c. milk
3/4 c. honey
3 eggs
1 c. raisins
1/2 tsp. cinnamon

Combine rice, milk and honey in bowl. Add eggs; mix well. Stir in raisins. Place in greased casserole. Sprinkle with cinnamon. Bake at 300 degrees for about 1 hour. Serve with whipped cream. Yield: 6-8 servings.

Alma Bartlet

RICE PUDDING

1/2 c. minute rice
1/2 c. raisins
1/4 tsp. salt
2 c. milk
1 sm. package vanilla pudding
*   and pie filling mix*
1 c. whipped topping

Combine rice, raisins and 1/2 cup hot water in saucepan. Let stand, covered, for 10 minutes. Add salt, milk and pudding mix. Cook according to pudding package directions; cool. Fold in whipped topping. Spoon into individual serving dishes. Chill in refrigerator. Garnish with nutmeg. Yield: 6-8 servings.

Jean Zeller

GINGERY PUMPKIN CRUNCH

4 oz. marshmallows, chopped
1 c. pumpkin
1/4 tsp. cinnamon
1/8 tsp. ginger
1 pt. vanilla ice cream, softened
1 c. ginger cookie crumbs

Combine marshmallows, pumpkin and spices in double boiler. Cook over hot water until marshmallows are melted, stirring occasionally. Cool slightly. Stir in ice cream. Sprinkle 3/4 of the crumbs in 9 x 9-inch pan. Spoon pumpkin mixture into prepared pan. Sprinkle with remaining cookie crumbs. Freeze. Let stand at room temperature for 10 minutes before serving. Cut into squares. Yield: 9 servings.

Patricia Rowan

RHUBARB CRUNCH

1 c. flour
3/4 c. oats
1 c. packed brown sugar
1 tsp. cinnamon
1/2 c. melted butter
1 c. sugar
3 tbsp. cornstarch

1 tsp. vanilla extract
4 c. chopped rhubarb

Combine first 5 ingredients in bowl; mix until crumbly. Mix sugar and cornstarch in saucepan. Add 1 cup water gradually, mixing well. Simmer for 1 minute or until clear, stirring constantly. Stir in vanilla. Press half the crumb mixture into 9-inch square baking pan. Cover with rhubarb. Pour syrup over rhubarb. Top with remaining crumb mixture. Bake at 350 degrees for 1 hour. Serve warm or cold with ice cream.

Sheryl Ginn

COCONUT SAUCE

1 can sweetened condensed milk
2 egg yolks, beaten
1/4 c. margarine
1/2 c. flaked coconut
1/2 c. chopped pecans
1 tsp. vanilla extract

Combine sweetened condensed milk, egg yolks and margarine in 1-quart glass measure. Microwave on Medium-High for 3 minutes; stir. Microwave for 1 to 2 minutes longer. Stir in remaining ingredients. Serve warm over ice cream or cake. Yield: 2 cups.

Ruth Freeman

HOT FUDGE SAUCE

2 oz. semisweet chocolate
2 tbsp. unsalted butter
1/4 c. corn syrup
1 c. sugar
1/8 tsp. salt
1 tsp. vanilla extract
6 oz. semisweet chocolate chips

Combine chocolate, butter and 1/3 cup water in heavy saucepan. Cook over low heat until chocolate has melted, stirring constantly. Stir in corn syrup, sugar and salt. Cook over low heat for 10 minutes or until smooth. Remove from heat. Stir in vanilla. Stir in chocolate chips. Serve over ice cream. Yield: 2 cups.

Annette Warnack

PEANUT BUTTER SAUCE

1 can sweetened condensed milk
1/3 c. peanut butter
Chopped peanuts

Blend sweetened condensed milk and peanut butter in 1-quart glass dish. Microwave on High for 2 1/2 to 3 1/2 minutes or to desired consistency, stirring occasionally. Stir in peanuts. Store in refrigerator. Serve over ice cream. Yield: 1 1/2 cups.

Bettye Sellick

CREAMY PECAN SAUCE

1/4 c. margarine
1 can sweetened condensed milk
1/2 tsp. rum flavoring
1/4 c. chopped pecans

Melt margarine in saucepan over medium heat. Add remaining ingredients. Cook for 10 minutes or until slightly thickened, stirring constantly. Cool for 10 minutes. Sauce thickens as it cools. Serve warm over baked apples, fruit or ice cream. Yield: 1 1/2 cups.

Carolyn Marston

EASY SUNDAE SHORTCAKE

1 20-oz. can pie filling
1 qt. ice cream
2 4-count packages
shortcake cups

Heat pie filling in saucepan over low heat. Spoon ice cream into shortcake cups. Spoon pie filling over top. Yield: 8 servings.

Mary L. Beien

MAKE-AHEAD SHORTCAKE

1 loaf angel food cake, sliced
1 lg. package vanilla instant
pudding mix
1/2 c. milk
1 pt. vanilla ice cream, softened
1 lg. package strawberry gelatin
4 c. sliced strawberries

Place cake slices in 9 x 13-inch dish. Combine pudding mix and milk in large bowl; mix well. Add ice cream. Beat until blended. Pour into prepared dish. Dissolve gelatin in 1/2 cup boiling water. Stir in strawberries. Chill until partially set. Spoon over pudding mixture. Chill until firm. Yield: 12 servings.

Evelyn Hebert

STRAWBERRY SHORTCAKE BOWL

2 pt. fresh strawberries, sliced
Sugar to taste
1 1/2 tsp. ground cinnamon
1/4 c. sugar
1 pkg. refrigerator flaky biscuits
1/4 c. melted butter
1/2 c. chopped pecans
1 pt. vanilla ice cream, softened

Combine strawberries and sugar to taste in bowl; mix well. Chill for 30 minutes. Combine cinnamon with 1/4 cup sugar in small bowl; mix well. Set aside. Separate each biscuit into 2 by pulling layers apart. Brush both sides with butter. Dip in sugar mixture. Place 1 inch apart on buttered baking sheet. Press pecans into tops of biscuits. Bake at 400 degrees for 10 to 12 minutes. Line large serving bowl with half the biscuits. Spoon half the strawberries over biscuits. Spoon in ice cream and remaining strawberries. Top with remaining biscuits.

Marti Kellogg

STRAWBERRY PRETZEL DESSERT

2 c. crushed pretzels
3 tbsp. sugar
3/4 c. melted margarine
3/4 c. sugar
8 oz. cream cheese, softened
8 oz. whipped topping
1 6-oz. package strawberry gelatin
2 c. boiling pineapple juice
2 10-oz. packages frozen strawberries

Toss pretzels, 3 tablespoons sugar and melted margarine in bowl. Press into 9 x 13-inch baking dish. Bake at 325 degrees for 10 minutes. Cool. Cream remaining 3/4 cup sugar and cream cheese in mixer bowl until light. Blend in whipped topping. Spread over cooled layer. Chill. Dissolve gelatin in boiling pineapple juice in bowl. Stir in strawberries. Chill until partially set. Spoon over cream cheese layer. Chill until set. Yield: 12 servings.

Lisa Bartley

FROZEN STRAWBERRY FLUFF

1 c. flour
1/2 c. butter
1/4 c. packed brown sugar
1/2 c. chopped nuts
2 egg whites
1 c. sugar
2 tsp. lemon juice
1   10-oz. package frozen
*   strawberries, thawed*
1 c. whipping cream, whipped

Mix first 4 ingredients in bowl until crumbly. Press into 8 x 8-inch pan. Bake at 350 degrees for 20 to 25 minutes. Cool. Stir until crumbly. Sprinkle half the mixture into greased 9 x 9-inch pan. Combine egg whites, sugar, lemon juice and strawberries in mixer bowl. Beat for 20 minutes or until mixture triples in bulk. Fold into whipped cream gently. Spread in prepared pan. Top with remaining crumbs. Freeze until firm. Yield: 8 servings.

Florence Gilmore

STRAWBERRIES AND WHITE VELVET

1 pt. heavy cream
1/2 c. sugar
Dash of salt
1 tbsp. unflavored gelatin
1 pt. sour cream
1   16-oz. package frozen
*   strawberries*

Scald cream in saucepan. Stir in sugar and salt until dissolved. Soften gelatin in 2 tablespoons cold water in small bowl. Add to cream mix-

ture; mix well. Stir in sour cream; pour into glass serving bowl. Chill until firm. Top with strawberries. Yield: 6-8 servings.

E. Denley Rafferty

ENGLISH TRIFLE

6 egg yolks, slightly beaten
1/2 c. sugar
2 1/4 c. milk
1 c. whipping cream
1/4 c. orange juice
2   11-oz. jelly rolls, cut into
*   12 slices*
1 c. whipping cream
Red candied cherries, slivered

Beat egg yolks and sugar together in top of double boiler. Stir in milk and 1 cup whipping cream. Cook over simmering water for 25 minutes or until thick, stirring constantly. Strain custard into bowl; cool slightly. Stir in orange juice. Line crystal bowl with jelly roll slices. Pour warm custard over slices. Cover with foil; chill thoroughly for 3 hours to overnight. Beat remaining 1 cup whipping cream until stiff. Decorate top of trifle with puffs of cream. Garnish with candied cherries. Yield: 8 servings.

Irina Mihalega-Maldonado

FRESH FRUIT TORTE

1   10-oz. pound cake
2 bananas, sliced
1/4 c. lemon juice
1 c. ricotta cheese
1/4 c. confectioners' sugar
1 tsp. vanilla extract
1 1/2 c. sliced fresh strawberries

Cut cake into 3 layers. Coat banana slices with lemon juice. Combine ricotta cheese, confectioners' sugar and vanilla in mixer bowl; beat until smooth. Alternate layers of cake, bananas, cheese mixture and strawberries on cake plate, ending with cheese mixture. Chill for 45 minutes. Garnish with additional banana slices and whole strawberries. Yield: 12 servings.

Sue Ellen Green

Beverages

APPLE COOLER

1 qt. apple juice, chilled
1 pt. vanilla ice cream, softened
1   8-oz. can crushed pineapple,
    drained
1/2 tsp. cinnamon

Combine all ingredients in blender container. Process until frothy. Pour into glasses. Garnish with pineapple cubes on skewers and mint sprigs. Yield: 2 quarts.

Marlene Arnold

BLENDER BANANA NOG

1 banana, chopped
1 egg
3/4 c. milk
1 tsp. sugar
1/2 tsp. vanilla extract
Dash of nutmeg

Combine banana and remaining ingredients in blender container. Process until smooth. Pour into serving glass. Yield: 1 serving.

Sharon Fracassi

ICED CHOCOLATE

4 sq. unsweetened chocolate, broken
1 c. sugar
Dash of salt
1 tsp. vanilla extract
1 pt. whipping cream, partially whipped

Combine chocolate, 4 cups hot water, sugar and salt in saucepan. Boil for 5 minutes. Add vanilla. Pour chocolate over whipped cream. Beat until frothy. Pour into glasses half filled with crushed ice. Garnish with whipped cream. Yield: 6 servings.

Barbara Meteyer

SOUTHERN COFFEE PUNCH

2 qt. strong cold coffee
1 pt. cold milk

2 tsp. vanilla extract
1/2 c. sugar
1 qt. vanilla ice cream
Nutmeg to taste

Combine coffee, milk, vanilla and sugar in punch bowl; stir until sugar is dissolved. Chill thoroughly. Add scoops of ice cream. Sprinkle lightly with nutmeg. Yield: 20 servings.

Janie Carpenter

DAIRY FRUIT PUNCH

1   12-oz. can frozen lemonade
    concentrate, thawed
1   6-oz. can frozen limeade
    concentrate, thawed
1/2 gal. vanilla ice cream
1/2 gal. lime sherbet
1/2 gal. milk
2 qt. ginger ale

Combine juice concentrates and 1 quart water in pitcher; mix well. Scoop ice cream and sherbet into large punch bowl. Stir in milk. Add the juice mixture and ginger ale, mixing gently. Yield: 50 servings.

Shirley Ringdahl

GLOGG NOG

6 eggs, beaten
1/4 c. sugar
1/4 tsp. ground cardamom
1/4 tsp. cinnamon
1/4 tsp. ground cloves
1 qt. vanilla ice cream, softened
6 c. orange juice
1/4 c. lemon juice
1 qt. ginger ale, chilled

Combine eggs, sugar and spices in mixing bowl. Beat at medium speed until sugar dissolves. Beat in ice cream and juices at low speed. Chill, covered, until serving time. Pour into punch bowl. Add ginger ale slowly; fold gently to mix. Float ice ring with orange slices in punch. Garnish each serving with nutmeg. Yield: 36 servings.

Lisa Ann Wilcox

1 liter ginger ale
Mint leaves

Mix fruit juices in bowl. Place ice cream in punch bowl. Add juices. Pour ginger ale into bowl just before serving. Garnish with mint leaves. Yield: 12 servings.

Betty Ruby

FRUITY FLOATS

1   6-oz. can frozen fruit punch
1 pt. vanilla ice cream

Dilute punch concentrate using package directions. Chill well. Place small scoop of ice cream in a chilled tall glass. Add 1/2 to 3/4 cup chilled punch; stir slightly. Top with additional ice cream. Yield: 4 servings.

Photograph for this recipe on this page.

LIME FLOAT

1 qt. lime sherbet, softened
1 c. pineapple juice
1 qt. vanilla ice cream, softened
1 c. 7-Up

Blend first 3 ingredients. Stir in 7-Up just before serving. Yield: 8-10 servings.

Barbara C. Nelson

CREAMY CITRUS COOLER

1 qt. orange juice, chilled
1 bottle of lemon juice, chilled
1/2 gal. vanilla ice cream

PINA COLADA FLIP

1   46-oz. can pineapple juice, chilled
1   16-oz. can cream of coconut
1 qt. vanilla ice cream, softened
1   28-oz. bottle of club soda, chilled

Combine pineapple juice and cream of coconut in punch bowl; mix well. Spoon in ice cream. Add club soda gradually just before serving. Yield: 12 servings.

Beverly Stallins

PINEAPPLE MINT COOLER

3 c. cold milk
2 c. pineapple juice, chilled
3/4 c. cream
1/4 c. sugar
1 1/2 tsp. lemon juice
1/8 tsp. salt
12 drops of peppermint extract

Combine all ingredients in 2-quart shaker. Shake until foamy. Pour into tall glasses. Garnish with mint leaves. Serve immediately. Yield: 6 servings.

Carolyn Huber

STRAWBERRY MILK PUNCH

6 c. fresh strawberries, sliced
3 c. sugar
1 gal. cold milk
2 qt. strawberry ice cream, softened
2 qt. mint ice cream, softened

Beat strawberries and sugar in mixing bowl until smooth. Combine with milk and ice cream in punch bowl. Yield: 25 servings.

Claire Ranier

CRANBERRY PUNCH

1/2 c. lemon juice
2 c. orange juice
3/4 c. sugar
1 1/2 qt. cranberry juice
2 28-oz. bottles of ginger ale, chilled
2 pt. raspberry sherbet

Combine lemon juice, orange juice and sugar in large container. Stir to dissolve sugar. Add cranberry juice. Chill in refrigerator. Pour into punch bowl. Add ginger ale; blend well. Spoon sherbet on top of punch. Yield: 30 servings.

Debbie Stanley

FROSTY FRUIT PUNCH

1 6-oz. can frozen lemonade
   concentrate, thawed
1 6-oz. can frozen orange juice
   concentrate, thawed
1 6-oz. can frozen pineapple
   juice concentrate, thawed
1 12-oz. can apricot nectar, chilled
1/2 c. lemon juice
1 qt. lemon sherbet
2 lg. bottles of ginger ale, chilled

Add water to frozen concentrates according to can directions. Mix with chilled apricot nectar and lemon juice in punch bowl. Spoon in sherbet just before serving; add ginger ale. Pineapple or orange sherbet may be substituted for lemon sherbet if desired. Yield: 20-25 servings.

Mary Schreiner

LIVELY SHERBET PUNCH

2 c. sugar
1 1/2 c. fresh mint
3/4 c. lemon juice
1 12-oz. can apricot nectar
1 6-oz. can frozen limeade
   concentrate, thawed
1 6-oz. can frozen orange juice
   concentrate, thawed
1 6-oz. can frozen pineapple
   juice concentrate, thawed

2 qt. ginger ale, chilled
1 qt. lemon sherbet

Combine sugar and mint with 2 cups boiling water in bowl. Cool; strain. Add lemon juice, apricot nectar, limeade, orange juice and pineapple juice concentrates; mix well. Chill in refrigerator. Mix with ginger ale and lemon sherbet in punch bowl just before serving. Garnish with sprigs of mint. Serve in punch cups. Yield: 20-25 servings.

Jeanne Lipman

BANANA PUNCH

4 c. sugar
1 32-oz. can pineapple juice
1 6-oz. can frozen orange juice
   concentrate, thawed
1 6-oz. can frozen lemonade
   concentrate, thawed
6 bananas
2 to 3 qt. ginger ale

Bring sugar and 6 cups water to a boil in saucepan; mix well. Chill in refrigerator. Combine with juices in large freezer container. Mix bananas with a small amount of juice mixture in blender container. Process until smooth. Add to juice mixture. Freeze until slushy. Thaw for 1 hour before serving. Combine with chilled ginger ale in punch bowl; mix gently. Yield: 2 gallons.

Diana Allen

CITRUS FIZZ

1 6-oz. can frozen orange juice
   concentrate, thawed
1/4 c. frozen grapefruit juice
   concentrate, thawed
1/4 c. frozen limeade concentrate,
   thawed
1 qt. ginger ale

Blend concentrates in large pitcher. Add ginger ale and ice. Pour into 6 tall glasses. Garnish with orange wedges. Yield: 6 servings.

Freda Stanley

GOLDEN FRUIT PUNCH

  2 3-oz. packages apricot gelatin
  2 c. sugar
  1 46-oz. can pineapple juice
  1 1/2 c. orange juice
  1 c. lemon juice
  3 to 4 lg. bottles of ginger ale

Dissolve gelatin in 1 cup hot water in punch bowl. Add sugar; stir until well mixed. Stir in 7 cups cold water and remaining ingredients. Yield: 40 servings.

Mary Allen

MOCK CHAMPAGNE PUNCH

  1 c. sugar
  1 qt. cranberry juice
  1 20-oz. can pineapple juice
  1 c. orange juice
  2 7-oz. bottles of lemon-lime soda

Combine sugar and 3 cups water in saucepan. Bring to a boil, stirring constantly; cool. Add to fruit juices in large container; mix well. Freeze, covered, until slushy. Add soda just before serving. Yield: 10 servings.

Rosemary Stewart

GRAPE JUICE CRUSH

  1 6-oz. can frozen orange juice
     concentrate, thawed
  1 6-oz. can frozen grape juice
     concentrate, thawed
  1 6-oz. can frozen lemonade
     concentrate, thawed
  1 qt. ginger ale, chilled

Combine fruit juice concentrates and 4 cups water in large container. Chill until serving time. Add ginger ale gradually. Serve over crushed ice; garnish with frosted Tokay grapes. Yield: 16 servings.

Janis Nielson

PICNIC LEMONADE

  1/2 c. light corn syrup
  1/2 c. sugar
  2 tbsp. grated lemon rind
  1 1/4 c. lemon juice

Boil corn syrup, sugar, 2/3 cup water and lemon rind in saucepan for 5 minutes; strain. Cool. Combine with lemon juice and 7 cups water in ice-filled pitcher; mix well. Garnish with maraschino cherries and lemon slices. Yield: 8 servings.

Helen Grimes

RECEPTION PUNCH

  4 12-oz. cans frozen orange juice
     concentrate, thawed
  1 12-oz. can frozen lemonade
     concentrate, thawed
  2 lg. cans pineapple juice
  1 lg. can grapefruit juice
  1/2 c. sugar
  4 bottles of ginger ale

Reconstitute frozen fruit juices, using package directions. Combine with pineapple and grapefruit juices and sugar in large punch bowl. Add ginger ale just before serving. Yield: 40 servings.

Henrietta Johnson

FROZEN TROPICAL PUNCH

  4 c. sugar
  5 bananas, mashed
  1 1/2 to 2 c. orange juice
  6 tbsp. lemon juice
  1 lg. can pineapple juice
  Ginger ale or 7-Up

Combine sugar and 6 cups water in saucepan. Bring to a boil. Boil for 3 minutes. Cool. Combine bananas and juices in bowl; mix well. Stir in sugar syrup. Pour into 1-quart freezer containers. Freeze until firm. Place frozen fruit juice mixture in punch bowl. Add ginger ale; mix gently. Ladle into punch cups. Yield: 40 servings.

Diane Weeks

FRUIT SLUSH

2 c. honey
1 6-oz. can frozen orange juice
  concentrate, thawed
1 46-oz. can pineapple juice
1/4 c. lemon juice
3 ripe bananas, mashed
3 qt. ginger ale

Combine honey with 3 cups water in large saucepan; bring to a boil. Prepare orange juice according to can directions. Stir orange juice, pineapple juice and lemon juice into honey mixture. Add bananas; blend thoroughly. Pour mixture into two 9 x 13-inch baking dishes; freeze. Remove from freezer 1 hour before serving. Chop into small pieces; place into punch bowl. Add ginger ale. Serve immediately. Carbonated lemon-lime beverage or sparkling water may be substituted for ginger ale, if desired. Yield: 36 servings.

Alice Barrett

WEDDING PUNCH

1 c. sugar
2 cans frozen orange juice
  concentrate, thawed
1 lg. can apricot juice
1 lg. can pineapple juice
1 c. lemon juice
2 qt. ginger ale
1 qt. tea

Combine sugar and 2 cups water in saucepan; boil until syrupy. Chill all ingredients well. Pour into punch bowl; serve immediately in punch cups. Yield: 46 servings.

Mrs. Thomas M. Parker

FOUR-FRUIT TEA PUNCH

1 c. instant tea
1 6-oz. can frozen limeade
  concentrate, thawed
1 6-oz. can frozen lemonade
  concentrate, thawed

1 6-oz. can frozen pineapple
  juice concentrate, thawed
1 pt. cranberry juice cocktail

Combine all ingredients and 2 quarts water in punch bowl; mix well. Add ice at serving time. Yield: 25 servings.

Dorothy Droste

FRUITED SUMMER TEA

8 tea bags
2 c. sugar
2 c. orange juice
3/4 c. lemon juice

Bring 1 quart water to a boil in saucepan. Add tea bags. Steep for 5 minutes. Bring 2 cups water and sugar to a boil in small saucepan, stirring to dissolve sugar. Combine tea, sugar mixture, juices and 2 quarts cold water in large pitcher. Serve over ice in glasses. Yield: 20 servings.

Jenny Hungerbuhler

FRENCH MINT TEA

4 lg. tea bags
Rind and juice of 3 lemons
1/2 c. fresh mint leaves
2 46-oz. cans pineapple juice
2 c. sugar
1 1/2 tsp. vanilla extract
1/2 tsp. almond extract

Steep tea bags and lemon rind in 2 cups boiling water for 15 minutes. Remove tea bags and rind. Combine with lemon juice, remaining ingredients and 4 cups cold water in large container; mix well. Serve over crushed ice; garnish with sprigs of fresh mint. Yield: 12 servings.

Margaret Hanson

GINGER ALE TEA

2 c. tea
Juice of 2 oranges

Juice of 1 lemon
1/4 c. sugar
2 c. ginger ale

Combine tea, fruit juices and sugar in pitcher; mix well. Chill until serving time. Add ginger ale. Serve over crushed ice. Yield: 4 servings.

Helen Walton

TEA COOLER

1/4 c. instant tea powder
1/2 c. instant lemonade powder
3/4 c. sugar
2 c. white grape juice

Combine all ingredients in 1-gallon container. Add enough water to measure 1 gallon. Chill until serving time. Yield: 16 servings.

Janice Hall

MAKE-AHEAD TOMATO COCKTAILS

1 tsp. salt
1/2 tsp. coarsely ground pepper
1 tbsp. minced instant onions
1/2 tsp. celery salt
2 tbsp. lemon juice
1 tbsp. lime juice
3 tbsp. Worcestershire sauce
Steak sauce to taste
2 beef bouillon cubes
Tomato juice

Combine first 9 ingredients in 1-gallon container. Add enough tomato juice to fill container. Let stand overnight. Serve over ice. Yield: 24 servings.

Donna Rouse

SPICED CIDER

1 tsp. whole allspice
2 2-in. cinnamon sticks
12 whole cloves
2 qt. cider
2/3 c. packed brown sugar
Dash of nutmeg

Tie whole spices in cheesecloth. Bring cider and brown sugar to a boil in 4-quart saucepan, stirring until brown sugar dissolves. Add spice bag; reduce heat. Simmer for 10 minutes. Remove spice bag. Pour into cups. Sprinkle with nutmeg. Yield: 12 servings.

Maudie Richie

VIENNESE COFFEE

1/2 c. heavy cream
1 tbsp. confectioners' sugar
1/2 tsp. vanilla extract
3 c. hot strong coffee

Combine cream, confectioners' sugar and vanilla in mixer bowl; beat until stiff. Pour hot coffee into 4 coffee mugs. Spoon whipped cream on top. Garnish with orange rind and cinnamon stick. Serve at once. Yield: 4 servings.

Norma Jennings

CAFE AU CHOCOLAT

1 c. instant cocoa mix
1/3 c. instant coffee
1/2 pt. heavy cream, whipped
Nutmeg

Mix cocoa, coffee and 4 cups boiling water in large pan. Pour into coffeepot. Heat to serving temperature. Serve in demitasse cups topped with whipped cream and dash of nutmeg. Yield: 6 demitasse servings.

Charlene Webster

HOT CHOCOLATE MIX

2 c. nondairy coffee creamer
1 1/2 c. sugar
3/4 c. unsweetened cocoa
1/2 c. nonfat dry milk powder
1/4 tsp. salt

Combine all ingredients in bowl; mix well. Store in airtight container. Combine 2 to 3 teaspoons dry mix with 1 cup boiling water for each serving. Yield: 4 3/4 cups mix.

Jane Surber

MEXICAN HOT CHOCOLATE

1 qt. milk
1/4 c. cocoa
1/4 c. sugar
3/4 tsp. cinnamon
Dash of salt
3/4 tsp. vanilla extract
1/4 c. light cream

Heat 1 cup milk to the boiling point in saucepan. Stir in combined dry ingredients; beat until smooth. Bring to a boil over low heat, stirring constantly. Add remaining milk. Heat to boiling point. Stir in vanilla and cream. Heat to serving temperature. Beat with rotary beater until frothy. Yield: 6 servings.

Roberta Sawyer

INSTANT TEA MIX

1   18-oz. jar instant orange
     breakfast drink mix
1 c. sugar
1/2 c. sweetened lemonade mix
1/2 c. instant tea
1   3-oz. package apricot gelatin
1 c. sugar
2 1/2 tsp. cinnamon
1 tsp. cloves

Combine all ingredients in large bowl; mix well. Store in airtight container. Combine 1 1/2 tablespoons mix and 1 cup hot water in mug for each serving. Yield: 50 servings.

Carla Stark

HOT SPICED PERCOLATOR PUNCH

3 c. unsweetened pineapple juice
2 c. cranberry juice
1/3 c. packed brown sugar
1 1/2 tsp. whole cloves
1 stick cinnamon
1/8 tsp. salt

Combine juices and brown sugar in 10-cup percolator. Place spices and salt in basket. Brew as for coffee for 5 to 6 minutes. Yield: 8 servings.

Margaret Mead

HOT CRANBERRY TEA

4 c. fresh cranberries
2 1/2 c. sugar
Juice of 1 lemon
Juice of 3 oranges
1/2 c. red hot cinnamon candies

Combine cranberries with 4 cups water in saucepan. Cook until cranberries pop. Strain into saucepan. Add 2 quarts water and sugar. Bring mixture to a boil. Cook until sugar is dissolved, stirring constantly. Add lemon and orange juice and red hots. Heat until candies are dissolved. Serve hot or cold. Yield: 1 gallon.

Betty John

RUSSIAN TEA

3 tea bags
Juice and rind of 2 oranges
Juice and rind of 3 lemons
1 slice (or more) pineapple
1 c. sugar
4 whole cloves

Combine all ingredients with 2 quarts boiling water in saucepan. Let stand, covered, for 1 hour. Strain tea into refrigerator container. Store in refrigerator for up to 5 days. Serve hot. Yield: 2 1/2 quarts.

Johnnie Templeton

PINEAPPLE WASSAIL

4 c. unsweetened pineapple juice
1   12-oz. can apricot nectar
2 c. apple cider
1 c. orange juice
6   1-in. cinnamon sticks
1 tsp. whole cloves

Combine all ingredients in large saucepan. Bring to a boil; reduce heat. Simmer for 15 minutes. Strain into large punch bowl or pitcher. Serve hot. Garnish with orange slices. Yield: 16 servings.

Shirley Berrard

Substitution Chart

	INSTEAD OF:	USE:
BAKING	1 tsp. baking powder	1/4 tsp. soda plus 1/2 tsp. cream of tartar
	1 tbsp. cornstarch (for thickening)	2 tbsp. flour OR 1 tbsp. tapioca
	1 c. sifted all-purpose flour	1 c. plus 2 tbsp. sifted cake flour
	1 c. sifted cake flour	1 c. minus 2 tbsp. sifted all-purpose flour
DAIRY	1 c. buttermilk	1 c. sour milk OR 1 c. yogurt
	1 c. heavy cream	3/4 c. skim milk plus 1/3 c. butter
	1 c. light cream	7/8 c. skim milk plus 3 tbsp. butter
	1 c. sour cream	7/8 c. sour milk plus 3 tbsp. butter
	1 c. sour milk	1 c. sweet milk plus 1 tbsp. vinegar or lemon juice OR 1 c. buttermilk
	1 c. sweet milk	1 c. sour milk or buttermilk plus 1/2 tsp. soda
SEASONINGS	1 tsp. allspice	1/2 tsp. cinnamon plus 1/8 tsp. cloves
	1 c. catsup	1 c. tomato sauce plus 1/2 c. sugar plus 2 tbsp. vinegar
	1 clove of garlic	1/8 tsp. garlic powder OR 1/8 tsp. instant minced garlic OR 3/4 tsp. garlic salt OR 5 drops of liquid garlic
	1 tsp. Italian spice	1/4 tsp. each oregano, basil, thyme, rosemary plus dash of cayenne
	1 tsp. lemon juice	1/2 tsp. vinegar
	1 tbsp. prepared mustard	1 tsp. dry mustard
SWEET	1 2/3 oz. semisweet chocolate	1 oz. unsweetened chocolate plus 4 tsp. sugar
	1 1-oz. square chocolate	3 to 4 tbsp. cocoa plus 1 tsp. shortening
	1 c. honey	1 to 1 1/4 c. sugar plus 1/4 c. liquid OR 1 c. molasses or corn syrup
	1 c. granulated sugar	1 c. packed brown sugar OR 1 c. corn syrup, molasses or honey, minus 1/4 c. liquid

Equivalent Chart

	WHEN RECIPE CALLS FOR:	YOU NEED:
BAKING ESSENTIALS	2 c. butter	1 lb.
	4 c. all-purpose flour	1 lb.
	4 1/2 c. sifted cake flour	1 lb.
	1 square chocolate	1 oz.
	1 c. semisweet chocolate pieces	1 6-oz. package
	4 c. marshmallows	1 lb.
	2 2/3 c. brown sugar	1 lb.
	2 2/3 c. confectioners' sugar	1 lb.
	2 c. granulated sugar	1 lb.
	3 c. tapioca	1 lb.
CEREAL AND BREAD	1 c. fine dry bread crumbs	4-5 slices
	1 c. soft bread crumbs	2 slices
	1 c. small bread cubes	2 slices
	1 c. fine cracker crumbs	24 saltines
	1 c. fine graham cracker crumbs	14 crackers
	1 c. vanilla wafer crumbs	22 wafers
	1 c. crushed cornflakes	3 c. uncrushed
	4 c. cooked macaroni	1 8-oz. package
	3 1/2 c. cooked rice	1 c. uncooked
DAIRY	1 c. freshly grated cheese	1/4 lb.
	1 c. cottage cheese	1 8-oz. carton
	1 c. sour cream	1 8-oz. carton
	1 c. whipped cream	1/2 c. heavy cream
	2/3 c. evaporated milk	1 sm. can
	1 2/3 c. evaporated milk	1 tall can
FRUIT	4 c. sliced or chopped apples	4 med.
	1 c. mashed banana	3 med.
	2 c. pitted cherries	4 c. unpitted
	3 c. shredded coconut	1/2 lb.
	4 c. cranberries	1 lb.
	1 c. pitted dates	1 8-oz. package
	1 c. candied fruit	1 8-oz. package
	3 to 4 tbsp. lemon juice plus 1 tsp. grated rind	1 lemon
	1/3 c. orange juice plus 2 tsp. grated rind	1 orange
	4 c. sliced peaches	8 med.
	2 c. pitted prunes	1 12-oz. package
	3 c. raisins	1 15-oz. package
MEATS	4 c. diced cooked chicken	1 5-lb. chicken
	3 c. diced cooked meat	1 lb., cooked
	2 c. ground cooked meat	1 lb., cooked

	WHEN RECIPE CALLS FOR:	YOU NEED:
NUTS	1 c. chopped nuts	4 oz. shelled 1 lb. unshelled
VEGETABLES	2 c. cooked green beans 2 1/2 c. lima beans or red beans 4 c. shredded cabbage 1 c. grated carrot 1 4-oz. can mushrooms 1 c. chopped onion 4 c. sliced or diced raw potatoes 2 c. canned tomatoes	1/2 lb. fresh or 1 16-oz. can 1 c. dried, cooked 1 lb. 1 lg. 1/2 lb. fresh 1 lg. 4 med. 1 16-oz. can

COMMON EQUIVALENTS

1 tbsp. = 3 tsp.	4 qt. = 1 gal.
2 tbsp. = 1 oz.	6 1/2 to 8-oz. can = 1 c.
4 tbsp. = 1/4 c.	10 1/2 to 12 -oz. can = 1 1/4 c.
5 tbsp. + 1 tsp. = 1/3 c.	14 to 16-oz. can (No. 300) = 1 3/4 c.
8 tbsp. = 1/2 c.	16 to 17-oz. can (No. 303) = 2 c.
12 tbsp. = 3/4 c.	1-lb. 4-oz. can or 1-pt. 2-oz. can (No. 2) = 2 1/2 c.
16 tbsp. = 1 c.	1-lb. 13-oz. can (No. 2 1/2) = 3 1/2 c.
1 c. = 8 oz. or 1/2 pt.	3-lb. 3-oz. can or 46-oz. can or 1-qt. 14-oz. can = 5 3/4 c.
4 c. = 1 qt.	6 1/2-lb. or 7-lb. 5-oz. can (No. 10) = 12 to 13 c.

Metric Conversion Chart

VOLUME

1 tsp.	=	4.9 cc
1 tbsp.	=	14.7 cc
1/3 c.	=	78.9 cc
1/8 c.	=	29.5 cc
1/4 c.	=	59.1 cc
1/2 c.	=	118.3 cc
3/4 c.	=	177.5 cc
1 c.	=	236.7 cc
2 c.	=	473.4 cc
1 fl. oz.	=	29.5 cc
4 oz.	=	118.3 cc
8 oz.	=	236.7 cc

1 pt.	=	473.4 cc
1 qt.	=	.946 liters
1 gal.	=	3.7 liters

CONVERSION FACTORS

Liters	X	1.056	=	Liquid quarts
Quarts	X	0.946	=	Liters
Liters	X	0.264	=	Gallons
Gallons	X	3.785	=	Liters
Fluid ounces	X	29.563	=	Cubic centimeters
Cubic centimeters	X	0.034	=	Fluid ounces
Cups	X	236.575	=	Cubic centimeters
Tablespoons	X	14.797	=	Cubic centimeters
Teaspoons	X	4.932	=	Cubic centimeters
Bushels	X	0.352	=	Hectoliters
Hectoliters	X	2.837	=	Bushels

WEIGHT

1 dry oz.	=	28.3 Grams
1 lb.	=	454 Grams

CONVERSION FACTORS:

Ounces (Avoir.)	X	28.349	=	Grams
Grams	X	0.035	=	Ounces
Pounds	X	0.454	=	Kilograms
Kilograms	X	2.205	=	Pounds

Cheese Chart

CHEESE	GOES WITH	USED FOR	FLAVOR, TEXTURE
Bel Paese (Italy)	Fresh fruit French bread	Dessert Snack	Spongy, mild, creamy yellow interior
Bleu (France)	Fresh fruit Bland crackers	Dessert Dips, Salads	Marbled, blue-veined, semisoft, piquant
Brie (France)	Fresh fruit	Dessert Snack	Soft, edible crust, creamy
Brick (U.S.)	Crackers Bread	Sandwiches Snacks	Semisoft, mild, cream-colored to orange
Camembert (France)	Apples	Dessert Snack	Mild to pungent, edible crust, yellow
Cheddar (England)	Fresh fruit Crackers	Dessert Cooking, Snack	Mild to sharp, cream-colored to orange
Cottage (U.S.)	Canned or fresh fruit	Fruit salads Cooking	Soft, moist, mild, white
Cream (U.S.)	Crackers and jelly	Dessert, Cooking Sandwiches	Soft, smooth, mild, white
Edam (Holland)	Fresh fruit	Dessert Snack	Firm, mild, red wax coating
Feta (Greece)	Greek salad	Salad, Cooking	Salty, crumbly, white
Gorgonzola (Italy)	Fresh fruit Italian bread	Dessert Snack	Semisoft, blue-veined, piquant
Gouda (Holland)	Fresh fruit Crackers	Dessert Snack	Softer then Edam, mild, nutty

CHEESE	GOES WITH	USED FOR	FLAVOR, TEXTURE
Gruyere (Switzerland)	Fresh fruit	Dessert Fondue	Nutty, bland, firm, tiny holes
Liederkranz (Germany)	Onion slices Dark bread	Dessert Snack	Edible light orange crust, robust, soft
Limburger (Belgium)	Dark bread Bland crackers	Dessert	Soft, smooth, white, robust, aromatic
Mozzarella (Italy)	Italian foods	Cooking Pizza	Semisoft, delicate, mild, white
Muenster (Germany)	Crackers Bread	Sandwiches Snack	Semisoft, mild to mellow
Parmesan (Italy)	Italian foods	Cooking	Hard, brittle, sharp, light yellow
Port Salut (France)	Fresh fruit Crackers	Dessert Snack	Buttery, semisoft
Provolone (Italy)	Italian foods	Cooking Dessert	Salty, smoky, mild to sharp, hard
Ricotta (Italy)		Cooking Filling	Soft, creamy, bland, white
Roquefort (France)	Bland crackers Fresh fruit	Dips, Salads Dessert	Semisoft, sharp, blue-veined, crumbly
Stilton (England)	Fresh fruit Bland crackers	Dips, Salads Dessert	Semisoft, sharp, blue-veined
Swiss (Switzerland)	Fresh fruit French bread	Cooking, Snack Sandwiches	Sweetish, nutty, holes, pale yellow

Herb & Spice Chart

Allspice   Pungent, aromatic spice, whole or in powdered form. It is excellent in marinades, particularly in game marinade, or in curries.

Basil   Can be chopped and added to cold poultry salads. If the recipe calls for tomatoes or tomato sauce, add a touch of basil to bring out a rich flavor.

Bay leaf   The basis of many French seasonings is nice added to soups, stews, marinades and stuffings.

Bouquet garni   A must in many Creole cuisine recipes. It is a bundle of herbs, spices and bay leaf tied together and added to soups, stews or sauces.

Celery seed   From wild celery rather than domestic celery. It adds pleasant flavor to bouillon or a stock base.

Chervil   One of the traditional fines herbes used in French-derived cooking. (The others are tarragon, parsley and chive.) It is particularly good in omelets or soups.

Chives   Available fresh, dried or frozen, chives can be substituted for raw onion or shallot in any poultry recipe.

Cinnamon   Ground from the bark of the cinnamon tree, it is important in preparing desserts as well as savory dishes.

Coriander   Adds an unusual flavor to soups, stews, chili dishes, curries and some desserts.

Cumin   A staple spice in Mexican cooking. To use, rub seeds together and let them fall into the dish just before serving. Cumin also comes in powdered form.

Garlic   One of the oldest herbs in the world, it must be carefully handled. For best results, press or crush garlic clove.

Marjoram   An aromatic herb of the mint family, it is good in soups, sauces, stuffings and stews.

Mustard (dry)   Brings a sharp bite to sauces. Sprinkle just a touch over roast chicken for a delightful flavor treat.

ALLSPICE	**BASIL**	**BAY LEAF**	**CELERY SEED**	**CHERVIL**	**CHIVES**
CINNAMON	**CORIANDER**	**CUMIN**	**GARLIC**	**MARJORAM**	**MUSTARD**
OREGANO	**PAPRIKA**	**ROSEMARY**	**SAGE**	**TARRAGON**	**THYME**

Oregano	A staple herb in Italian, Spanish and Mexican cuisines. It is very good in dishes with a tomato foundation; it adds an excellent savory taste.
Paprika	A mild pepper that adds color to many dishes. The very best paprika is imported from Hungary.
Rosemary	A tasty herb important in seasoning stuffing for duck, partridge, capon and other poultry.
Sage	Perrennial favorite with all kinds of poultry and stuffings. It is particularly good with goose.
Tarragon	One of the fines herbs. Goes well with all poultry dishes.
Thyme	Used in combination with bay leaf in soups and stews.

Index

Simply Delicious!
Recipes with a Dash of Distinction.

Favorite Recipes Press

FOR ORDERING INFORMATION
WRITE TO:

FAVORITE RECIPES PRESS
P. O. Box 305142
Nashville, Tennessee 37230

OR CALL:

TOLL FREE Cookbook Hotline

1-800-251-1542